Jh. Howclle 4

INCAS

D0434311

Book One

The Puma's Shadow

INCAS

The Puma's Shadow

A. B. Daniel

Translated by Alex Gilly

POCKET
BOOKS

LONDON · SYDNEY · NEW YORK · TOKYO · SINGAPORE · TORONTO

First published in Great Britain by Simon & Schuster UK Ltd, 2001
This edition first published by Pocket Books, 2002
An imprint of Simon and Schuster
A Viacom company

– Original title
Inca
Princesse du Soleil

International rights management for XO Editions: Susanna Lea
Associates
© XO Editions, 2001. All rights reserved.

English translation copyright © Alex Gilly, 2001

This book is copyright under the Berne Convention.
No reproduction without permission.
® and © 1997 Simon & Schuster Inc. All rights reserved.
Pocket Books & Design is a registerd trademark of Simon &
Schuster Inc

The moral right of the author has been asserted in accordance with
sections 77 and 78 of the Copyright, Designs and Patents Act, 1988.

1 3 5 7 9 10 8 6 4 2

Simon & Schuster UK Ltd
Africa House
64–78 Kingsway
London WC2B 6AH

www.simonsays.co.uk

Simon & Schuster Australia
Sydney

A CIP catalogue record for this book is available from the British
Library

ISBN 0-7434-1604-X

This book is a work of fiction. Names, characters, places and incidents
are either a product of the author's imagination or are used fictitiously.
Any resemblance to actual people living or dead, events or locales is
entirely coincidental.

Typeset by Palimpsest Book Production Limited,
Polmont, Stirlingshire
Printed and bound in Great Britain by
Cox & Wyman Ltd, Reading, Berkshire

Antoine B. Daniel wishes to express his thanks to Bernard Fixot. Without him, his energy and sensitivity, this saga which he had the idea for would not have existed, and neither would our meeting.

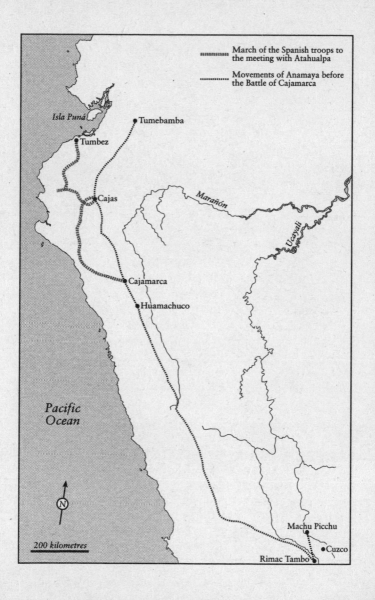

March of the Spanish troops to the meeting with Atahualpa

Movements of Anamaya before the Battle of Cajamarca

Isla Puná

Tumebamba

Tumbez

Cajas

Marañón

Ucayali

Cajamarca

Huamachuco

Pacific Ocean

Machu Picchu

Cuzco

Rimac Tambo

N

200 kilometres

PART 1

CHAPTER 1

Near Pocona, Bolivia, December 1526

CUDDLED AGAINST HER MOTHER, ANAMAYA AWOKE abruptly and listened to the rain falling on the roof of the hut.

It was still dark in the deep impenetrable night of the jungle. The rain fell heavily. It was deafening. She could hear nothing else, not the creaks of the roof beams, nor the cries of the monkeys and other beasts that normally haunted the forest.

Rolling over on the reed bed she reached for her mother's hand. Why couldn't she sleep?

If she opened her eyes, the shadows transformed the beams into snakes, and the earthenware jars into scowling monsters. If she closed her eyelids, the clamor of the rain became unbearable. The raindrops seemed to burst right through the thick palm thatched roof and strike her chest.

She was scared without reason. Her heart was troubled by a violent and incomprehensible sorrow. Trembling, she drew her knees up to her chest. Nestled close against her mother's belly, she sobbed silently.

And then, without even realizing, she fell asleep.

*   *   *

At dawn, Anamaya had forgotten her troubled night. Leaping from her bed she slipped between the hammocks and stepped silently into the deserted courtyard.

The place where she lived was a tiny village surrounded by the vastness of the jungle. A high wall built of wooden poles, their ends sharpened into spikes, enclosed and protected the four large communal huts that marked the boundaries of the central courtyard. It was empty in the early-morning hour. The rain had stopped, but the air hung still, hot and muggy. The sky, a uniform gray, was reflected in the puddles glistening among the tall grass.

Anamaya crushed a mosquito on her arm. The insects zigzagged in battalions through the humid air, like tiny furtive clouds.

She skipped a few steps to reach the wall of spikes, and joined the guard keeping watch at the entrance. Like all the *Chiriguanos* – 'those-who-fear-the-cold' – the young warrior was naked except for a woven loincloth around his waist. His chin and cheeks were painted in black and green arabesques and his forehead was shaved to the crown of his perfectly curved head. His skin was as ochre and as glowing as the muddy earth in the village, contrasting with the shine of the long turquoise necklace that hung down his chest.

Dozing, he woke with a start when Anamaya splashed a puddle. Instinctively, he grabbed for his spear. Then, upon seeing her he laughed.

'What are you doing out here at this hour, big mosquito?'

'I've come to help you guard the village,' replied Anamaya in a serious tone.

The warrior stopped laughing and nodded his head gravely.

'Good idea! If the Incas realize that you're with me, they will never dare attack us!'

'That's for sure! So, will you let me pass?'

The young warrior laughed brightly again and patted her

lightly on the nape. 'Go, mosquito. But not too far, or your mother will dunk my head in her jar of evil spells!' he joked, and loosened the liana creeper that held the reed gate shut.

Anamaya stole through the narrow opening and ran into the dense forest.

Ignoring the thorns that snatched at her loincloth, she bounded into a clearing, her bare feet flying through the multicolored flowers.

Arriving at the big pond, she dove in without hesitation, her arms outstretched, her young body as fluid and supple as the water itself. For a long moment, she reveled in the pleasure of bathing. Then, reaching for the low-hanging branch of a Cyssus tree, she grabbed hold and hung for a moment before hauling herself up in a single monkey-like swing. Down below, her reflection scattered and merged in the subsiding ripples – the reflection of a girl tall for her ten years. She wished she looked more like the other girls in the village. She was paler and had a flat forehead. Even her mouth was different: narrower, her lips well defined but thin. What she hated most, even more than her willful, almost pointy chin that added an atypical length to her face, was her long nose, much more delicate than those of the little *Chiriguanas* in the village. But, above all, there were her eyes.

Closing her eyelids, she slapped the water with her foot, erasing her reflection.

Why was she made differently from the others? She had heard the rumors whispered in the village, but her mother never spoke of these things.

Her mother . . . Anamaya had a sudden aching urge to see her, to touch her.

She hollered her name, laughing, and, while her cry echoed through the emerald jungle, she jumped down from the Cyssus tree. She ran towards the village as fast as her legs would carry her, her heart pounding with long-ing.

Mid-morning, the clouds scattered, and sunlight slipped through over the forest and reached the huts. When it touched Anamaya's shoulders she burst into laughter.

She danced, her arms outspread. Her heavy black hair bouncing in rhythm, she offered her body to the sun and the rain.

'Anamaya!' her mother called.

Of all the villagers, she was the only one wearing clothes, a long woven gown reaching down to her knees. Its colors were faded; the checkered design of carefully arranged crosses and diamonds was barely discernible. Rips in the cloth had been mended with agave fiber.

'The sun!' shouted the child, spinning in its warmth, 'Come on, Mummy!'

Anamaya ran to her mother. She grabbed her hand and tried to drag her along. Her mother resisted at first but, with a smile, surrendered to the child's obvious joy.

Together they danced. Mud squelched between their toes and spattered them while they yelled out loud in high-pitched tones. Suddenly, Anamaya slipped. Her mother lifted her by the arm and held her close. They almost fell, wrapped together. Their laughter subsided and they recovered their balance.

'C'mon, Mummy, again!' murmured Anamaya against her mother's neck; her mother looked into her eyes tenderly.

'Have you forgotten our promise?' she whispered, attempting to sound stern.

Anamaya frowned. No, she hadn't forgotten.

'Do we really have to help the old witch?'

'Anamaya! She's not an old witch, she's the Spirit Mother.'

'So what? I still don't like her.'

Her mother smiled as she led her along. Hand in hand, they circled around one of the great communal huts and crossed the central courtyard. Now the sun reflected in the puddles while a fine, steady rain sprinkled down.

It was so hot that layers of fog, supple and transparent, rose from the jungle, splitting into streams around the spikes of the village wall.

At the corner of a hut, near a little fire, holding a long flat spoon of iroko wood, an old woman stirred a thick green liquid in a wide-necked pot. Anamaya couldn't help but scowl.

'I've brought the cloth, Spirit Mother.'

Skeptically, the sorceress examined the patch of silk. It was so worn that it was almost translucent, and its pink lacing had faded to white.

'It'll do, I suppose,' she grumbled.

Anamaya lifted herself onto the balls of her feet to see what was in the pot.

'How do you know there are spirits in there?' she asked the old woman.

'Because I put them there, little twit.'

'I'm not a twit! I don't see anything—'

'Quiet, Anamaya,' commanded her mother, without conviction.

'How come you see them and I don't?' insisted Anamaya.

'Because I have the gift and you don't!' The old woman was annoyed. 'Now, be quiet. Obey your mother, child. We shall now proceed . . .'

Anamaya sighed. They stretched the fabric across the mouth of a smoke-blackened jug. The old woman slowly filtered the liquid through the silk. A green residue gathered on its surface. It smelt strong, like the deepest part of the jungle where the sun never reaches.

Anamaya watched for the spirits, but heard only the liquid dripping to the bottom of the jug, a diminishing trickle.

The child would have liked to ask another question but didn't dare. Suddenly she felt a coolness on her burnt shoulders. She looked up to a shadow in the sky. The girl let go of her corner of the silk filter.

The green dregs fell into the container. The old woman uttered a harsh cry.

'Anamaya!' yapped her mother. 'What are you doing?'

'Look, Mummy! Look at the bird!'

It was enormous, almost as big as a hut, and was flying so low that it looked like it was about to land. They heard its shiny black wings flapping through the air. It turned its long, down-covered neck to point its menacing beak at them before rising up with a single stroke of its wings.

'Mummy, look how beautiful it is!'

In the courtyard, the naked children stopped playing. The adults stood still. The shaven foreheads of the men were lined with worry. Even the old emerged from the communal huts and raised their gaze to the sky, shielding their eyes from the sun and rain with their hands.

At the ends of its wings, spread like fingers, the bird's long white feathers quivered. It looped back over the villagers, and they saw its huge claws, larger than a man's hand. Anamaya sensed the bird's stony glare. For an instant, its round beady eyes looked straight into hers. She became oblivious to everything around her. The child heard only an increasingly violent sound, like a din in the dark night, a trampling, as if hundreds of men were running together. She wanted to scream but felt her mother's hand rest gently on her shoulder – a hand that wanted to reassure her, but that was trembling.

'The condor,' said her mother, closing her fingers tighter.

'The harbinger of the Incas,' added the Spirit Mother.

Anamaya held her mother tight and whispered:

'The condor . . . but the condor doesn't live here – he never comes down from the mountains to the lowlands . . .'

Anamaya looked at her mother. She saw her face pale with fear.

'Mummy!' she cried. 'Mummy! What's wrong?'

The creature rose in the sky. Turning to the east, it climbed even higher, above the clouds of fog, then pivoted suddenly, as if to dive on the village, before continuing to climb and climb. The clouds parted for it: the great bird flew through the gap towards the western hillsides, and the blue sky appeared.

Anamaya shivered, her words remaining stuck in her throat as if a thousand screams were suddenly echoing through her.

In the village courtyard, all eyes still looked to the sky, and everyone was still. Nothing moved. Even the jungle fell silent.

And then the blare of a howling trumpet cut through the air.

'The Incas! The Incas!'

The guard had jumped over the village wall and was running like a madman.

'The Incas! The Incas are here!'

The instant his shriek left his pierced lips he crumpled to the ground. His turquoise necklace broke and the little blue beads spilled to the ground and drowned in the mud. Dark blood flowed from his temple and mixed with the black and green paint on his cheeks. The sling stone had buried itself in his skull.

Anamaya felt a shudder run through her mother's body. The trumpet roared continuously like a savage animal, and the vibrations of loudly beating drums shook the jungle. Screams shredded the air. The village men rushed to their huts for their weapons. Others were already at the wall, their bows in their hands, double-stemmed arrows sticking out of their quivers. The uproar was horrendous.

Anamaya pressed her cheek against her mother's stomach; her mother caressed her hair feverishly to reassure her, stroked her cheeks, her hands.

The condor had disappeared into the mountains. Clouds shut out the sky. The *Chiriguano* warriors crouched at the foot of the village wall. For an instant everything was frozen.

And then, suddenly, it was as if the whole world had begun to ring. Anamaya saw the sky ablaze with projectiles, darts and sling stones, like an immense black cloud of insects. Hundreds of arrows flew and slammed into the courtyard.

'Mummy!' she screamed again.

The mother gathered her child to her breast. They shut their eyes as darts pierced the warriors' flesh and the mud with equal ease. Blood darkened the puddles and grown men were crying like children.

The old woman's jug of green lees lay overturned.

Anamaya's mother sang softly to reassure her cowering little daughter, to tell her that Mummy was there, that it was all right, that she mustn't be scared. But Anamaya didn't hear.

When she reopened her eyes, she saw the courtyard strewn with a rainbow of colors. On the bodies of the fallen warriors, the dazzling shafts seemed like flowers grown from magic seeds.

'Come,' gasped her mother.

She dragged her child by the hand into the field of arrows at the same moment as the invaders breached the village wall. Men in multicolored helmets swarmed over its useless spikes. The slingshots whirled, the leather strips of the *ayllos* whistled through the air. Overwhelmed by the superior numbers and weapons of their enemies, the *Chiriguano* warriors fell, their short clubs worthless.

'Quickly! Quickly!' cried her mother.

They ran straight ahead, ignoring the darts on the ground

that lacerated their feet. The sling stones whistled past their ears and they ran as fast as a puma's prey. An old man with black teeth opened his mouth to say something to them, but a stone struck his chest. He fell backwards, gasping.

'Quickly, Anama—'

Anamaya felt the impact in her hand. The blow shook her arm. She stumbled roughly in front of her mother, fell and then dragged herself to her knees.

'Mummy! C'mon! Please get up!'

Her mother didn't move. Anamaya wouldn't look at her face. She found her mother's hand, so warm and reassuring. It had held hers safely only a moment before – already so long ago. She tugged at that hand. Her mother's body barely slid along the muddy ground.

'Mummy! Hurry up! They're coming . . .'

She could sense the soldiers in their bright tunics approaching behind her back. In the background, the child could hear wailing – and laughter.

Finally she brought herself to look at her mother's face.

A red petal of blood lay in the center of her mother's forehead. The woman's eyes were closed and a brown liquid trickled from between her lips.

Anamaya knew.

She looked at the silk rag still clutched in her mother's grasp, still damp from the Spirit Mother's green liquid. The girl prized open the dead clenched fingers and took the fabric. She didn't hear the laughing conquerors, or the moaning of the dying, or the crying of an orphaned baby, abandoned in its hammock. She didn't see the last of the warriors fall, or the flames engulf the village wall and its huts. She heard only silence, as if each door in her heart had closed, one after the other.

Surrounded by the raging fire, the child fell forward softly and lay on her mother's stomach.

She was breathless, lifeless; Anamaya felt nothing but

bottomless grief as the warmth of her mother's body ebbed from beneath her.

That was when the soldier found her.

When he tried to lead her away, Anamaya resisted silently, straining to remain where she was.

He had to loosen the grip of her fingers, her entire body pressed against her mother's, trying to force life back into it.

At last, he succeeded in separating her, and dragged her away through the mud and dust, her body limp and lifeless.

The Inca officer held a *chuqui* in his right hand, a spear with a bronze tip and a hardwood staff adorned with condor feathers. A leather breastplate protected his chest. He still had his headpiece on, a finely woven rush helmet with a red and yellow plume.

An acrid smoke tinted the air. Anamaya kept her eyes lowered obstinately, her fingers clutching the silk rag. She sensed the tall, thin figure of the Inca approaching her.

'Have we finally destroyed those damned *Chiriguanos*?' he asked the soldier who had captured Anamaya.

'Yes, Captain Sikinchara, except for a few who managed to escape into the jungle.'

'Good.'

He turned to look at Anamaya. Her face and body were covered in dirt.

'And her? Who is she?'

'I don't know, Captain Sikinchara. She was near a dead woman. I brought her to you because—'

'Look at me, child,' interrupted the officer.

Anamaya didn't move. Her fingers tightened around the silk. The soldier was about to grab her when Sikinchara stopped him with a quick order.

'Look at me, little one,' he said, an unexpected gentleness in his tone.

She remained motionless. Sikinchara handed his spear and helmet to the soldier, and approached her. He knelt down and took her chin in his long fingers. He tilted her face towards his. His intelligent gaze caught the light of her blue eyes.

The Inca officer almost fell over backwards in amazement.

Anamaya saw the face of a man with a proud long nose, and well-defined thin lips.

She saw his surprise.

And his fear.

CHAPTER 2

Quito, October 1527

THAT MORNING, AMANAYA WOKE WITH A START IN the great dormitory.

Most of the girls had already risen from their straw mats, but one face remained, looking down on her curiously, with knit eyebrows and a smirk. It was a young girl with the high cheekbones and hard black eyes of a Cuzco princess. Her name was Inti Palla. She was older than Anamaya, and didn't mind showing that her body was already that of a woman.

But above all, Inti Palla was a daughter of Emperor Huayna Capac, Unifier of the Four Cardinal Directions.

How many children did he have? As many as there were plates of silver and gold in his temples. Two or three hundred; no one knew for sure.

Their eyes met, and Inti Palla's smirk grew into a quizzical smile.

'Anamaya,' she chuckled, 'why are you so ugly?'

Since Anamaya's arrival at the Temple of Virgins in Quito – the Emperor's northern city – Inti Palla had often spent time with her and seemed to revel in goading her. Anamaya had tried to teach herself to ignore the hurtful words.

'I know what's going to happen to you today, Anamaya!'

Anamaya stretched her limbs in feigned indifference. Inti Palla jangled the bracelets on her wrist.

'Don't you want to know?'

'Of course I do.'

'Well, I'll tell you later.'

Typical! Anamaya stifled an angry mumble but the princess, undeceived by her restraint, continued to taunt her.

'C'mon, tell me, why are you so ugly?'

This time Anamaya sat up and pushed her angrily away.

'I don't know! I don't know anything! But I'm sure *you* do – you know everything, don't you!'

Inti Palla's laughter crackled like a pile of seashells.

'My poor, hopeless friend! You've been here almost four seasons and you still won't admit that you'll never be like us!'

Anamaya turned away, carefully folding her woven blanket to mask her hurt. If there was one thing that she had to admit it was that. Not only was she not a blue-blooded princess, but her body was developing differently from those of the young Inca girls. Her legs and thighs had begun to stretch, growing long and thin instead of thick and plump. Her face also, lengthening rather than widening, her forehead refusing to bulge, her lips stubbornly thin, her eyebrows wispy. But most of all, her eyes . . .

They were almost as wide as the other girls', but sapphire blue – the same color as the sky seen reflected in a mountain lake on a clear afternoon.

Hers was a mineral stare, one that repulsed the gaze and invited derision but actually mostly inspired fear. Anamaya's eyes forbade affection and hindered friendship – during the last year spent in the *acllahuasi* no girl had really dared to become her friend. Even the matrons addressed her as if she were barely human. Only Inti Palla braved the taboo that surrounded her like a contagion – but only the more easily to mock her.

With tears in her eyes Anamaya hugged her blanket to her chest:

'If I'm so ugly, why do you hang around me all the time?'

The young princess smiled, revealing fanglike teeth.

'Because you're weird to look at!'

'Well, you've got all the time in the world to stare at me later – now leave me alone . . .'

To prevent Anamaya from leaving the room Inti Palla jingled her bracelets again and switched to a soft honeyed tone:

'Anamaya, I'll tell you what's going to happen to you today . . .'

'Tell me or don't tell me, I don't care!'

'Today is an important day for you. Today, my father, the Emperor Huayna Capac, will inspect you . . .'

Anamaya froze and held her breath. She had been expecting this, but somehow it still took her by surprise . . .

She turned and looked directly at Inti Palla, and saw in her eye a hateful joy.

'Today, he will decide how you are to die.'

The previous night Anamaya had dreamed of the village in the forest, as she did whenever the moon was new. She could feel her mother's hand holding hers and could hear echoing screams. A breath of fire set her chest ablaze. The instant her mother fell she was overwhelmed by a terrifying feeling – a fusion of shock and unbearable pain. She thought she saw words form on her mother's lips – words from behind the veil of death – but she could not hear them. The girl woke in tears, overwhelmed by loneliness, her arms seeking out an absent mother. As the gray dawn peeled the darkness from the tapestries on the wall, she steadied her breathing. Anamaya closed her eyes to banish fear and death. Her mother's gentle voice was so close . . .

But no one must see her grief: she must bury it deep within herself.

Whispers rustled through the Temple of the Virgins. As they washed her hair and then combed it into fine plaits, the matrons shot Anamaya reproachful glances. Anamaya remembered Inti Pallas's cruel words and a dread rose in the pit of her stomach: If the Emperor decided that she must die without the right of entry to the Other World, she knew that they would feed her to the puma.

Her hair finished, the matrons swathed her in an ankle-length silk wrap. They tightened a plain red belt roughly around her waist and laid a *lliclla*, a long purple cape, lined with a white collar and fastened with a single cedar wood pin, on her shoulders. Finally they handed her a pair of brand new straw sandals that Anamaya had trouble fitting.

The matrons stepped back to scrutinize her.

Their repugnance was visible. Clearly, they felt that her fine new clothes had not lessened her ugliness. They didn't look her in the eyes.

She waited for a long time in a dark, tiny room.

Her fear had plenty of time to grow.

The sun was at its zenith when Anamaya was finally led from the Temple of the Virgins. Two soldiers were waiting for her. It was the first time in many moons that she had left the *acllahuasi*.

The soldiers led her silently through narrow lanes flanked by high walls to the Great Square of the Palace. They met no one along the way, and Anamaya wondered if people had deserted the streets because of her.

From the Great Square they made their way to a narrow entrance, a door crowned by a stone carving of the Snake of Eternal Life. The soldiers knocked with their spears and stood to attention as Anamaya held her breath.

Anamaya instantly recognized the splendidly dressed officer who emerged at the threshold. She even remembered his name – Sikinchara. She would never forget his face – he had been the one in command of the men who had murdered her mother.

This time, he looked at her without fear or surprise. He appeared handsome and commanding. A solid gold breastplate covered his chest, and a headpiece of yellow wool topped by two large green feathers covered his head and emphasized his strong manly features. Large silver orbs covered his ears, held in place by finger-sized silver tubes pierced right through his stretched earlobes. The jewels swayed and sparkled as he moved, producing a kaleidoscopic effect.

Silently, he motioned Anamaya to come forward. When she didn't move one of the soldiers encouraged her with a jab from his spear. And so she joined Sikinchara in entering the Palace. He bid her with a look to follow him quietly.

They crossed an inner court edged by long, low walls. White orchids, purple *cantutas* and pink azaleas bloomed in splendid rectangular thickets along both sides of the paved walkway, but Anamaya scarcely noticed the flowers.

They passed under a matted roof and followed a wall; magnificent objects of gold and painted wood glittered from alcoves carved into its enormous smooth stones. Finally they reached a narrow door set in a perfectly hewn stone frame. Anamaya barely had time to glimpse another court, this one much bigger and with a colossal basin at its center, when she heard Sikinchara order her in his dry voice:

'Prostrate yourself, child, and grovel before your great Lord!'

She fell to her knees and bent towards the ground, watching from the corner of her eye as Sikinchara went through the door. She followed him as best she could, scraping her palms and knees on flagstones burnt by the sun's heat.

It was almost better this way, she thought, for now that she felt the gaze of the Sun King, she felt as if she had already begun dying.

Anamaya heard noises, low voices whose words she could not make out. Suddenly, a cane struck her shoulder. She froze. She heard Sikinchara's voice again as he announced:

'My lord, here is the girl I told you about.'

No reply. Only the sound of splashing water. Finally, a weary, remote voice:

'I'm tired of bathing. Give me my clothes.'

Anamaya saw the skirt hems of a dozen scurrying women, their fabrics patterned with beautiful dazzling colors. She knew what was happening. She'd had it explained to her enough times at the Temple of the Virgins. The servant girls were to give the Emperor new clothes that no one had ever touched since their making. The Sun King personally selected a maiden to help him into his vicuña-pelt tunic, another to fasten his sash, a third to place his cape. Finally he chose the young girl who had the honor of placing a crown upon his royal head . . .

Anamaya squeezed her eyes shut and fought to recover her breath. Her heart beat so loudly that she barely heard the feeble voice say:

'Captain Sikinchara, raise up that girl.'

She felt him hit her in the back and say in his deep voice:

'Rise before your Great Lord!'

Anamaya struggled to stand, as if she was carrying a massive weight upon her shoulders. Once upright, she kept her gaze down towards the flagstones, but the Great Lord ordered:

'Raise your eyes to mine, child.'

She looked at him.

Him, the Emperor Huayna Capac, the Inca of all the Incas, the Sun King and the Unifier of the Four Cardinal Directions!

He was an old man, an ancient man . . .

Despite the extraordinary beauty of his clothes, despite the gold bracelets that adorned his wrists, despite the cape of multicolored feathers around his neck and the huge gold orbs that distended his earlobes, despite his breastplate of seashells, he appeared as fragile as a man built of bird bones. His stretched cheeks shone like the glaze of old pottery, his hands so wrinkled they seemed to belong to another body.

From his elevated throne of cushions, he looked Anamaya straight in the eye. He appeared neither astonished nor fearful.

A high-pitched and peremptory voice abruptly snapped:

'My lord! You see her eyes! No Inca woman, ever, has had blue eyes!'

'Silence, Villa Oma, and let me look at her.'

Anamaya couldn't see the owner of that voice. It came from a man on her right, a good distance from the Great Lord. He too wore the ear baubles reserved for Inca blue-bloods; the green juice of the coca leaves he chewed dribbled from his thin lips.

Without removing his gaze from Anamaya, Huayna Capac asked:

'She's from the forest, then, Sikinchara?'

'Yes, my Lord. We destroyed a village of *Chiriguano* savages. She was found near her mother.'

'Where is the mother?'

'Dead, my Lord. Killed by a sling stone during the attack. We could tell it was her by her Inca tunic.'

'A Cuzco woman, then?'

'Most likely, my Lord.'

'An impure child,' bleated Villa Oma.

'And the father?' continued the Emperor.

Villa Oma pursed his thin green-tinted lips in disgust. Huayna Capac turned to look at Sikinchara.

'What information do you have?'

The captain remained silent and lowered his head. The Emperor looked again at Anamaya, and she saw the distress in his eyes. His lips were trembling and he suddenly grabbed the armrests of his throne to steady himself. Pearls of sweat glistened on his forehead.

Anamaya felt the fear of death twist anew in her stomach; but the sight of this old man's suffering inspired within her another ill-defined feeling, as if she felt his suffering with him, or suffered for him.

For a moment the Emperor shuddered, and his eyelids trembled. But he stiffened his back to control himself. In a subdued voice he asked:

'Villa Oma, what do the soothsayers say of her?'

Green Mouth waved contemptuously and growled:

'She's ill-omened, my Lord. She has hideous blue eyes, and is misshapen, as you can see. She's thinner and taller than our own girls. She may have Inca blood through her mother, but she's impure! She's from the Under World and must be returned there!'

'Another omen,' murmured the Emperor listlessly.

He looked at Anamaya quietly. Curiously, she sensed a benevolence in his gaze.

Almost unwillingly, Villa Oma continued:

'But not all the soothsayers are in agreement, my Lord . . .'

'What say the others?'

'That she augurs well for your reign, my Lord, and has been sent by Quilla, our Moon Goddess, and that her blue eyes are Quilla's promise of your passage to heaven.'

The Emperor's breathing became faster. Despite his effort to mask his suffering, Anamaya was not deceived.

She realized he was dying and in her mind's eye she saw the Sun King lying still and lifeless. Soon the Emperor would join his father in the invisible Other World.

She had trouble holding back her tears.

The Emperor held his gaze upon her:

'What is she called?'

'Anamaya.'

Sikinchara had barely answered when the Emperor doubled over, coughing. Anamaya perceived the fright that startled the captain. But after a moment the Unifier of the Four Cardinal Directions recovered himself, and spoke in a barely audible voice:

'What is your opinion, Villa Oma?'

'She must be thrown back into the Under World, my Lord, and quickly. We should offer her to the puma, so that he is fed and she disappears. She must not curse you any longer, my Lord. Not in this world or the next. Our god Inti does not approve of her.'

'And what if she is Quilla's messenger?'

'Well, then, we could offer the Moon Goddess her heart, but—'

Villa Oma never finished his sentence. The Emperor uttered a cry and doubled over in pain, vomiting bile onto the armrests of his throne. His agony was so unbearable that he fell off his seat onto his knees. Everybody around him, whether noblemen or servant girls, froze in terror.

The law allowed no one to touch the Sun King.

Sikinchara grabbed Anamaya by her shoulders to draw her away. But the Emperor, his features distorted by pain, looked at her and cried:

'Help me, child, quickly, help me!'

Then, suddenly, there were no more noblemen or servants, no more laws, no more taboos – and she was no longer fearful of death. At last she could allow her tears to flow.

CHAPTER 3

Quito, December 1527

THE ROOM WAS DARK AND BLEAK, DESPITE THE gold glimmering from the walls. Smoke rose from the coca leaves burning in the fire-pan.

For three days, the Emperor had lain under blankets of vicuña and llama wool. He had slept fitfully. The rest of the time, during the long, silent vigils, his eyes searched the shadows for answers to the questions that haunted him.

How would the Sun God receive him in the next world if he died without naming a successor?

What would happen to the Empire that he, Huayna Capac, had built up from its beginnings at Cuzco – now so vast that one needed many, many moons to cross it?

What was the meaning of the strange omens that had appeared in the sky and the mountains over the past season?

Was it the wrath of Inti, the Sun God? Or the fear of Quilla, the Moon Goddess?

This litany of questions succeeded one another in his febrile mind, until, exhausted, he succumbed to feverish sleep. Pain filled his head and penetrated into his bones; an unbearable pain that an Emperor should have been spared.

He dreamed of the extraordinary blue irises of the girl

captured in the southern lowlands; blue like the water of Titicaca, the sacred lake as old as time; a blue that soothed his soul each time he looked at them.

The Emperor heard trumpets sound at the Palace entrance, then footsteps and voices echoing from the courtyard. But only one man appeared at the doorway, instantly dropping to his knees and lowering his head. A stone as big as a child was placed on his shoulders; thus encumbered he approached the Emperor on his sick bed.

The Sun King sat up with a groan. His voice was weakened by fever:

'Atahualpa? Is it you, my son?'

From a sunless corner Villa Oma spoke:

'Yes, my Lord, it's him.'

'Stand up!'

The Emperor fell back, exhausted. Once a servant had removed the stone, Atahualpa stood upright.

A royal headpiece girdled his perfect head, and he wore the tunic and cape decorated with the motif of the governing clan. An aquiline nose sat at the center of his symmetrical face. The whites of his eyes were flecked with a web of red blood vessels, eyes so bloodshot they seemed to be reining in a bursting fury, but his expression remained inscrutable. His powerful good looks, notwithstanding his disfigured right ear, deeply impressed everyone he met.

But today he was the one affected by a face. He looked at his old father, the Emperor, the Inca of all the Incas, dying.

Huayna Capac was in a worse condition than his son had imagined. His eyes were glazed like those of someone who had abused the coca leaf. He had aged monstrously since his son had last seen him. Atahualpa almost stepped back in shock; suddenly he was uncertain whether he should break the bad news to his father. The Emperor noticed his son's misgivings:

'I can bear it, Atahualpa my son. Tell me what you know.'

Atahualpa glanced at Villa Oma, who nodded his assent.

'My Lord,' said Atahualpa cautiously, 'I have bad news.'

Huayna Capac motioned with his hand to continue.

'Some traders on the coast have told of a strange encounter. Some . . . strange-looking beings arrived from the ocean on a floating wooden mountain . . .'

Huayna Capac scrutinized his son through fevered eyes:

'Were they many?'

'No more than ten or twenty. They left after kidnapping some sailors and stealing a shipment of balsa wood out of Tumbes.'

'Were they human?'

'We're not sure, my Lord. Some had torsos made of silver, others were completely covered with hair, even on their faces. They walked upright like us, but they stank horribly and spoke a strange language.'

'When did this take place?'

'Not three seasons ago.'

'And they left immediately?'

'Yes, my Lord, on the floating mountain on which they had come.'

Villa Oma stepped forward, interrupting:

'They could have been Viracochas. Have you thought of that?'

'What do you mean?' replied Atahualpa harshly.

'Viracocha, Father of our world, came out of Lake Titicaca to bring life to the mountains and plains. Viracocha the Almighty, who caused Inti to bring us light and Quilla to guard the night—'

'Villa Oma, you talk too much! I know who Viracocha is.'

'Well then, you will know that once he had completed

his task he disappeared into the ocean and went to rest on the western horizon; and that he promised to return to us one day—'

'And you think that he's returned to us,' Atahualpa interrupted angrily, 'on a floating mountain, disguised as a bunch of stinking men, covered in hair and tarnished silver?'

Villa Oma returned Atahualpa's angry look, then turned towards Huayna Capac.

'It is not impossible, my Lord. Viracocha can take any form he chooses. He can be one or many, human or animal, mountain or forest. He is omnipotent.'

Huayna Capac's eyes were closed, his breath so loud and labored that his voice was barely audible:

'Do you not believe that they were Viracocha returning to us, my son?'

Atahualpa shrugged his shoulders:

'I don't know, my Lord. But I think it's too early to tell. We know that impure humans can look strange. During the wars, you yourself saw all kinds in the forests and in the southern mountains. And why would Viracocha return to us now? Our Empire is great and powerful. We have order, the rule of law . . .'

'But I'm dying,' whispered the Emperor, 'soon to join Inti. And I haven't named the one who will wear the royal *borla* after me.'

A heavy silence followed.

The sick old man propped himself up on a shoulder and continued in a stronger voice:

'Why do you refuse, Atahualpa, my boy? You know that you are closer to my heart than any of my other sons. You know that you are the wisest and most capable. Why do you sadden me so as I leave for the Other World?'

'My Lord, my father, we both know the answer to that question. The Cuzco clans will never accept me. You may be my father, but my mother is from a minor clan. If I were to wear the crown, they would wreak havoc, and the peace and order of the Empire would fall apart! I cannot allow that.'

'My Lord!' cried Villa Oma, 'you must decide! You cannot leave for the Other World without naming a successor! You will offend the gods, and your offence will rebound onto us all!'

'Villa Oma!' yelled Atahualpa. 'Recollect yourself!'

'But we face disaster! Have you forgotten the omens, Atahualpa? The other night the moon split into three circles over the palace. The first was blood red. The second was both black and green. And the last was smoke!'

Huayna Capac collapsed onto his sickbed, exhausted. He breathed with great difficulty, but Atahualpa barely noticed. He said to the Sage angrily:

'And what was Quilla's message then?'

'The first circle told that once the Emperor is at Inti's side, his clan's blood will flow in rivers. The second predicts massacres and wars that will dig an abyss between the North and South of the Empire. The third circle was only smoke, because once we commit these sins the wrath of Inti and Quilla will be so great that we will be reduced to smoke, utterly destroyed! That is her message, my noble Lord!'

'Bah!' cried Atahualpa furiously. 'Feeble-minded stupidities! Villa Oma, I thought you were smarter than that. You listen too closely to foolish soothsayers who can't hold their tongues. It's all just idle talk. You know full well that they all contradict each other!'

'Who is the fool?' asked Villa Oma, squinting. 'He who looks for the omens to better understand? Or he who sticks his head in the sand and refuses to see?'

'Wise is the man who knows when to hold his tongue, my dear Villa Oma!'

'Atahualpa! Atahualpa!' whispered Huayna Capac, lifting a trembling hand. 'My son, Atahualpa, don't be angry! I like your quick mind, and your strength. But maybe Villa Oma is right. He has always advised me well. I want you to listen to him after I'm gone . . .'

The old man shuddered as a new wave of pain seared through his chest. He spoke with great effort:

'Quilla, my mother . . . she has sent me another sign – Villa Oma, bring me the blue-eyed girl!'

Another dawn rose on the Temple of the Virgins. Inti Palla slipped noiselessly under the wall hanging, startling Anamaya. The anguish of the past few days remained with her. Inti Palla crouched beside her and smiled conspiratorially.

'Here!' she murmured. 'Take this, it's for you . . .'

The princess then astonished Anamaya by handing her a magnificent solid gold bracelet, consisting of two intertwined serpents so lifelike that they seemed to cling to her arm.

'Take it!' insisted Inti Palla, it's for you.'

'It's so beautiful . . .'

Inti Palla slipped the bracelet gracefully onto Anamaya's wrist.

'Never lose it, Sister. It will always protect you.'

Sister? Anamaya was not sure whether to take these words seriously. Could this be the same Inti Palla who had cheerfully announced that she was to die?

But she had a forgiving nature. Timidly, she leaned against Inti Palla and whispered:

'Thank you.'

Inti Palla opened her arms and held her close. Anamaya felt the heat of that strange embrace, and the beat of Inti Palla's young heart. She thought, *It's been over a year since anyone's hugged me, since anyone's stroked me*. Despite herself, she held Inti Palla tight, and felt a lump in her throat. She wondered if it meant anything when they shivered together, as if one.

Inti Palla broke the embrace first. She looked straight into the blue of Anamaya's eyes and said solemnly:

'Don't ever forget that I'm your friend.'

Anamaya's eyes shone with appreciation, yet she was still not sure whether to believe her.

'Hurry up,' added Inti Palla, getting up. 'Captain Sikinchara has come to fetch you. The Emperor has asked for you again.'

The old fear returned, but this time Anamaya felt something more: a sort of excited curiosity, a feeling that something important was about to happen.

Even a sense of pride.

Before prostrating herself at the entrance of the darkened room, Anamaya had just enough time to glimpse a strange tiny figure draped in red. It was a man with a body smaller than a child's. His powerful hands gripped the edge of the Emperor's sickbed. His piercing eyes fixed upon hers. His countenance bore an expression of quiet desperation.

Sikinchara prompted her forward. The air in the room soon irritated her throat and eyes – burning coca leaves mixed with the smell of disease. She sensed others lurking in the shadows, but did not see them, although she recognized the tunic of the green-mouthed Sage.

She crawled to the sickbed on her hands and knees. The dwarf stepped back to make room for her, but remained close to the Emperor. She sensed the closeness of his deformed body, but didn't mind it. Then the Emperor called her, his voice as dry as firewood:

'Sit up, my child, and look at me.'

Sitting up, what she saw made her nauseous.

The Emperor's face seemed to be rotting. A foul rash covered his forehead and temples, and the same blemish stained his violently trembling hands. He murmured:

'Atahualpa, see her eyes . . .'

The young prince approached to look at her.

Anamaya restrained her instinct to jump back. She sensed the power of this man. He looked straight into her blue gaze and she was shocked by the blood vessels that so reddened his eyes. Despite this, she saw that he was remarkably handsome.

She didn't dare look at him for too long and so turned away. What she saw then sent a chill through her body and she fought back a scream. A pair of dark eyes set above a black snout shone at her from the Emperor's bed. She caught sight of a flash of gleaming fangs.

Anamaya realized with a shudder that the puma wasn't alive; it was only a pelt spread over the Emperor's feet. But its head was so lifelike that she felt the creature's eyes piercing her own.

Atahualpa asked:

'Who is she and where does she come from?'

'Villa Oma will explain it all to you,' whispered the Emperor. 'Come closer, child.'

Reluctantly, Anamaya edged closer to his sickbed. The foul odor constricted her throat. She wondered if witnessing his suffering was not harder than confronting wild beasts. The dwarf drew near, and she stiffened with fright. But when he whispered in her ear, 'Don't be afraid of him', she felt steadied by his simple reassurance. With immense effort, the Emperor reached for her with his trembling hand.

'Take my hand, child.'

She heard a bleat of surprise from behind her. Villa Oma carped:

'My Lord! Be careful!'

Anamaya didn't dare lift her hand to the Emperor's. Terrified, she stared at the outstretched, emaciated hand, blotched and putrid like a rotten vegetable. No one, except the Chosen Women, ever touched the Unifier of the Four Cardinal Directions!

But his feverish eyes continued to stare into hers. Huayna Capac ordered again:

'Take my hand, child!'

Her head spinning, she put her tiny pale fingers into the convulsing hand of the Inca of all the Incas.

His arm jerked uncontrollably as he held her, a death rattle. Then his eyes closed and his head fell back onto his sweat-soaked cushion.

Nobody dared speak.

Anamaya was trembling as much as the Emperor. She waited, listening to the anxious breathing of his entourage.

Eventually, a tiny grin, almost a smile, appeared on the Sun King's shriveled mouth. His eyelids fluttered and his gaze was as glazed as a drunk's. His hoarse voice crackled from his dry throat:

'She has the blue waters of Titicaca in her eyes, my son. The waters of heaven! O Quilla, thank you for having sent her to me. I see clearly now. I understand . . .'

'My Lord, my father . . .'

'Hush, Atahualpa. All is well. She was sent by the gods to accompany me to the threshold of heaven. Her eyes soothe me. Do you hear my voice, my son? It is softer already. My pain ebbs; Ah, thank you, Quilla!'

Anamaya stood unsteadily. She didn't understand what the Emperor meant, but she felt the tightness of his grip. She sensed that his pain was indeed ebbing, and she wanted to smile with him.

After a long silence, she heard sandals brushing on stone. She heard Villa Oma and the young prince Atahualpa leave the room. She remained by the Inca of all the Incas, her hand in his, with the dwarf squatting somewhere behind her.

'Is my eldest son still near?' asked the Emperor weakly. The dwarf spoke in a deep bass, like the echo from a giant:

'I am here, beloved father.'

'We must be left alone now, my son.'

Questions burned Anamaya's mind as she heard the dwarf shuffling away. Could the Sun King really have fathered such a grotesque being? And yet, she had detected a profound tenderness in their brief exchange.

The Sun King gripped her hand in both of his with an unexpected strength. Anamaya bit her lips. In a low voice he told her:

'Be patient, child, I've a long tale to tell you.'

Through that long night, the Emperor never let go of Anamaya's hand.

He talked and talked. He spoke in a low voice, hardly pausing, as if speech was all he had left.

He told her of the past, of the birth of the world, of the founding of Cuzco by the first Inca king, and of the subsequent conquest – carried out with infinite patience – of the mountains, the plains and the lakes by the Sun Kings.

He told how he himself, Huayna Capac, the twelfth in the line, had extended the Empire of the Four Cardinal Directions to the burning mountains of Quito in the North, and far beyond Lake Titicaca to the South, to the land of eternal ice and snow.

He told of his great battles and sieges, and of the peoples he had conquered.

He told of the power and the wisdom and the greatness of all the Sun Kings. His breathing grew ragged and his lips became dry because of the length of his epic tale.

He talked passionately of how the Moon Goddess had smiled upon him, and of the joy he felt to be joining Inti, the Sun God, at last.

But he admitted to being apprehensive at meeting his ancestors in the next world; they would surely upbraid him for imperiling the Empire's future by failing to name a successor.

He explained that he hoped to become a stone, like the Ancients, and to rest on a lush green hillside near Cuzco.

And finally he shared with her a great secret – he whispered the future to her. But he did not deliver his message with words. Instead, he passed it on directly through the ruins of his hands to her tender young palms.

And Anamaya was overcome by all that she'd learned. She couldn't listen any longer. She was unaware of all the nobles thronging in the great torchlit courtyard and pressing at the threshold of the room.

All were finely dressed. Their gold ear-jewelry shone through the night as if all the stars had congregated together. But they remained in absolute silence; only the murmurs of the dying Emperor could be heard, like the buzzing of a fly.

And throughout the night the Inca noblemen watched this unheard-of scene: a Sun King, lying on his deathbed, holding the hand of a kneeling, exhausted half-blooded girl. She, an impure child with eyes the color of the sacred lake, and not even a member of the lowliest clan. And he was telling her everything! All the secrets previously guarded only by Sun Kings! All the knowledge of the Ancients!

Many wanted to cry out against this heresy. And yet, no one dared.

As the sun returned to the horizon, Anamaya felt drained, as if her heart had been emptied. She had almost nodded off a hundred times. A hundred times she had scratched her thighs with her free hand to keep herself awake. A hundred times the puma's yellow eyes had bored into hers, and frightened away her drowsiness.

At dawn her body was as numb as a snow-covered statue.

Her spirit was blank, and the sentences the Emperor had spoken to her were erased from her consciousness.

Then, just as the last of the nobles still standing awake in the courtyard were falling asleep, their heads drooping with tiredness, the Emperor fell silent.

Anamaya shuddered, her neck stiff, her eyes open wide. She felt a burning sensation through her numb fingers. The Emperor had begun shivering again, and was breathing quickly. His old face appeared crumpled, as if his jawbone and skull were dissolving. His eyes, although as opaque as the night, burned with enough heat to melt gold, and his gaze seared into Anamaya's own blue orbs. She wasn't scared but, even so, she felt as if her heart had been torn open and filled with all the grief of the world. She saw in the old dying man's face her mother lying dead in the village. An agonizing cry came from deep inside her chest. Tears welled in her eyes.

Her anguished wail was heard even at the far side of the great courtyard, and terrified everyone in it.

But the Sun King gripped her hand one last time, so strongly that she fell forward onto the edge of his bed. He said to her:

'Anamaya, daughter of the sacred lake, child of Quilla: May you live a long life in this world; for I will remember you lovingly when I am seated besides Inti, the sun god, in the other world.'

And with these last words, he died.

A tremor ran through the crowd gathered in the court-yard.

Like a teardrop, Anamaya fell to the floor.

CHAPTER 4

'ARE YOU SUCH A BRAINLESS CHILD? DO YOU understand nothing I tell you? The Emperor himself talks to you throughout the night and his words slip through your mind like sand through fingers?'

The Sage, Villa Oma, had been grilling her with the same questions for hours. And for hours she had meekly given the same answer over and over:

'I don't know, Noble Lord, I didn't understand . . . he spoke and spoke, he spoke words I'd never before heard . . . I tried to understand . . . but the black puma was eyeing me and my mind went blank—'

'The puma looked at you so your mind went blank!'

There was so much bitter sarcasm in his sneering face that Anamaya had to look away.

'Calm down, Villa Oma,' interrupted Atahualpa dryly.

Villa Oma beat his gold breastplate with his clenched fist, as if this action would quell his rage, and stepped away furiously.

The air was stifling in the darkened room. It was small and bare except for a couch and a big empty pot. Villa Oma gathered his cape and turned to Anamaya and Atahualpa again, shaking his hand sadly.

'Most Virtuous Lord Atahualpa, my beloved brother by descent,' he began. 'I respect you greatly, but I don't think you've grasped the gravity of the situation. Already a moon has come and gone since your father rose to the Other World. He left without naming a successor. Perhaps, in his fevered agony, he confided his last wishes to this young girl. But a puma skin looked at her and so she can't remember!'

With this, Villa Oma threw Anamaya a look of disgust. She felt her knees give way in shame.

'And so,' continued the Sage acidly, 'the Empire is in darkness. No Inca can claim the imperial *borla* as his own. The Empire of the Four Cardinal Directions has no center. Inti has no son on Earth, and we've no Sun King. Do you not realize the peril we face? Atahualpa! My Lord Atahualpa, you could be crowned Emperor—'

'You know why I've forfeited the throne, Villa Oma. There's no point talking about it.'

'But your refusal forced Huayna Capac to make bad decisions at a time when he was so sick that he was already halfway to the Other World!'

'Villa Oma! Beware of what you say!'

'But isn't it the simple truth? Whom did he nominate in your place? His youngest child, less than a year old! A newborn! And the oracles foretell ill. All the soothsayers agree that it's an abominable decision. But alas, your father, consumed by fever, persisted—'

'You are harping on, Villa Oma. You are disrespectful, and in any case you have told me nothing that I don't know.'

'Well then, My Lord, allow me to tell you some news that arrived only this morning . . .'

'Go ahead.'

'The priests went to Tumebamba to crown the baby, the Emperor-elect. But when they arrived, they learned that the baby had died, like his father!'

The ensuing silence chilled them like a cold gust of wind.

Despite herself, Anamaya had been listening closely. She remained as still as possible. She could hear Atahualpa's slow breathing and the Sage grinding his teeth. Villa Oma said:

'What are we to do now, Atahualpa? You seem to know everything: tell me, what will happen to us now?'

'No doubt the powerful Cuzco clans will place the royal band on my brother Huascar's head,' admitted Atahualpa gravely. 'He was designated second in line—'

'No doubt! But the omens are as bad concerning him as they were concerning the newborn! And no matter how much the clans want him as leader, you know Huascar as well as I do, Atahualpa. He is unpredictable. For the moment he follows the wishes of his uncles and aunts in Cuzco, who crave power and who feel nothing but hate for the northern clans. No one can know how he will rule the Empire, but one thing is for sure: blood will flow. He is cruel and violent! And he will see us as his enemies. That is what to expect if he takes the throne. Is that what you want? I tell you: I fear the fury of our Lord Inti; I dread the tear of Quilla and Illapa's lightning! Atahualpa, only *you* can maintain order across the Empire!'

In a measured tone, Atahualpa replied:

'No. Huascar will wear the *borla*. That was the last wish of Huayna Capac, my father.'

Enraged, Villa Oma stamped his foot so violently that Anamaya jumped. The Sage pointed a finger at her like a spear blade. His green teeth and lips, stained by coca leaves, appeared black in the shadows of the room, and his words seemed to come out of a terrible black hole:

'How do you know? His last words were to this little girl! He spoke to her for an entire night! We must find out what he told her. All she has to do is remember! Ah, Atahualpa! Let me have her. I'll skin her alive if need be. I promise you that before sunset—'

'No, Villa Oma,' interrupted Atahualpa sharply. 'You'll do no such thing.'

For an instant the two men glared at each other. Anamaya was on the verge of collapsing when the Sage turned and headed for the narrow door. Atahualpa recalled him sharply.

'Listen to me closely, Villa Oma. I know that you have my interests at heart and I won't forget it. But I will respect my father's last wish, even if I don't like it. If he felt that this girl was a messenger from the moon goddess, then he had good reason. If he confided the future to her yesterday, and then had her forget it today, he did so for a purpose.'

Villa Oma sighed. He paused for a moment before backtracking to ask:

'What do you want me to do?'

'What must be done. We both heard my father say, "Anamaya, daughter of the sacred lake, child of Quilla: May you live a long life in this world . . ." He chose her as the guardian of his Sacred Double. We will ensure that it is so.'

Villa Oma shook his head, his face weary. As if speaking to a child, he said:

'It's impossible, it doesn't happen. A Sacred Double never has a wife.'

'Well, it's possible from now on. You will tell the priests yourself: this girl will be the Sacred Double's *Coya Camaquen*.'

'They'll never accept! Please, I can make her remember, I'll throw her into the puma's pit—'

'No! The Emperor Huayna Capac wants her close to him and here in this world. The nobles present on his night of passing heard him as clearly as we did.'

'But the child is a savage!' insisted Villa Oma. 'She doesn't even know what a *Camaquen* is, and she's never seen the Sacred Double!'

'Then you are to see to it that she learns, and learns quickly.'

'Atahualpa! What are you saying! She's not a true Inca, she cannot learn our secrets! It would be against our tradition, against our law – if you are wrong, do you know what will happen to us?'

'I cannot go wrong by following my father's wishes.'

'Who can tell? If our mistake is too great, then the sun won't rise over the eastern mountains! Do you want us to live in the same darkness as the Underworld? Do you want time to stop and us with it?'

His words struck fear in Anamaya's heart. But Atahualpa ordered calmly:

'Stop moaning, Villa Oma, and do as I command.'

The Sage stood still for a moment with his eyes closed; but then he bowed, defeated. Suddenly he grabbed Anamaya by the chin, his fingers as calloused as old wood. He lifted her head and stared at her with eyes as dark as a moonless night.

'You heard, Anamaya. From now on you will obey me completely. That is the will of my brother Atahualpa. And I promise to you that should you suddenly recover your memory and your tongue, and then tell someone other than me what the Emperor told you before he died, I'll cut your heart into little pieces!'

Villa Oma thrust her face away so roughly that it felt almost like a blow. He left the room without a look in Atahualpa's direction. Anamaya's knees gave way and she collapsed onto the narrow couch. Her pride abandoned her – she gasped in terror. Prince Atahualpa looked at her for a moment, hesitating, before stepping forward and bending over her. He touched her shoulder with the tips of his fingers, almost a caress.

'Look at me, girl,' he ordered gently.

The whites of his eyes were redder than ever following the argument with the Sage, but a faint smile appeared on his handsome face.

'Don't cry, Anamaya,' he said softly. 'Be strong and proud. Don't be scared of the Sage. He speaks harshly but is not as nasty as he pretends. He wants the best for our people . . .'

He scrutinized her closely, as if looking for an answer in her enigmatic blue eyes. He stopped smiling and his face hardened when he said:

'Fear no one. I will protect you as my father commands me to from the other world.'

'Anamaya, my sister . . .'

Inti Palla had come in furtively after Atahualpa had left. She kneeled beside Anamaya and stroked her hand. Her fingers ran over the serpent bracelet. Her eyes burned with curiosity.

'Is it true what they say?' she whispered.

Anamaya looked at her, not understanding.

'That you don't remember anything!' added Inti Palla peevishly, 'that you can't remember a word the Emperor told you . . .'

Anamaya hesitated to answer. She still felt the echo of Villa Oma's threat. But she didn't want to seem to keep secrets from her new friend.

'The Emperor spoke to me and his words are within me,' she said cautiously.

'But do you remember them?' insisted the princess impatiently, squeezing her wrist.

'When the Emperor wishes it, I'll remember . . .'

Inti Palla groaned with exasperation, but she saw something in Anamaya's eyes that prevented her from persisting. Her fingers relaxed, and she stroked Anamaya's arm lazily. A smug smile curled her lips.

'Too bad – if you don't want to trust me . . .'

'Inti Palla, I can't! I'm not allowed to!'

The young princess shrugged and toyed with the gold pin holding her cape together. In that fraction of a second she had readopted the haughtiness and disdain that Anamaya hadn't seen for so long.

'It doesn't matter, anyway,' she said. 'I came here to tell you something more important. Since you haven't left this room since the Emperor's death, there's no way you that would know . . .'

'I'm not allowed to leave,' murmured Anamaya, looking resentfully at the door hanging.

'Exactly!' continued Inti Palla. 'And I'd better not hang around here for too long. But you should know that as soon as the fast for the Emperor's passing is over, I will become Prince Atahualpa's concubine!'

'Oh!'

'Yes – are you surprised?'

'No! You're beautiful, I understand why . . .'

'Yes,' laughed Inti Palla, self-importantly. 'I believe he finds me beautiful. And so you see, it doesn't matter if you won't tell me anything. I'll find out anyway. When standing, the nobles are all pride and reticence, but lying in bed in the arms of their concubines . . . now, that's another story!'

And with that Inti Palla left the room, the rustling of her finely woven wool tunic just audible beneath her cascading laughter.

'Don't believe her,' said a deep voice, which Anamaya immediately recognized.

'Inti Palla is a cruel liar!'

The dwarf's head and shoulders appeared out of the mouth of the big pot, followed by his torso and legs. His thick hair was speckled with yellow flecks of maize. He perched himself on the edge of the mouth of the pot and looked at Anamaya, wearing a serious expression on his face.

'She's a liar and as mean as a cut snake,' he continued, shaking the maize grains from his head. 'The first time she laid eyes on me, she kicked the life out of me. She bends over for the strong and steps on the weak. Just listening to her is dangerous.'

But for her surprise, Anamaya would have burst into laughter at the sight of this puny squit popping out from the pot like a monkey, his head sprinkled with the grain of the sacred plant. But instead she knit her brows in an attempt to appear offended:

'Well, it's none of your business. Anyway, what are you doing here?'

'I'm watching over you, Princess.'

'I don't need you to know who my friends are!'

'Ah? And are you sure?'

The dwarf chortled. Nimbly, he leaped from the pot and prostrated himself before Anamaya, who was having trouble containing her amusement.

'My Princess!'

'Stop playing the fool!'

'I'm not playing the fool, Princess,' protested the dwarf with a sorrowful look. 'On the contrary. My master has died, and I ask nothing more than the honor of serving you.'

'You want to serve me? But I'm so ugly, and—'

'And have you had a close look at me, Princess?'

Anamaya could no longer control herself: she burst into a profound, ringing laughter that lifted her anguished soul. She hadn't laughed for so long and had suffered so much that now she couldn't stop. As she laughed and laughed, the dwarf stood up and looked at her impassively.

'Forgive me,' she stuttered when she finally calmed down, 'but I don't even know who you are . . .'

'Didn't you hear the Emperor call me his son?'

'Yes, but—'

'But you thought that the fever had demented his mind?'

'I . . . I don't know. I was very frightened and maybe I—'

'Don't worry about it,' said the dwarf without rancor. 'You didn't hurt my pride . . .'

Through the door, its cover lifting slightly in a breeze, she saw signs of busy activity in the palace. The dwarf perceived her anxiety and waved his arm as if to brush it away.

'No one will come in here,' he whispered conspiratorially.

'How do you know?'

'I know these things,' he said with comic assurance.

They stopped talking and faced each other, Anamaya slowly getting used to his strange appearance. His disproportionate head reached her chest, and the hem of his long red tunic gathered mud and dust as it dragged along the ground. He had been wearing the same tunic the day she first saw him, crouched at the foot of the Emperor's deathbed.

'Do you never change your clothes?'

'I was wearing this the day the Great Lord Huayna Capac captured me and anointed me his son . . .'

'I don't understand.'

'My people are a tribe of *Canaries* who have always warred with the Incas. One day Huayna Capac had chased us to the shores of Lake Yaguarcocha and had destroyed most of our houses, and I had hidden under a pile of thick wool blankets, trembling . . .'

As he spoke, the dwarf's expression changed as frequently as the sky during the wet season. Extreme fear and wry jocosity played in turn across his face.

'I heard his wrath explode into words like fat black storm-bearing clouds. I was terrified of dying, a terrible and undignified fear. When I felt a hand probing through the pile, I thought, "That's it for me."'

'You must've really begged for mercy!'

'Not at all, Princess. I still don't know why I did, but I suddenly yelled, "Go away, whoever you are. Just let me sleep!" and I repeated this several times as I slowly sat up,

yawning as if I'd just been woken from a long slumber. "Just
let me sleep!"'

Anamaya laughed again, her heart filled with lightness.

'What did the Emperor say?'

'He laughed, just like you are laughing, Princess. He
laughed heartily. And everyone around him laughed – generals, soldiers, noblemen – they laughed despite the predatory
gleam in their eyes, they laughed because he was laughing.
The only one who didn't laugh was his red-eyed son—'

'Atahualpa? Why not?'

The dwarf fell silent for a moment.

'I know the reason, along with a select few – but, believe
me, it's better for you not to know . . .'

'So, you also keep a dangerous secret.'

He pretended to cut his throat with his hand.

'That's what would happen to me. If the Sun King Huayna
Capac hadn't declared me his son, his eldest son, I would've
been dead long ago. But now that he's gone to the Other
World . . .'

The dwarf stopped talking. Anamaya's mirth dried up.

'I've lost my father,' he continued sadly, without a trace of
his earlier humor.

Anamaya's heart beat heavily. In a deep and measured
voice, the dwarf added:

'And they hate me as much as they hate you.'

Anamaya understood his unspoken meaning.

'You're as alone as I am, aren't you?' she whispered.

'It seems that way.'

The ensuing silence united them. Anamaya no longer felt
the fear of being a child. Ancient, primeval emotions, feelings
that she didn't try to understand, made her shiver. A wave of
tenderness knotted her stomach and dimmed her eyes with
tears. She wanted to tell him about her most private demons;
she wanted to reveal to him the shreds of her memories. But
all that came out of her mouth were garbled, meaningless

sounds. And as her tears fell and her breathing grew short, the dwarf reached out to her, his large, disfigured hands holding hers with uncommon tenderness.

'Princess, say nothing. It's all right, everything is all right.'

'I want to . . . I would like to . . .'

But the words wouldn't come. Anamaya huddled against the dwarf and suddenly she felt minuscule, tinier even than he; she felt utterly lost and helpless. Nevertheless, for the first time in many moons, she felt a spark of hope and gratitude.

For she had finally found a friend.

The dwarf would hide whenever anyone visited.

As the night progressed he lay beside her on the straw mat, and they talked.

Anamaya told him about her village, about the Incas' attack and her mother's death, about Captain Sikinchara, about the strange, hateful passion that Inti Palla showed for her, about the fear she had acquired along with Huayna Capac's secret, the secret everybody wanted.

He spoke of the royal court and its intrigues, the jealousies of the concubines and the tyranny of the aristocrats. He told her the secret that Atahualpa was guarding in his heart, the real reason he could not be Emperor. He told her to trust nobody with the words hidden in her breast, the ones that Huayna Capac had placed there and that lay dormant within her.

They admitted to one another that they never wanted to be separated now that they had met, and promised to look out for each other.

He made her laugh quietly and she called him 'My Lord' and he called her 'Your Grace' or else 'Princess'. In the privacy of night they laid aside their terrible loneliness, and peeled back the layers of their accumulated fears.

In the gleam of the pre-dawn gloaming, the dwarf told Anamaya that he expected them to murder him soon.

And she held him with all her strength, and asked him not die, not to leave her.

CHAPTER 5

Quito, January 1528

'C OYA CAMAQUEN! COYA CAMAQUEN! WAKE UP,
please!'

Anamaya woke with a start and propped herself
up on her elbow, flabbergasted by what she saw. Six or seven
young women were busying themselves about her room.
And before she even got out of bed they were prostrating
themselves and shuffling back, according her all the signs
of respect usually reserved for high-ranking ladies.

The eldest of them, about twice Anamaya's age, kneeled
before her with her head lowered. She spread her palms on
the beaten-earth floor and said respectfully:

'*Coya Camaquen*, please follow us.'

Coya Camaquen!

So, the powerful will of Lord Prince Atahualpa had tri-
umphed after all, despite the resistance of the Sage, Villa
Oma.

Coya Camaquen!

If only she knew what it actually meant. What was her
new role? What were her new duties?

But she hadn't the time to ask herself questions.

The tapestry covering the doorway had been lifted, and
outside the sun was shining brightly. Finally, she was going

to leave this room that seemed to her more of a prison cell than a bedroom.

She hadn't seen the dwarf since the night he had eased her loneliness by offering her his own. Sometimes she wondered if she hadn't dreamed that whole evening . . .

She rose and followed the servant girls, none of whom dared look at her directly. She had only walked a few steps into the sunshine when she heard an awful sound and shuddered.

Wailing echoed through the great palace. The flowers had all been cut and lay fading on the ground. All the Emperors' wives wandered about aimlessly, their faces marked by grief, their voices wailing, their eyes vacant.

The servant girls led her into a courtyard where she'd never been before. There she saw men, also grieving, gathered into small groups. She recognized them as noblemen from their clothes and the gold disks on their ears. They turned away from her when she came in and remained still until she had passed them by.

Finally she entered a large stone edifice. Its walls were covered in sheets of gold and high alcoves contained llamas carved from stone, pottery, and delicately painted wooden vases. A magnificent set of clothes was laid out on a wooden bench. The *lliclla*, a dark red cape, was distinguished by a large V-shaped motif in light blue and bright yellow. She ran her trembling fingers over the weaving, which felt as soft as a baby's skin.

Then there was the *acsu*, the finest tunic she'd ever seen. Dyed the same red as the *lliclla*, it was decorated with two bands of geometric motifs, one yellow and white, the other blue and red. And so finely woven that some strands of color were as narrow as a hair . . .

'It is Huayna Capac's imperial motif,' growled a voice that she knew well.

Absorbed in the beauty of the clothes, she hadn't heard the

Sage, Villa Oma, come in. The servant girls had retreated and bowed before him. Villa Oma pointed his finger at the cape and tunic:

'I suppose I have to teach you everything, girl. From now on, you belong to the dead Emperor's clan. At certain ceremonies you will wear only white, but the rest of the time you will wear his colors, *Coya Camaquen* . . .'

The Sage spoke these last two words with doubt in his tone, as if still finding the situation difficult to accept. He looked at Anamaya and sighed, showing her the green coca leaves he was chewing. Then he shook his head and continued, speaking mostly to himself:

'"*Coya Camaquen*" . . . That is what you now are — Atahualpa wishes it and I couldn't persuade the priests to defy his will . . . oh, may Inti forgive our folly!'

'My Lord—'

'Don't bother me with your questions now, girl. I'll explain everything to you only when you'll need to know.'

He turned to the servant girls and ordered severely:

'Dress her quickly! Don't make me wait!'

When Anamaya reappeared in the central courtyard, the noblemen stopped talking again. But this time they did not turn away.

This time they fixed their gazes on the young girl, observing with distaste her non-Inca features. Mostly, they were deeply affected by her extraordinary blue irises. Indeed, it occurred to more than one of them that her shining eyes were the ultimate jewels to be added to the wealth of Huayna Capac.

Embarrassed by so much attention, Anamaya concentrated as best she could on advancing towards the Sage, Villa Oma.

He stood near the porch of the adjoining courtyard, holding a heavy ceremonial spear, a gold-tipped *chuqui* adorned with green and red feathers. He waited for her motionlessly, and watched her walk through the crowd of noblemen gathered in the massive court. But from the corner of his eye he noticed the stupefied looks that followed her.

When she was within whispering distance he murmured to her:

'Listen to me carefully: do everything I tell you, as I tell you. Speak only when I command.'

Villa Oma turned and walked briskly towards the porch, where some soldiers stood guard in front of a huge blood-colored tapestry. Upon reaching them he stopped and solemnly tapped the ground with his *chuqui*. The soldiers stood aside and he passed between them, drew aside the tapestry and passed beyond it. Her heart beating rapidly, Anamaya followed him.

Inside, she froze, unable to take another step.

Before her was a massive, delicately paved courtyard. Low buildings stood along three sides, their entrances covered by hangings made of blue and yellow feathers. All the walls were covered in gold sheets so fine that they shivered with the slightest breeze.

This place was dazzlingly beautiful. The intense midday sun bounced off the sheets and encircled them in a fluid gold light. It was hypnotic and violently iridescent.

For an instant she was blinded, hypnotized.

She had entered the earthly eye of Inti, the Inca Sun God. The atmosphere was heavy here, and the air harder to breathe.

Villa Oma didn't wait for her but continued right into the center of the gold-lit courtyard, where there stood a roofless room enclosed on four sides by tapestries, these with many gold orbs hanging from them.

He stopped before it and turned to Anamaya. He gestured imperiously for her to approach.

The sun's rays and its reflections off the walls of gold lit her bare face. She felt feverish, and was sweating profusely. She shuffled along, barely lifting her feet from the sun-scorched flagstones.

Once she had arrived beside him, he turned away and thrust his spear up towards the sun. He threw his head back and said in a deep, hollow voice:

'Oh, Inti! Oh, Inti, Lord of day! Here is the *Coya Camaquen* of your favored son Huayna Capac. Here she bows before you. May you accept her and not be offended by her ignorance!'

Then the Sage lifted the gold tapestry with his spear and had Anamaya follow him in.

There he was – the one whose hand she had held throughout the night as he lay dying. He was stretched out on a thick layer of grass and cinchona leaves spread on straw mats. Large solid-gold llama statues stood guard around him. Coca leaves were burning in great shallow bowls made of clay. A gold statue with emerald eyes stood on a polished granite stand a few paces from him.

The corpse's skin was dark and taut. His stomach was an open pit filled with a sort of black paste, smelling of burned meat. Anamaya dug her nails into her palms to prevent herself from screaming and running away. Never in her life had she seen such a horrible sight, not even when her mother had been killed right beside her.

Villa Oma bowed and murmured some words that she didn't understand. She wondered if she should do the same, but as he had not ordered her to, she remained upright, petrified with fear.

She looked at the Inca's face so as not to have to look at his open stomach or throat. His eyelids had been pinned up and revealed two hollows where his eyeballs should have been. The skin was stretched tight over his high-set cheekbones, and his long ear lobes hung there, strangely distorted without the gold disks that had once decorated them. Still, she had only seen the Emperor when he had been grimacing in great pain, and she had to admit that in death his expression seemed beautifully calm.

The emerald-eyed statue was watching over him with a lifelike gaze. As big as a child, it was a statue of a man with his hands spread open on his thighs. She recognized its face – the dead Emperor's.

Anamaya felt faint, overwhelmed by emotion. Indeed, she might well have crumpled to the ground at that very instant had Villa Oma not hissed into her ears, pointing at the statue:

'Child, you see before you the Emperor's Sacred Double. The Emperor selected you to be his eternal companion. For as long as you live, you will remain close to his golden brother. That is why from now on you will be known as *Coya Camaquen*. The Emperor will speak to us through his Sacred Double and your mouth, and he will tell us his will, and protect us—'

Anamaya convulsed suddenly.

She didn't understand the meaning of the Sage's words. She felt an urge to run away and cry like the terrified child that she was.

But then, as if an invisible hand had appeased her fear and calmed her, she listened to the Sage speak. She remained patiently still and felt reassured by the Emperor's calm expression.

'Now,' continued Villa Oma slowly, 'repeat after me: My Lord, I am betrothed to your twin soul . . .'

She had difficulty unclenching her jaw. All her muscles were so tense that they felt as if they would crack. Her stomach felt as hollow as the one in the dried cadaver before her.

'Say it!' ordered the Sage, still looking directly at the statue.

'My Lord, I am betrothed to your twin soul.'

'My Lord, I will watch over you in this world, while you are in the other.'

'My Lord, I will watch over you in this world, while you are in the other.'

'My Lord, I will serve your Sacred Double as his loyal wife.'

'My Lord, I will serve your Sacred Double as his loyal wife.'

'Now, *Coya Camaquen* Anamaya, prostrate yourself before your new master!'

CHAPTER 6

Quito, February 1528

OVER THE FOLLOWING TWENTY DAYS, THE SAGE, Villa Oma, led Anamaya five more times into the forbidden golden courtyard.

Five more times she watched the Emperor's body mummify. Sometimes he was covered in a coating of grass and saltpeter and left to dry in the hot sun. Sometimes blocks of ice brought down from the mountain were covered in hay and placed around his body to freeze it overnight.

His body was no longer laid flat but set upright upon a pile of reeds. His legs were folded and his heels had been pushed under his mummified thighs, thighs no thicker than his bones. The very last time she went she saw that he had been dressed in a magnificent vicuña-pelt tunic. A diadem of feathers crowned his restful face.

For a terrifying instant Anamaya thought she saw his lips move and his eyes look at her.

With each visit the Sage lost a little of his crabbiness. His voice was patient as he led her through the evocations she repeated in front of the golden Sacred Double. And he reminded her calmly how the world was divided into three realms. The one she could see and touch was *Kay Pacha*. Here were the mountains and the lakes, the animals and mankind. In this world humans made war and peace, gave birth and became ill. This world contained the Law of the Cuzco Incas, the princes of the Empire of the Four Cardinal Directions and the only humans that the Sun considered as his own.

'The Sun God lives in the Upper World. There he is sometimes joined by his wife-sister the Moon Goddess and by his brother *Illapa*, the Lightning God. And beneath your feet, *Coya Camaquen*, is the realm of our ancestors . . .'

'But where is the Emperor now?' asked Anamaya, confused.

'He is everywhere, child. He is close to Inti our Father in the Upper World. He is with his ancestors in their Under World. And he is here with us, through his Sacred Double and you who can hear him – if you're up to it!'

Villa Oma smiled slightly. But this time he teased her without sarcasm or contempt.

'That is why we say that he's in the Other World,' he continued. 'The Other World is a place of happiness. But to reach it, one must have lived here without breaking any Cuzco law. And one must have died well.'

The Sage chewed on his coca leaf in silence for a moment and then concluded with a nod of his head:

'You must not die unless told to by Huayna Capac. And you must never leave his Sacred Double. Do you understand?'

Did she really understand? Anamaya wasn't sure.

That evening she saw Prince Atahualpa again for the first time since his father had died. He came into her room as she ate alone. She almost knocked over her bowl of potato soup in surprise.

She quickly bowed her head and knelt on the ground, but Atahualpa said gently:

'You may stand and look at me, *Coya Camaquen*.'

She obeyed timidly. But Atahualpa's kind gaze gave her confidence. He appeared as handsome and strong as when she had first seen him, despite the unease that lined his face. He said:

'Anamaya, I'm pleased with you. The Sage tells me that you are a fast learner, that you are obedient and that you are strong.'

She blushed, bowing slightly in appreciation. He immediately asked:

'*Coya Comaquen*, do you remember yet what the Emperor told you?'

She shook her head sadly.

'No, My Lord. I don't remember . . .'

'Not one word?'

'No – but . . .'

'But?'

She straightened herself and looked into his eyes:

'I know that his words remain within me. But I feel that the Emperor doesn't want me to remember them yet.'

Atahualpa contemplated her silently for a moment before moving closer to her. He glanced quickly at the doorway before whispering:

'Are you sure?'

'No,' replied Anamaya just as quietly. 'No, I'm not sure. But when I'm with his Sacred Double, I feel confident that his words are within me. It's just that I'm not free to remember or speak them yet.'

Gladness lit up Atahualpa's reddened eyeballs. With astonishing gentleness he stroked Anamaya's arm with his fingertips.

There was a long silence before he murmured:

'Be careful, *Coya Camaquen*, be very watchful. I can protect you here, but other clans may wish you harm.'

'Why, my Lord? Why would they want to hurt me?'

'Because the words you hold within you may decide the

future of the Empire. Be careful, Anamaya, and watch what you say, especially after the great ceremony.'

'The great ceremony?'

'You'll find out later. But I've faith in you. I think my father made a good decision, albeit an odd one. But be on your guard, especially with my brother Huascar and his clan. They too want to hear the secret you have within you.'

When she was alone again later that night, Anamaya was hit by a wave of panic. She felt lost in a chasm of silence and mystery.

A silence that seemed to freeze the palace.

A mystery that gripped her soul.

Was it true what Prince Atahualpa had told her: that she held the future of the Empire within her? Why? What words were they?

And above all, why her?

The young girl was rooted to the spot with terror.

Why *her*?

She was so young, had lived so few years. How was she supposed to carry such an enormous responsibility?

And what if her instinct was wrong? What if she didn't have the words sleeping inside her after all, or if she'd simply forgotten them, and had been too exhausted that night to listen to Huayna Capac's endless talking?

Tears welled in Anamaya's eyes. Through her tears the flame on her bedside lamp seemed to fragment into tiny pieces.

The girl was petrified! And she felt so alone, with no one to help her. Since she had become *Coya Camaquen*, the dwarf had not visited her once. Perhaps he was scared of her . . . she felt completely alone in this world, alone in all three worlds that the Sage had told her about.

Suddenly Anamaya jumped with fright.

From the darkest corner of the room she thought she could see the bright yellow gaze of a puma fixed upon her.

Anamaya bit her lips to stop herself from screaming. Her fingers gripped her blanket.

Yes, there they were, two golden eyes shining at her from the darkness. She imagined the beast's round ears, his quivering snout and the shine of his fangs. The girl couldn't breathe. She was unable to speak the words that leapt to her mind:

'Don't kill me, mountain lion. Don't kill me, for I am to live a long life and watch over the Emperor's Sacred Double. I beg of you, noble puma, don't eat me, let me live and I'll never forget what I owe you . . .'

The beast vanished as easily as he had appeared. The shadow in the corner returned to being just a shadow.

Much, much later, still sitting upright and trembling, Anamaya fell asleep.

Dawn, and a cacophony of terrible wailing resonated throughout the palace.

Anamaya went into the courtyard, expecting to witness another catastrophe. What she saw bewildered her. All the Emperor's servant girls and wives were walking in a vast circle between the buildings in the courtyard. They were following one another around, their crying faces turned down to the dusty ground. Suddenly, as if possessed, they all threw their arms to the sky and cried:

'Viracocha! Viracocha! Save us!'

Tears streamed down their faces from eyes wide with fear. They wailed:

'O Inti, save our Sun King! Uphold him, oh Lord! May he be patient, for soon we shall join him once more . . .'

Anamaya trembled at the sight of this awful procession. Her arms were cold with goose bumps. She backed away from the sight into the shadow of the building, intent on returning to the sanctuary of her little room. But then the girl

heard a louder din from outside the palace walls. Hundreds
of thousands of cries rose into the cloudless sky.

Anamaya curled up on her bed, shivering in fear, hugging
her legs against her chest. She waited for hours, consumed
by anxiety. No one came to fetch her. She wondered if she'd
been forgotten in the heart of the great, terrible wailing all
around her.

Her fear and pain ran so deep that when she began to speak
to the Emperor's Sacred Double she didn't realize what she
was doing. Anamaya whispered to him with her eyes closed,
reassuring and comforting the gold statue.

'I'll keep my promise!' She told him, 'I will never, ever
abandon you, Sacred Double. I'll do whatever you ask of
me . . .'

At last, just before midday, Villa Oma came into Anamaya's
room. He was dressed more splendidly than ever. He wore
an immense red-and-blue cape and a beautiful headpiece of
long, colorful feathers. A finely worked gold plate covered
his torso. His face was serene.

The Sage was followed by two matrons from the Temple
of the Virgins. One carried a long white tunic and the
other a headpiece of white cloth topped with a gold crown.
Two blood-red feathers rose from green stone clasps on
the crown.

The matrons silently and expertly dressed Anamaya in the
white tunic, and then fixed the headpiece on her rich black
plaited hair.

Once finished, they backed respectfully out of the room,
their eyes downturned. Villa Oma looked at Anamaya for a
moment. She felt that she saw approval in his eyes, that he
was happy with what he saw.

'Come with me,' he said.

They went into the courtyard. There, four soldiers carried
the Emperor's Sacred Double on a palanquin. The gold statue
shone as bright as the sun itself!

The servant girls and wives were still circling around the courtyard wailing their grief, but Villa Oma led Anamaya right through them as though they were invisible. He indicated with a movement of his eyes her place in front of the palanquin. He carried his ceremonial spear pointed at the sky.

As the strange procession slowly prepared to leave the palace confines, Anamaya again heard the enormous cry from outside. But Villa Oma continued as if he hadn't heard it. The sun was higher now, and their shadows shorter.

At last they reached the palace door. The noise from outside was deafening. Two trumpeters holding coiled shell horns preceded them. Villa Oma shook his spear, and the door opened.

Anamaya froze in her tracks.

She saw before her an unimaginably huge crowd crushed into the great courtyard. Men, women and children, all of them wailing and throwing their arms to the sky, entreating Inti.

The trumpeters sounded long, vibrating notes from their horns; the wails lessened at the sound and the enormous mass of people turned to look at the small group standing at the palace door.

Thousands of eyes looked at the Sage, the *Coya Camaquen* and the golden statue on its palanquin. A moan began and spread through the crowd like a wave, ending at those immediately in front of Anamaya. Villa Oma led the procession forward and the crowd divided. On both sides faces lowered respectfully as they advanced. Terrified, Anamaya urged herself forward, concentrating on every step. She looked beautiful, tall and straight in her long white tunic, her clear blue eyes fixed straight ahead.

Again the horns sounded.

Ten thousand people and more now stood absolutely silent. Not one person looked directly at the white-clad virgin. The crowd parted to let them pass, and from afar the effect was of wind rippling through a stand of cinchona.

They reached the other side of the great place where the doors of Viracocha's Temple stood open, guarded by a double rank of soldiers.

Again the trumpets sounded. Villa Oma went through the doors first. They came into a perfectly round room where the walls were covered from floor to ceiling with delicate seashells. Smoke from burning coca leaves danced in the air and obscured the light.

The palanquin bearers lowered the Sacred Double in the center of the room while Villa Oma waited to the left. Instinctively, Anamaya stood to the right of the statue.

The Sage waited for the soldiers to leave the room. Then he raised his arms and exclaimed in a clear voice:

> 'Nothing exists in vain, O Viracocha!
> All begin on the shores of Lake Titicaca,
> All return to the place of your choosing.
> You are the inventor of the universe, Viracocha,
> You hold the stick of origin.
>   O Viracocha, hear me . . .
>   O Venerable Lord, Ruler of all three worlds,
>   Accept Huayna Capac's double brother,
>   Accept the Emperor's Coya Camaquen,
>   Her maiden name is Anamaya, O Viracocha,
>   If you reveal yourself she will humbly worship you,
>   With her eyes turned down modestly.
>   Venerable Lord of all three worlds,
>   May she live long by your grace,
>   May she not die before you wish it.'

The last words hung suspended in the silent temple, echoing through Anamaya's soul.

The Sage asked Anamaya to repeat the prayer after him.

They lifted their arms thrice in invocation to the sky above. Then the Sage fetched a jug of sacred beer and poured it on the ground around Anamaya and the statue. Only then did the priests join them inside. One after another, they recited the prayer before pouring beer upon the temple floor.

Much time passed, and as the sun retreated to the western horizon the shadows grew as long as the soldiers' spears.

At last the trumpeters blew their shells again. The somber procession made its way back out into the courtyard.

Which was now completely empty. Anamaya was stupefied.

And as she followed the golden statue back to the palace, she found that each courtyard they passed through was now completely empty. Not one person was to be seen, not one of the thousands of men, women and children who had thronged there earlier. They had vanished like soundless ghosts.

'Where are they?' she asked in a strangled voice. 'Where did they all go?'

She saw Villa Oma look at her intensely, his mouth stained green by coca-leaf juice. With a satisfied expression, he replied:

'They have joyfully joined their Emperor to serve him in the Other World!'

That night Anamaya could not sleep. She felt crushed by the great empty silence that occupied the palace.

She cried and cried.

How many had they been? How many had offered their hearts at the sacred stone altars that surrounded Quito, how many had offered their lives to their Emperor Huayna Capac?

Thousands had died.

All his wives, all his concubines and servant girls, all his captured eunuchs, all his slaves, all had given their lives for him. Their blood infected the air and grieved the lonely girl. She recognized that nauseating odor from the day the Incas had annihilated her lowland village.

In the early hours of the morning she went out into the courtyard to escape her sad thoughts. The round moon shone brightly and threw inky shadows across the flagstones. For an instant Anamaya felt completely alone in a deserted world.

And then, suddenly, she heard ten thousand whispers reverberate softly through the still night, as if all those departed souls had returned briefly to wish her farewell.

CHAPTER 7

Tumebamba, December 1528

ALMOST FOUR SEASONS HAD PASSED SINCE Huayna Capac's desiccated body and its escort had left the northern capital of Quito to embark on the long journey to Coricancha's Temple in Cuzco. Since the beginning of *Inti Raymi*, the Inca harvest-feast month, they had been in the North's second great city, Tumebamba, where the Emperor had enjoyed the company of his northern wives and concubines in the city's mild climate.

Tumebamba was only a provincial capital, but its layout and magnificent architecture were so similar to that of Cuzco that the northern lords sometimes called it 'the Other Cuzco'.

At its center was the great square of the Temple of the Sun. Around this lay long straight streets bordered by the walls of the *canchas*, often perpendicular to one another and criss-crossed by carefully maintained irrigation canals. The nobles lived in palaces near the great central court. These buildings were surrounded by imposing walls far better built than those of their humbler neighbors.

The high walls, constructed of immaculately fitted stones, guarded fine houses set around meticulously tended court-yards, with flower beds and vegetable gardens and patches dedicated to sacred plants. Water flowed constantly through magnificent stone fountains fed by hidden conduits.

Dozens of busy servants kept stock of the food stores, as well as the supplies of wool, dyed cotton, pottery, carpets, tapestries and fabrics, all produced by hard-working artisans and peasants for their noble Inca masters.

Since the arrival of the mummified corpse of the Emperor, the city had temporarily expanded, a forest of tents having appeared to accommodate all the clans for whom there was not enough room in the palace. The city was alive with singing and dancing, with grand ceremonies, with endless carousal and with great communal feasts celebrating the sons of the aristocracy – for this was the time of the summer solstice initiation rites, the *huarachiku*.

By completing this long series of trying challenges, these male children of the nobility would pass to manhood. The bravest would be lionized by all, including their ancestors in the Other World. The last challenge, known simply as The Great Race, would produce the next generation of great warriors and venerated priests, while all the rest would have to content themselves with being loyal servants to the Empire.

All those who survived the course would have their ears pierced by a gold needle, and would receive their first mark of rank – admittedly only a modest wooden disk, which still might one day become the gold insignia worn by the most powerful Incas.

Strictly obeying Villa Oma's command, Anamaya hadn't left the golden Sacred Double's side. But a lot else had changed.

Now no one dared make fun of her or mock her blue eyes. Both the lords of the northern clans and those from Cuzco treated her with the utmost respect. But despite this they couldn't hide their impatience and worry: everyone was waiting for Anamaya to recall the Emperor's last words, or for him to manifest himself through her, and thus to confirm or deny Huascar's ascendancy.

Perhaps due to her situation, the *Coya Camaquen* had changed distinctly over the last few months. Anamaya was now more self-assured, and was no longer astonished when servants bowed to her or when she felt unknown eyes looking at her. She had grown used to waiting during long ceremonies, both night and day, and to enduring patiently the endless arguments between soothsayers, and to her countless other duties.

What was more, she had changed physically. While dressing in the mornings she had noticed that her legs were growing longer and her hips rounder. Every day she seemed to shed a little more of her girlish figure, and her woman's body became more evident as her heart and spirit hardened; she minded loneliness less now, and cried fewer tears.

She had noticed that the dwarf had followed the procession from Quito, but they had had too few opportunities to talk. Sometimes she recognized him in a crowd, and her heart warmed.

She endured Inti Palla's mood swings patiently; as before, the princess was sometimes as affectionate as a sister, sometimes as wounding as a slingshot.

The nights she had spent with Prince Atahualpa had done little to soften Inti Palla, but she had nevertheless become a young woman. The princess was also as beautiful an Inca woman as had ever been, a very great beauty. She had developed an opulent form, with supple, firm features, and had a round face with a prominent forehead over a long nose. Her mouth curved in a seductive wide bow. And since arriving in Tumebamba, she had been basking in all the attention her beauty attracted.

Occasionally, Anamaya envied Inti Palla her beauty, and wished that she could be as arrogant and chameleon-like as the carefree princess . . . but more often than not she thanked Inti that she wasn't.

That day was a big day, the day of the *huarachiku* Great Race. For once, Anamaya would be just another young girl, free of her duties to the mummy, thanks to Inti Palla. The princess had urged Prince Atahualpa to insist before the Council of Elders that Anamaya be one of the virgins who helped the competitors. Each was assigned one boy to assist and encourage during the terrible race.

Anamaya had been greatly looking forward to it, until that night, when Inti Palla had managed to spoil her happiness. One morning a few days previously, Inti Palla had been explaining to her the details of the forthcoming ceremonies when she had suddenly pointed at the steep slopes and peaks that overlooked the city. She had had a ruthless gleam in her eye:

'The Great Race, of course, will be the hardest of all the challenges. Only the bravest and hardiest will finish it. And of them only those right at the front will be honored as greatest of the great. They'll have to suffer the cold and rain; they'll have to conquer the mountain . . . and their fear. They'll only get a little uncooked maize to eat. They'll be so tired that they'll hardly be able to stand, and yet still have to carry on . . .'

'But they've been fasting this past week!' exclaimed Anamaya. 'They'll never make it!'

'Oh yes, they will. They'll have to conquer the three peaks, ignore their weakness and pain and trust themselves to Inti . . .'

'And what if they fail?'

A cruel smile spread across Inti Palla's face:

'Then they'll amount to nothing, and bring dishonor upon their clans . . . unless they still have enough energy to throw themselves into a ravine, or at least die of asphyxiation before the finish line!'

Anamaya remained subdued as the princess laughed heartlessly. But in her own heart she knew that Inti Palla was right: it was the way things worked in the Empire of the Four Cardinal Directions. One had to constantly triumph in this world, or face unhappiness in the next.

After a while the princess reflected:

'You know, this year the boys from the Cuzco clans must not win. If they did it would only reinforce their appetite for power. I can't help our men because I'm no longer a virgin. But you, on the other hand . . .'

'You think I could help them?'

'I could ask for special dispensation for you.'

'No way, that's impossible! What about the Sacred Double? Villa Oma would never accept that I leave him, even for just one day!'

'Nothing's impossible,' insisted Inti Palla. 'And in any case you wouldn't really be abandoning your position – the statue will oversee the race from the top of the temple. He'll be able to see you and you him . . .'

Inti Palla threw out a sprightly laugh as she developed her plan:

'Trust me, Atahualpa will accept it. I know how to ask for things that I really want.'

And, in point of fact, she got what she wanted.

Inti Palla woke Anamaya in the middle of the night to tell her the news:

'Anamaya! Anamaya! Prince Atahualpa accepted! You're going with Guaypar!'

'Who's Guaypar?'

'He's my uncle's son, Atahualpa's brother!' He's the bravest boy in our clan – and the most handsome!'

Anamaya joyfully wrapped herself around Inti Palla and nestled her forehead against hers. They were giggling girlishly when Inti Palla abruptly broke off:

'In return for what I've done for you, I'd like you to promise me something.'

Blinded by her enthusiasm, Anamaya replied without thinking:

'Anything you want!'

'Don't let Manco or his brother Paullu win the race.'

Anamaya's heart missed a beat. Instinctively she retreated, breaking the embrace.

'But why?' she asked weakly, 'I don't know them any better than Guaypar!'

'Anamaya, don't be such a fool! Sometimes you're a real idiot! Guaypar is one of us, whereas Manco and Paullu belong to Huascar's clan, Huascar the Cuzco madman! If Manco or his brother win, the Cuzco people will take it as a sign—'

'Inti Palla! You know very well that Prince Atahualpa himself refused—'

'I know what I know! And I know a lot more than you about certain things!'

'And anyway, how do you expect me to prevent Manco or Paullu winning the race if they're the strongest?'

The princess's eyes burned fiercely:

'By asking the Sacred Double! Everyone knows you have special powers – that's why we accepted you among us, Anamaya. Don't you forget it!'

Anamaya's face flushed scarlet as she protested:

'No, that's not true! I don't have any powers!'

'Of course you do. Aren't you the *Coya Camaquen*? All you have to do is tell the Sacred Double not to accept them as winners!'

'You're crazy, Inti Palla!'

'I'm not! If you like, you could also tell him that it displeases

Huayna Capac to see them win. The Emperor speaks to you, doesn't he?'

Trembling with both outrage and shame, Anamaya drew herself up:

'Has Prince Atahualpa asked for this ridiculous lie or is it your own doing?'

'What's it to you?'

'Because if it is him I want to hear it from his own mouth!'

Her face made ugly by bile, Inti Palla looked as if she was about to slap Anamaya:

'You're such an idiot! It's a present I want to surprise him with. And you should want it for him, too. You owe him a lot, if I'm not mistaken.'

For a prolonged moment they faced each other like two warriors on the battleground. Finally, Inti Palla murmured:

'Anamaya, don't make me regret being your friend, or remind me that you're not pure Inca . . .'

Now, as the first light of dawn revealed the peaks that the boys would have to cross, Anamaya shivered, her face somber.

Inti Palla's poison had taken effect. What should have been a moment of joy became a dark shadow across the future.

'Don't make a sound. Keep your eyes shut.'

Anamaya woke with a start in the dark, her heart beating furiously. She felt a large hand on her shoulder, a hard-callused hand.

Despite the deep-throated order, she opened her eyes. The dwarf's silhouette was as spine-chilling as a ghost.

'You're hard to get to, princess . . . O exalted *Coya Camaquen* . . .'

'I'm in no mood for laughing, first-born son! And I hate being woken up like that!'

She sat up, a shadow of anger crossing her blue eyes. But the dwarf ignored her bad mood and sat on the mat beside her.

'You're right not to laugh, princess,' he said, nodding his head. 'War is coming.'

'War?'

'I can feel it. I know it. During tomorrow's *huarachiku*, it isn't the young warriors who are competing, but the clans. Atahualpa and the northern families versus Huascar and the Cuzco clans . . . brother against brother, a blood-feud . . .'

'Your friend Inti Palla asked me to "use my powers" to prevent the Cuzco boys from winning. She seemed especially worried about Manco . . .'

'She's acting on behalf of Atahualpa.'

Anamaya shook her head.

'She said she wasn't. And I believe her. Atahualpa has too much integrity to lower himself like this. And remember, he himself declined the imperial *borla*.'

'But others want it for him. What did you tell our charming princess?'

'That I had no magic powers . . .'

The dwarf sighed.

'I know them, I've watched them long enough. Noble Incas, worshipers of the Sun God, the Moon Goddess, the God of Thunder: Hah! What a joke! Bloodthirsty like a pack of savage dogs, power-hungry, tyrannical, ferocious . . .'

'Quiet, don't be blasphemous.'

'I'm not blaspheming, gentle princess. It's just that I don't want to die . . .'

The dwarf fell silent. She felt his breath not far from her face and his hand on her shoulder was the hand of a friend. *Coya Camaquen* . . .

There was nothing to do or say, and the time for tears had passed. She remembered their first night when she'd been terrorized by loneliness, and she'd found refuge in his arms.

So Anamaya took the trembling dwarf in hers, and sang to him softly, as if he were a child who needed shelter from the storm.

CHAPTER 8

Tumebamba, December 1528

A LOW, GRAY SKY RAINED DRIZZLE OVER THE TOWN. From where he stood at the base of the cliff, Manco could see the palaces and huts of Tumebamba. They wafted in and out of view through the shifting fog and the many plumes of smoke rising from the offerings burning for the gods. In the great central place, before the Temple of the Sun, he could see the motley crowd of notables huddling around Huayna Capac's desiccated body, lying serenely beneath its feather canopy.

The Emperor's golden Sacred Double gleamed on the nearby temple steps.

That was where the finish line was, for those who managed to finish the Great Race.

It seemed impossibly far away.

'No, not that far,' said Paullu, standing beside him, as if he had read his brother's thoughts. 'Not too far for you, Manco, if you want it enough . . .'

He laughed easily and poked Manco playfully in the ribs:

'. . . But it's true that your legs are a little short! Bah, I'll wait for you!'

Manco smiled. They both knew that he ran twice as fast as Paullu. Still, they would try to run as much of the race as possible alongside each other. They had been born under the same moon, and their friendship was indestructible.

Both were sons of the dead Emperor, born on almost the same day. But this wasn't the key to their friendship: after all, Huayna Capac had as many sons as there were stars in the sky.

In truth, neither had met their shared father – or at least, they couldn't remember if they had. Each of their mothers had been born of the highest clans in Cuzco, and had been among the many wives whom the Emperor had left behind when he had moved to Quito, to lie there each night with any number of his concubines and spread his seed like pollen to the wind.

But their mothers had raised them together. And from the very beginning, from when they had spoken their first words, Manco and Paullu had been inseparable.

Firmly gripping Manco's shoulder, Paullu said confidently: 'You're going to win, I know it. And I'm going to win too, because I'm not letting you out of my sight! Now come along, it's time we drank some *chicha* and offered tribute to the gods.'

The priests had lit a fire at the foot of the *huaca Anahuarque*, an ancestor reincarnated in stone who, like the original in Cuzco, was reputed to have run as fast as a falcon flew. Clumps of uncombed alpaca wool, coca leaves and maize fruit burned as offerings on the fire. The sacrifice of llama kids was to follow.

But Manco didn't pay much attention to these goings-on. He was starving, and his stomach hurt. He could see the same anxiety as his on the hollow faces of the other boys, their eyes feverish and circled with exhaustion.

But they all strained to stand tall; none wanted to betray weakness.

They each watched for their uncles, who were moving to and fro through the ill-smelling smoke. For before the start of the race came the whipping ritual: each boy was to be whipped by his uncle, as a reminder of the nature of Inca law.

Manco dreaded this event more than the race itself, but not because of the pain; the anticipated ignominy made him swell him with rage.

Luckily his uncle was feeble: Manco doubted he would feel much when the leather whip came down on his arms and legs. The same could not be said for the other initiates.

He stood up and smiled an embarrassed smile. 'I'm only fourteen,' he thought to himself, 'but I'm stronger than him. I'm stronger than all of them.'

He had to believe his brother. He had to be as confident as Paullu. Today, he was going to win.

Trumpets sounded the start signal, and their notes echoed from the valley floor to the peaks around it. Manco released all his tension; he forgot all his self-doubt and his fatigue, he forgot about the enormity of the task before him, and he ignored the cold rain as he settled easily into his pace.

He raced down the first slope as nimbly as a puma, powerful, happy and free. He would have cried out in joy if he hadn't had to save his breath.

The path's first stretch lay true North: after the initial (too short) descent, the competitors had to climb a black peak, moderate enough in appearance but which in reality had an awkward surface of rocks and stones that made each step a grueling trial. It was only beyond this that the path turned to the West and led them down a long, gentle slope to the base of Huanacauri, the *apu*, the God-mountain that watched them defiantly. If they reached his summit and survived the descent, a loop would then lead them by the plateau of the Temple of the Sun, and then to the severely testing final climb, through a ravine where the virgins were waiting, until they returned to the first peak of the race.

Paullu stayed right on his heels. Together, they easily passed the pack on the first few bends of the path. Once they reached the ghastly rock field, however, they struggled heavily with their weary legs. And on this dismal summit, open and unprotected, the wind lashed the rain across their faces far more stingingly than their uncles' whips had done earlier.

Manco's breath shortened much sooner than he had expected. His lungs burned and his legs stiffened. He could hear Paullu's raucous panting falling further behind. Further still, he could hear the faint sound of the rest of the competitors looming up behind them, their indistinct cries swallowed up in the immense valley. His own body ached and resisted his efforts.

He paused to glance back and saw Paullu wincing with pain. He signaled for him to go on, not to wait for him . . .

Just then a group suddenly appeared from around a bend: boys from the northern clan. Manco noticed Guaypar, the bravest of them all, throw him a disdainful look as he sped ahead to take the lead.

Hatred spurred Manco on, and he surged onward heedless of the sharp stones that cut through the soles of his sandals.

He quickly made up ground and felt his breath steady. But Guaypar was racing easily across the rocks, lifting his feet high.

Manco ignored the pain from his quivering muscles and burning lungs; he shut out the feelings of his body completely, and relied on his spirit to drive him on.

Soon he had caught up with Guaypar, and together they reached a narrow path barely wide enough for two abreast.

They ran side by side, straining to overtake each other, both their faces taut with effort. But then Guaypar fell back and yielded.

As Manco overtook him, Guaypar, jerking awkwardly in a

desperate effort to keep up, lost his balance and rammed his elbow into Manco. For a suspended instant, the young prince wavered and snatched at the emptiness in front of him before darting ahead.

Almost unwillingly, he shouted triumphantly, the sound bouncing off the stones.

Guaypar couldn't keep up.

Manco didn't have to look back to know that the rest, including Paullu, were far behind. Despite his confidence, Manco knew that his fragile friend could never keep up with him. Nevertheless, he was sure Paullu wouldn't be last, and so wouldn't have to wear the ill-famed black shorts given to that luckless person.

He reached the stony summit and rushed down the other side. He stretched his stride to the full, intent on increasing his lead. He kept his eyes fixed intently on the next peak.

He felt elated, his feeling of strength over all the living things around him amplifying into an epiphany: he was Man amid the stones, the insects, the souls. *'I am the wind, I am the rain, I am the light.'*

He had the impression that a benevolent eye was watching over him, watching from the sky and from behind each rock, from everywhere.

Although the race seemed endless, his breathing steadied, and he felt strangely calm. He slowed before the first steep rise up Huanacauri. Up high, the trail ran along a ridge with sheer drops on both sides, a giddy tightrope pass.

Manco knew the crippling power of vertigo. He knew that on steep slopes, his heart could stop, that he could become paralyzed, unable to take another step. He had trained himself for this and had practiced forcing himself through that moment of absolute terror, which could freeze him on the spot.

But as he approached the precipice, he did exactly what he shouldn't have done: he looked down into the abyss.

In his mind's eye, he saw himself falling to his death on the rocks far below. His legs trembled. And as he ran along the narrow ridge, the hairs on the back of his neck rose, and an icy fear gripped him. The void seemed to grow deeper with each step he took, and seemed to take on a bizarre life of its own, as if smiling to him and pulling him in.

A great boulder blocked the way, leaving only a narrow strip of path past the sheer cliff. Manco plastered himself flat against the boulder, digging his panicked hands into its pitifully shallow crevices.

Only a few paces on, the path left the ridge and trailed away up a gentle grassy slope. But to get there he would have to let go of the boulder and face the void. He would have to accept his fear, confront it.

He couldn't.

Raindrops mixed with tears of rage on his cheeks. Through the fog, he heard the sounds of the other competitors approaching: the cries of those falling and hurting themselves, and of those calling to and encouraging each other.

Suddenly Guaypar appeared and sniggered at him as he flew by:

'Manco! Manco, you're going to fall off, and you won't even have the black shorts to hold you up! You're a coward, Cuzco boy!'

Guaypar was right. Just as earlier he had been filled with courage, so now he was gripped by fear. He hid behind his shame as he had behind his earlier feeling of invincibility. He could stay stuck where he was until nightfall, or until his hands let go. Then they would find his body broken on the rocks below. Where was his ancestor, now so silent? Where had his soaring bravado gone?

Only panic remained. His heart beat as fast as a humming-bird's wing.

'Manco!'

Paullu's familiar voice. He had immediately realized what was happening. Gently, he said:

'Here, give me your hand . . .'

Manco obeyed blindly. He retreated step by step until he reached the trail where his brother stood waiting. His limbs were quivering.

'Breathe easy. Trust me. I'll go first, you follow me.'

Paullu went ahead and stepped around the boulder nimbly. He turned and looked back.

'Your turn now.'

'I can't.'

'Yes, you can. If I can do it, you can do it.'

If I can do it, you can do it. It was the sentence that had held them together since childhood, the bonding catchphrase of soul brothers.

Manco inched forward. His brother's voice reassured him, although he couldn't understand the words he spoke. But when he was poised on the edge of the cliff, he felt himself pull back – and he began to slip . . .

Paullu grabbed his wrist.

'Stay with me, brother.'

Then Manco was safe.

He saw that many runners had passed them and were not far from the peak. Paullu didn't give him the opportunity to regret the time they had lost:

'Run, Manco, run! You're the fastest, and I'm proud of you!'

'No, I'm a coward . . .'

'You're brave and strong, Manco, and you've a brother who loves you and will do anything he can to help you . . . so go on, win the race for the two of us!'

His heart started beating again, and he swept the rain from his face.

I am the wind . . . he thought as he lifted his feet, heavy as granite.

*   *   *

He ran on towards the summit, and one by one overtook all those who had passed him earlier during his moment of terror. He willed himself on, ignoring his pain and pushing his shame into a corner of his soul. He ran, gritting his teeth.

He thought of the honor of being first – 'the falcon' – and of the pleasure of watching those behind him arrive exhausted.

He would secretly enjoy watching Guaypar's vexation, he thought as he overtook him for the second time in the race, although this time without even bothering to look at him.

He ran as if he had limitless breath. He barely noticed the path ahead of him, or the virgins gathered on the other side of the ravine. Everything danced magically before him: the mountains, the clouds, the bushes, the entire valley danced in time with his breath.

'Watch out!'

He heard the cry at the same time as he heard the hiss. He stopped dead: a long, gray snake with yellow stripes, its body, as thick as a human arm, reared up on the path ahead.

'Watch out,' repeated the mysterious voice, softer this time.

Then he saw her approach behind the snake as it slithered along menacingly, its pink mouth stretched open to reveal its pointed, venomous fangs.

'Don't move,' said the girl.

Manco's breathing became quicker as he looked into the girl's eyes. By Inti, was such a color possible?

They were bluer than the southern sky. Was she really a girl, of flesh and blood, and not a magic being?

Manco watched her bend gently, never taking her strange blue-eyed stare off the reptile. The snake coiled its length into a heap, its head and neck swaying as if about to attack.

Automatically, Manco picked up a stone.

'Put it down,' said the girl, without looking in his direction. 'Let me take care of it.'

Her commands were calm and self-assured. It didn't occur to him to do otherwise. She looked directly into the snake's dilated eye-slits, as if trying to hypnotize it. She squatted carefully . . .

The snake wound its coils even tighter and slipped its head in amongst them.

Manco heard someone approaching behind him: Guaypar coming down the embankment. Just then the snake uncoiled and flashed forward, vanishing into the bushes.

The blue-eyed girl stood up and smiled. Her shining face was like a beacon of hope amidst the gray mountains.

'The road is clear!' she said lightly.

Manco was aware that Guaypar had stopped to watch them. He hesitated for a moment. But the girl waved him on.

And so he took off and ran all the way to the great square in Tumebamba as if nothing could stop him.

Manco had finished first, and as he collapsed into the mud he could hear the cheering of his fellow competitors on the clifftop path, looking down at him in the town. He was half unconscious, but as he'd floated home to the finish he'd felt as if he was suspended in the unknown girl's blue eyes.

CHAPTER 9

Tumebamba, December 1528

A LONG GOLD-LACED CORD SURROUNDED THE great square, held up on solid gold and silver posts. Light rain fell on a fire at its center on which coca leaves and maize burned, spreading a sweet, heady odor.

Manco's mouth was clammy. His tongue and palate retained the bitter, throbbing taste of *chicha*. While he half listened to Villa Oma and a group of priests praising the courage of the initiates nearby, he reran the race in his mind. He remembered his strength, his terrible vertigo, and the giddiness of victory.

A rising eddy of coca-leaf smoke enveloped the gold Sacred Double, and briefly obscured the one they called *Coya Camaquen*. But when her strange face reappeared and they caught each other's gaze, Manco was mesmerized.

Sitting beside him, Paullu picked up on their covert exchange. He grinned:

'You think she's pretty?'

'I don't know . . . she's different from the others. Where's she from?'

'The jungle, apparently.'

Now the priests approached the initiates. With feathers

dipped in bowls of llama blood, they streaked lines across each boy's face. This prepared them for the oath-taking rite.

It seemed to Manco that the words coming from his mouth, swearing loyalty to the Sun and allegiance to the Inca, were not his own. Only one thing really mattered to him in this whole ritual: to hear the words that at last entitled him to be called an *auqui*, a warrior.

As the race winner, he was the first to be presented with the white shorts. Complementing that much-coveted garment were a pair of rush-soled sandals, a red tunic with a white stripe – and a glorious feathered headband hung with orbs of silver and gold.

A crowd looked on: parents, clan members, the nobility of Cuzco and Quito, all watching with open admiration and, occasionally, jealousy.

Manco stood tall with pride. The next to be honored, after the winner, were the runners-up, including Paullu and Guaypar. But while his brother glanced at him affectionately, Guaypar made clear his anger at the winner's somewhat arch grin. Far from lowering his head humbly, as were the losers now receiving the shameful black shorts, he exuded a defiant arrogance, and a barely veiled menace.

The hours went by, and singing was followed by dancing. The happy sounds of laughter and congratulations filled the square. Manco went to pay his respects to the veteran warriors, all of whom smiled benevolently as they held him by the shoulders in their grizzled hands.

But no matter to whom he was speaking, his thoughts were always returning to the young girl married to the gold statue.

When at long last the ritual was over, the virgins brought the boys jugs of *chicha*. They would offer it to the newly promoted young warriors to drink, and then remain near them through the last night of the *huarachiku*. Drunk on beer, the young men would affront the moon goddess Quilla's purity, and shame the spirits of their ancestors. It was traditional.

Manco was stupefied when he saw Anamaya carry her jug towards Guaypar. He pointed her out to Paullu:

'She supports that insect?'

'She would have had no choice, Manco. She belongs to Atahualpa's clan.'

'Clans . . . it's always about clans, Paullu. They were never an issue for the great Manco Capac, founder of our dynasty. And let me tell you that I certainly wasn't thinking about clans when I was running that race!'

'Well, the problem isn't you, brother. It's that others think about them.'

The girls assigned to them approached, smiling, their gazes lowered respectfully. They were very young, and pretty as dolls as they poured the *chicha* from their pitchers. Manco drank his *chicha* down in great big gulps. It had been brewed fresh that very morning, and its soft bite slaked his thirst and revitalized his tired body.

The virgins immediately replenished the emptied pitchers from enormous jugs with ropes attached that servants could tilt forward to pour. Like the others, Anamaya filled her pitcher from the mouth of one such *macca*, its earthenware elaborately painted. The *chicha* flowed in rivers, and its slightly nauseating bitterness permeated the air.

They invoked Inti for the final time. Gradually, the boys became increasingly drunk until they were staggering about, exhausted. In a short while their knees would buckle and they would close their eyes. They would be overcome by a desire to find some place to lie down and sleep. However, Manco felt the few sober ones were watching him from the corners of their eyes. He shut his eyes to concentrate.

'Manco?'

He felt Paullu tugging on his sleeve. He opened his eyes to find Anamaya in front of him.

'It's you!' he exclaimed, slurring his words – and instantly regretted all the *chicha* he had drunk. 'I want to thank you, Anamaya. You probably saved my life today.'

Anamaya made a vague gesture of denial:

'No, the snake would only have prevented you from winning by stopping you on the trail: he didn't want to kill you. Snakes slithered between my feet when I was learning to walk. I learned to make friends with them.'

To emphasize this she showed him the two intertwined golden serpents on her wrist bracelet. He barely noticed. Her blue eyes still made him nervous. He was privately admiring her strong, svelte figure.

'Isn't the snake a symbol of wisdom?'

'That's what they say.'

'Why do people all look at you, Anamaya?'

Anamaya smiled coyly.

'Not as much as they look at you today, noble warrior.'

At that point Anamaya noticed Villa Oma looking sternly in her direction. The Sage motioned haughtily for her to move away from Manco. She bowed to the brothers:

'I must leave you now. But I hope you both have a happy night, and may Mother Quilla bless you!'

Once she had gone, Manco turned playfully to Paullu:

'So what do you think, brother? Do we like her or not?'

'She's not like the others, at any rate. But did you see the Sage watching her like a jealous old husband? I don't think he approves of his protégée keeping our company.'

That night, Anamaya rediscovered fear.

A heartening fire glowed in the *cancha*'s courtyard. By the light of its blaze she could see the demented look in Guaypar's eyes. He had been drinking continuously since nightfall, drowning his humiliation in *chicha*.

His hands were trembling so much that he poured as much

chicha on his *unku* as he did down his throat. But inebriation didn't put him to sleep. He reeked of alcohol. He puffed his chest and outstretched his hand to the moon, as if trying to bury his fingers in her, and he mouthed inaudible words. And then he crashed back down, his hand searching for the pitcher of beer.

'It's empty,' Guaypar yapped. 'Get me some more, blue-eyed girl!'

'You've drunk a lot already,' replied Anamaya softly. 'Maybe you should rest now.'

'Go get me some *chicha*! Get me some *chicha*, and don't talk back.'

But as Anamaya rose he reached out his hand to grab her thigh. Anamaya dodged him, her tunic lifting as she spun away, but Guaypar managed to grab it and started pulling her to him. She kneed him hard and he let go, falling sideways and laughing:

'You like my dear brother Manco, don't you?'

'Guaypar . . .'

'I saw the two of you looking at each other! But you're only a girl from the jungle, and he is a from a noble Cuzco clan, after all. You'll never get him—'

'I am your father's Sacred Double's wife. Don't forget it!'

'I know, I know, the little *Coya Camaquen*! Hah! I bet Villa Oma had to make up a name just for you!'

Guaypar stumbled as he rose to his feet, his face twisted with rage.

'Manco is a cheat!' he said to no one in particular. 'Soon everyone will know it.'

Anamaya remembered Inti Palla's rant against Manco. Yet Manco had won the race!

Although it should have been a night of celebration, she felt its shadows threaten her soul. The animosity between the Cuzco and Quito clans hung thick in the air. Guaypar stood there swaying and pointed his finger at her:

'And you helped him cheat, *Coya*—'

'*Me?*'

'You let him win!'

'Don't be ridiculous. I just stopped him from stepping on a snake—'

'Inti put that snake there for a reason, and you removed it. Isn't that cheating? You helped that mangy dog win and he's not even Atahualpa's real brother, as I am. You betrayed us!'

'I didn't mean—'

But Anamaya decided to hold her tongue. There was no point in arguing. Guaypar was too drunk to hear reason. All she could do was wait for him to flounder in his *chicha* and pass out.

But Guaypar stayed upright, albeit unsteadily.

'Come,' he growled. 'Follow me.'

'Where?'

Guaypar stared at Anamaya with a renewed intensity. He sneered:

'You're not so ugly after all! I like the look of you, jungle girl. In fact, I prefer you to the other girls, although you're a bad seed!'

Anamaya bit her lip as she stepped away from him. But Guaypar grabbed her brutally by the arm and dragged her roughly across the square. She saw that he was heading towards the *cancha*'s exit and she resisted with all her strength. But he wouldn't let go and ignored her pleas.

Drunkenness reigned in the streets. No one paid them the slightest attention. From within each *cancha* they passed, they heard singing and merriment, sometimes the lilt of flutes or the thudding of drums. The many fires flung freakish, flickering shadows on the walls. At each crossroad lay semi-conscious figures writhing in their own vomit. The bitter smell of *chicha* pervaded the air.

Guaypar stopped in his tracks before a thin wall, recovered his balance and yelled:

'Manco! Paullu!'

He thrust Anamaya ahead of him through the brothers' *cancha*'s entrance.

'Guaypar!'

Anamaya was relieved to recognize Manco's noble figure silhouetted against the fire as he rose to his feet. He didn't seem drunk, although his eyes were bloodshot and he was breathing heavily.

'Let go of her,' he snarled. 'Let go of the *Coya*. You've no right to treat her so.'

Now Paullu got up. He walked slowly into the firelight and said calmly:

'Go back to your own *cancha*, Guaypar. You've still got to finish the—'

'Here they are!' Guaypar said scornfully and threw Anamaya violently to the ground, 'Here are the brothers you love so much! A pair of cheats, always together the better to hide their cowardice!'

'You're not wearing the black shorts, Guaypar? And yet they would suit you perfectly since they're as black as your own soul . . .'

Manco, gritting his teeth in anger, threw his cape back over his shoulder and stepped forward, fists raised.

'No, Manco,' protested Anamaya. 'He doesn't know what he's doing . . .'

Too late. With a roar, Guaypar plunged his right hand into his tunic; he pulled out a *tumi*, a sickle-shaped blade that glinted in the firelight. Guaypar sliced through the air twice before pointing the copper blade at Manco's face:

'Now you're *really* going to run fast, Manco, as fast as I want you to.'

Paullu sidled next to Anamaya, grabbed her by the shoulders and pulled her away from the action. Meanwhile Manco sidestepped the knife, moving as deftly as a desert ocelot.

'Well, look at this,' growled Manco, his voice strained. 'He accuses us of cowardice, but he himself wields a *tumi* against bare hands!'

'Cheat! You're a crew of Cuzco scoundrels! Everyone cheats in Cuzco! You pretend you're so noble, but you're just a fraud—'

There was movement in the darkness that encircled them; a crowd had gathered – servants, uncles, sisters, aunts – but no one said a word. A man was not held accountable for what he said in liquor. But Manco was sober and had been publicly insulted: it was for him to reply.

'This is it, Guaypar. I've waited a long time for this moment. Come on, then, try and cut my throat with your knife. Come on – do it, if you can!'

The two boys circled around one another by the light of the fire. Guaypar seemed to have sobered up slightly. But when he lunged across the burning embers, Manco dodged him easily. Both his hands shot forth simultaneously, and in a flash he had Guaypar's empty hand jammed against his shoulder while he grabbed the other that held the *tumi*. Seeing red, Manco stepped back a little and spun on his heel. His right hand, holding Guaypar's, swept around and brought the knife across Guaypar's face: a great crimson gash appeared on his cheek, and he retreated with a cry of pain. Blood flowed freely from his wound. Guaypar ran his fingers over his face and looked at his red hand, stunned.

'Go home, Guaypar!' said Paullu. 'While there's still time!'

'No, brother,' taunted Manco. 'There is no more time: this is it.'

Just then, as if being cut had woken him from a dream, Guaypar threw his *tumi* aside and dived at Manco, tackling him to the ground. Then it was a blur, the two boys rolling around beside the fire like savage dogs, a cloud of dust rising from them. Their legs kicked into the fire, scattering embers and a shower of sparks. Anamaya let out a cry, and Paullu had to hold her back from diving in and separating them.

'Leave them be, Anamaya. It must run its course.'

Manco and Guaypar battled in the dust, wrapped so close that the blood of one would streak the other. Their gasps were punctuated with cries of pain whenever a punch landed, or one or the other's fingers would manage to get a hold of an eye or neck. Suddenly, Anamaya saw Guaypar roll to the side, his *unku* tearing off him with a great cracking sound. Manco immediately stood up and jumped onto him, his knees landing on his stomach, and seized his blood-sodden throat.

'Didn't you swear to bear the warrior's courage?' asked Manco, his voice barely audible. 'To embody honor?'

Guaypar couldn't reply. He gasped for air, strangled. Manco said in a louder voice:

'Did you or did you not swear an oath to our sun god Inti and to Quilla the moon? To all our ancestors, and to the spirit of every Emperor that's ever been?'

Anamaya sensed that Manco was losing control of his rage. She shrugged off Paullu's hand:

'Manco, please, let him be . . .'

But Manco wasn't listening.

'Are you not the one who insulted the virgin whom my father chose to watch over his Sacred Double?'

His hands released Guaypar's throat and closed into fists, fists that came raining down on that hated face, the fists of a berserk warrior. Neither Anamaya's cries nor Guaypar's own pleas stopped Manco in his fury. The crowd of onlookers had gathered closer together, but still no one intervened. Anamaya wanted to grab hold of Manco's flailing arms, but she saw the flames dancing in the young Inca's black eyes. And in those flames she saw too all the hatred borne by Guaypar burning . . .

'That's enough!'

The order came abruptly out of the surrounding night. Anamaya turned to look just as Manco lifted his head, his fist suspended in the air. A man in priest's garb entered the ring of light around the fire and pointed his hand:

'That's enough, Manco. Don't kill him.'

Anamaya saw that it was one of Manco's uncles. He looked at her warily for a moment before adding:

'The lesson has been given, and nobody will forget it: no one insults the Cuzco clans and gets away with it.'

Breathing heavily, Manco disengaged himself and stood up slowly. Anamaya looked at Paullu who had stayed silent and motionless throughout the fight. She saw sadness in his eyes as he watched his brother recover his breath.

Also breathing hard, but spitting blood too, Guaypar rolled over and then weakly got up on his knees. He lifted himself a little, and he looked entreatingly for Anamaya's help. She kept her hands at her sides. With the last of his strength he straightened himself, his hands clutching his stomach, and said:

'You are damned, Manco. You'll burn before you reach the Other World. Your soul will never be free.'

Manco continued wiping the blood from his hands:

'Only the damned speak of damning.'

Anamaya hesitated as Guaypar stumbled out of the *cancha*. Her gaze became locked to Manco's.

'I must go with him,' she said after a while, 'I'm obliged to look after him tonight, although I know he's wrong about you.'

Manco glanced at Paullu, and then replied, his voice strangely gentle after so much violence:

'I know, blue-eyed sister . . .'

'Take care of yourself, Manco, and don't be afraid of snakes.'

'Alas, you won't always be by the side of the road to lure them away from me.'

But Anamaya's silhouette was already fading into the smoke-filled night.

CHAPTER 10

Tumebamba, December 1528

'WAKE UP, ANAMAYA.'

Her eyelids were heavy. She would have liked to have remained asleep on her mat. The girl wrapped her *manta* tighter around herself. Villa Oma looked at her sternly.

He had come in silently, as usual, his straw-soled sandals sliding noiselessly across the flagstones. And, again as usual, his tall figure and green-tinged mouth seemed menacing.

'Get up quickly!'

'What's happening?'

'Don't talk, just get up and follow me.'

It had been but two days since the boys' initiation rites had finished. Two nights had passed since Manco and Guaypar had fought and insulted one another. Only two days of peace for Anamaya.

She got up and looked regretfully at her warm bed. The dawn gave only the faintest light at the edges of the tapestry covering the door to the inner court.

'What have I done wrong?'

'I've no idea. I only know that your presence here in Tumebamba may not be such a good thing.'

'But I didn't want Manco to fight Guaypar—'

'Do you think I'm concerned with such nonsense?'

Villa Oma's serious tone dispelled the last vestiges of sleep and made Anamaya shudder.

In an alcove by the window sat a silver disk consecrated to Quilla, the moon mother. It shimmered delicately in the dark, as if shedding tears. Villa Oma's dry fingers clutched the door-hanging. His hollow voice echoed like a thunderclap:

'The Emperor's desiccated body is not in the temple. It cannot be found.'

Anamaya felt as if someone had punched her in the stomach. She had trouble breathing. In a tiny voice she said:

'What did you say?'

'You heard me. I said Huayna Capac's mummy has disappeared.'

Villa Oma raised his eyes in an expression of powerlessness. His face was creased with deep wrinkles brought on by worry and anger.

'At sunrise I went with the other priests to Inti's temple. The niche was empty. The body was gone from its bed.'

'But . . . who would have dared do such a thing?'

'Who? And how? Only one thing is for certain: they will accuse you of the crime, child.'

'Me? Why me? No one can say I could do such a thing, Villa Oma, you know that perfectly well!'

'I'm not the one accusing you, Anamaya,' he said with a listless sigh. 'But others will be only too happy to do so, alas. You are the *Coya Camaquen*: are you not therefore the one charged with protecting the mummy, with the Sacred Double's help? Isn't that what Huayna Capac ordered you to do from his deathbed? To look after him in this world after he had gone to the next?'

Anamaya's vision was blurred by tears. But she felt so wronged that presently she wiped them away with the back of her hand. She was no longer a terrified child brought before the Inca of all the Incas. Her voice trembled with anger:

'And why, exactly, would I have committed such a crime?'

Villa Oma brushed away her question with an irritated gesture:

'Who cares? You are Atahualpa's protégée. They'll make something up if they have to.'

'I don't understand . . .'

'Really? You haven't noticed that the Cuzco clans hate us and would do whatever it takes to be rid of us—'

Villa Oma broke off suddenly. People were shouting in the inner court. They were shouting Anamaya's name with hate in their voices, vilifying her.

'Well, they certainly didn't waste any time,' Villa Oma said calmly. 'Be prepared, my child. They are the ones you shall have to convince of your innocence.'

'There she is!'

'She's the one!'

'She's the one who made Lord Huayna Capac vanish!'

'Sacrilege! The mummy's been defiled! The world is doomed! Inti's wrath will fall upon us!'

'It's the baleful blue-eyed witch's fault! Inti wants her burned to ashes, Quilla would see her drowned in the river!'

Huayna Capac's palace had an immense inner courtyard. Even so, it was so packed with frantic Incas that the late arrivals remained bottlenecked at the door, waving angrily under the twin snakes carved into its lintel. Everyone present was a member of one or other of the Cuzco clans, all loyal to Huascar. Some had come armed, and bawled threats as they brandished their clubs, having previously polished the black stones of their weapons. Others waved spears, or whirled their slingshots, or brandished obsidian axes . . .

The heads of each clan had gathered in a circle in the courtyard's center and murmured amongst themselves, looking at one another gravely. And although their words may still have been civil, their glances told another tale – and no one received more glances than Anamaya, who stood buffered between Atahualpa and Villa Oma. They formed a still and silent trio.

'The omens have been terrible since that girl arrived,' yelled one old man.' She's a witch!'

'Everyone knows that you only protect her to taunt us, Atahualpa!' pronounced one richly dressed warrior. He pointed his colorfully feathered spear at her in emphasis, and those beside him muttered their agreement. The man wore the headpiece of a general. His *unku* was cut from the softest vicuña pelt and was decorated with the motifs of the highest clans. He smiled arrogantly:

'We've fathomed your deception, Atahualpa! You want to prevent Huayna Capac's mummy from reaching the Unique Temple at Cuzco! You don't want to see the Emperor take his place among our ancestors, because then Huascar, our Emperor-elect, would inherit his father's power to take the throne! That's why you asked this girl to make the mummy disappear!'

'Stick her feet in the fire, then she'll tell us where she's hidden him!'

Anamaya singled out Manco's eagle-like profile in the depths of the crowd. He stood beside noble Paullu. They looked down, embarrassed; for they too were Huascar's kin. They would be powerless, should they want to help her . . .

She saw Guaypar at the other end of the court, standing with Atahualpa's people and the Quito noblemen. His face was bruised, his left cheek plastered with healing herbs. His swollen lips winced in a grim smile.

Suddenly, Atahualpa's booming voice sounded loudly above the hum of the crowd:

'Have you all finished talking nonsense?'

His voice revealed nothing of his rage, which was evident only from the quivering of his fingers. Immediately everyone fell silent. He extended his arm straight out like a rod, his palm downturned, and pointed at the people from Cuzco:

'Do you really believe that the *Coya Camaquen*, the one my father chose to watch over his Sacred Double, is capable of such an outrageous sacrilege? Do you really think that I would contradict the will of Inti and prevent my father's return to Cuzco?'

The prince turned to his right and pointed out an old man wearing a headpiece topped with a disk of gold, the mark of a nobleman of the highest rank:

'Colla Topac was there, along with the other clan leaders, when the Emperor Huayna Capac ordained the *Coya Camaquen* before he died. Lord Colla Topac was entrusted by my father to make sure his last wishes were respected in accordance with our Law, before my brother Huascar assumed the *borla*. It is he who is to take my father to Cuzco. He is the one who will bring him to the Temple of Coricancha.'

'It's true,' replied the old nobleman. 'I was so appointed, and no one among us wishes the Emperor's return to his beloved city more than the prince. And neither do I believe that the *Coya Camaquen* is capable of what you accuse her of: the Sun King himself trusted her!'

'Those of you who cry "Treason" the loudest,' continued Atahualpa, 'would do well to weigh your words more carefully – for isn't "Treason" the traitor's loudest cry?'

A frozen silence; then came a high-pitched voice:

'Are you accusing us? Are you threatening us, Atahualpa? We are Huascar's clansmen! Your father's favorite son! How dare you!'

Atahualpa could no longer contain his rage:

'You dare to reply, you who dare to spit on the one ordained by my dead father!'

Amid the boiling tension, Anamaya stepped calmly to the center of the circle. She raised an open hand:

'Don't fight because of me!'

All eyes turned to her.

'Let me go to the temple where the Sacred Double, my betrothed, rests. He will tell me where to find the mummy.'

Both Atahualpa and Villa Oma looked at her, stupefied:

'Do you know what you are saying?' whispered the green-lipped Sage nervously.

Anamaya nodded. In truth, however, what she had just said had surprised her as much as it had the two men. She had no idea where the words had come from; they had flown confidently from her lips of their own volition. Now her heart tightened. Meanwhile, a surprised, newly respectful hum arose from the crowd. Manco and Paullu looked at her with shining eyes. Guaypar, however, had lost his smile. And then someone shouted:

'Atahualpa! If the girl doesn't find the Emperor's body, we'll cut out her intestines!'

The mob murmured its agreement.

Atahualpa watched anxiously as Villa Oma firmly took hold of Anamaya's thin arm. She sensed the pride in his voice, the almost doting pride, when he said:

'Threaten her all you like. But know that she has no fear of you!'

It was only a short walk from the palace to the temple. The heat was oppressive. Anamaya felt it weighing on the back of her neck, and she slowed her breathing. The entire city seemed gripped by a black fog. Gangs of men were pushing through its narrow lanes, their demeanour indicating a dangerous blend of anger and fear. Some muttered insults as she passed them by. Women stood at the doorways of the *canchas* and followed her progress with hate on their faces.

Anamaya walked tall, her gaze doggedly fixed on the cape streaming back from Atahualpa's broad shoulders. She felt comforted by the soldiers at her side and Villa Oma behind her.

They entered the temple and made their way into the room with nine alcoves, a room with no roof save the vault of the sky.

Anamaya detected the brisk murmur of water running through the drains and fountains. The low sun threw shadows on the walls, playfully suggesting animals or, more seriously, gods. The alcoves were carved in alignment with each other along the expertly built walls, and above them was a gold frieze with geometric forms hammered into it.

The Sacred Double resided in the central alcove. But next to him stood an empty pedestal where the mummy should have been. Anamaya could scarcely bear to look.

Villa Oma, however, stared into the space as if trying to conjure up the statue out of nothingness. Eventually he said to Atahualpa:

'I'm certain that it's Huascar's people who pulled this absurd crime!'

'Probably. They've lost their minds. Never has anyone so insulted my father.'

'It shows that Huascar and his people are consumed with fear.'

'Fear? How so? They know perfectly well that I would never contradict my father's wishes. They all know that I won't wear the sacred *llautu* on my head. I don't want to be Emperor. You know that as well as I do, Villa Oma, as well as they all do. The omens are against me . . .'

'Not all of them – you're trying too hard to convince yourself. And Huascar senses it. He's like an animal; he senses more than he thinks. But he sees some things that you don't; he's scared of the powers gathered around you. He's scared of her—' he pointed at Anamaya '—and they live in dread of the day she'll remember what the Emperor told her the night he died. They fear that the Sacred Double will tell her your father's true desire!'

Atahualpa took a moment to contemplate the Sacred Double's serene, inscrutable face. He moved as if to touch it, but changed his mind. The prince turned to Anamaya:

'What do you think, child? Do you agree with the Sage? Do you too think that I'm blind to my father's will?'

'I think that you don't know who you really are, my noble Lord.'

As soon as she had spoken the words, Anamaya stifled a cry and covered her mouth with her hands.

'I'm sorry! Forgive me! The words just came out by themselves. I didn't mean to say that!'

'Listen to her,' said Villa Oma. 'Listen to her, Atahualpa. Huayna Capac speaks through her, I can feel it!'

Atahualpa's bloodshot eyes switched from the Sage back to the girl. Anamaya, however, was looking at the Sacred Double just as a ray of sunlight landed with pinpoint precision on its gold face . . .

'Find the mummy, Anamaya,' whispered Atahualpa. 'Find it!'

And as he turned away, the sun's ray slipped from the statue's helmet to the disks in its ears. Anamaya felt the gold light bounce off it and penetrate her to the core, as if filling her with more secrets, more knowledge that she would carry without being able to tell.

CHAPTER 11

Tumebamba, January 1529

ANAMAYA WALKED WITH VILLA OMA IN THE square in front of the temple. Facing them, on the Tumebamba hills, the *canchas* stood in tidy grids, their high walls enclosing not only the palaces and courtyards of the rich but also the more humble dwellings.

The Sage walked in silence. Anamaya knew better than to pester him with questions. Across the valley she made out Huanacauri's black and blue summit. They were walking together on a paved path that led in a straight line from the temple to the mountaintop.

The day's heat was rising. Anamaya felt pearls of sweat form on her temples and on the back of her neck, and felt them trickle down her spine under her thick ceremonial tunic.

Without slowing the pace, the Sage's hand disappeared into his *chuspa*, his ubiquitous pouch. It emerged clutching a handful of coca leaves and a flask of white powder, lime ground as finely as talc.

'Take this.'

He handed her some coca, and then poured a little lime into her open hand. Anamaya rolled the thick green leaves into a tube, and began to chew on it slowly. Its bitter-sweet taste made her salivate.

Little by little, the town receded behind them. Soon the flagstone road became an unpaved path, lined by two roughly hewn stone walls. Anamaya walked effortlessly, without tiring. She felt uplifted by a kind of euphoria.

Over on the other side of the hill, a gentle slope led to a plateau. On it stood an enormous, crevassed, dun-colored boulder, its gnarled and twisted form giving the impression of both erupting from and driving into the ground.

Anamaya didn't need the Sage to tell her it was a *huaca*. An Ancestor Stone, one of the multitudes of sacred rocks that held up the entire Empire along lines known only to the High Priests.

The souls of all the ancestors and all the gods gathered at these sites to receive the prayers of men and women living in the material world.

Villa Oma came to a halt before the entrance, a space in a wall of stones so finely worked that in some places it blended indistinguishably into the rock itself. The gap was shaped to evoke the lightning bolt of Illapa, the god of thunder.

Villa Oma took another handful of coca leaves from his bulging *chuspa*. This time, however, he placed them in a niche in the wall, at the foot of a small gold statue. He drew a flagon of *chicha* from his travel bag, and poured a little onto the shrine and the ground. Then he stood up, tilted his head slightly, and raised his palms to the sky, imploring the gods.

This done, he turned and handed Anamaya the *chicha*, and told her to drink. She swallowed two long gulps that burned her throat.

'Now we wait,' said the Sage.

Anamaya sat down on a flat, sun-warmed stone, her legs tucked underneath her. The sun caressed her skin and spoke to her. A strange torpor weighed on her, and her eyelids grew heavy as her breathing slowed. Eventually her eyes closed altogether, and she became acutely aware of her body, experiencing each limb as a distinct part in itself. And then suddenly she was whole again, but now so incredibly heavy that she felt herself sliding, falling vertiginously to the center of the earth, an irresistible force pulling her down . . .

Perhaps she had fallen asleep.

When she awoke, dusk was sweeping away the last light of day. She could see a few fires that had been lit on the hillsides around the plateau.

'Villa Oma!'

Nothing but the echo of her call. The effect of the coca and *chicha* had waned. Anamaya was drained and exhausted, and felt enveloped by the spreading darkness.

'Villa OMAAaa!'

The mountains returned her own words to her.

Anamaya stood up, her thighs stiff and her knees creaking. She guided herself with her hands along Illapa's wall. At its end she found the beginning of a path, overgrown with thorn bushes but that seemed to lead around the *huaca*.

She walked carefully, making sure not to slip in her straw sandals. The two snakes on her bracelet flashed in the silver moonlight.

Anamaya stumbled into thick scrub, needled bushes blocking the path more effectively than a stone wall. A wave of panic overcame her, and her breath came faster. She turned abruptly to go back the way she had come – and tripped forward into the darkness. But instead of encountering the solid rock she had expected, she fell head first, arms flailing, through a gap, grazing her thighs on a sharp edge.

When she had recovered her balance, breathing hard and petrified by the silence and blackness all around her, she understood that the rock had opened to let her in.

It was freezing cold here inside, and blacker than the night outside.

Against her will, Anamaya's shoulders trembled. But she

knew, without knowing how she knew, that she had passed the point of no return.

She stood up, and with tiny, searching steps, she inched forward. She felt herself descending a gentle slope. She was going deeper into the earth, ineluctably following the path to its center. Her mouth was dry, and her chest felt bruised from the great thumps of her heart. The girl wanted to shout out loud that she preferred to stay in the world above, that she didn't want to go to the Under World.

Now she was in an immense space. The darkness felt lighter in the soft air. Her outspread arms encountered nothing. She moved forward into the darkness and still there was nothing. Whether she turned to the left or the right it was the same. There was no light, no noise, no walls, nothing but the ground beneath her. Yet she felt more and more certain of one thing: that she was not alone.

'V-Villa Oma?' she whispered, on the verge of tears.

There, in front of her, two yellow eyes shone:

The puma!

So Villa Oma's wish from the first day was to be fulfilled: Anamaya's heart would be fed to the puma, her flesh to the Under World, the universe cleansed of the impure blue in her eyes and rid of the embarrassment of her dubious birth.

The yellow eyes shifted to the left, as if examining her.

Suddenly Huayna Capac's voice resounded in her head. Huayna Capac, the one she had been waiting for all this time, the one for whom she had suffered all those insults and hateful words. His voice was clear and strong; it was not the voice of the dying old man who had spoken to her throughout that fateful night, and who had promised her that he would be with her again, but the voice of his earlier, triumphant self.

'Anamaya! Anamaya, my child, you whose eyes are the color of the sacred lake, how could you have thought that I wouldn't keep my promise? Come, Anamaya, come closer. Don't be afraid of me!'

Anamaya advanced towards the puma's yellow eyes. Although she remained convinced that the creature would devour her, she felt calm. She was resigned to her fate, and felt relieved to have met the Emperor again before she followed him in death.

'They tried to take me away,' he said gently. 'But I want to stay with you until the appointed hour when I shall take my final seat at Cuzco, beside the Sun God. They wanted to take me away, back where I always was . . .

'Anamaya, my child, do not lose your faith in me. Draw your breath from mine, and trust the puma . . .'

His words echoed off the stone and through her head.

Anamaya offered herself, her arms opened wide, to the puma's jaws. She didn't hesitate to offer it her flesh, her blood. But the yellow eyes had disappeared. She could see nothing but the infinite darkness . . .

Although—

Yes: through a crack in the rock above her head, she saw Quilla's silver light, the shining of the moon.

Anamaya touched her cheeks, and ran her hands through her hair.

She was still alive.

Anamaya burst breathless from the dark, near Illapa's wall. Villa Oma was there waiting for her, a white silhouette in the night. She stood before him, smiling.

'He spoke to you, didn't he?'

Anamaya nodded, her eyes ablaze.

'And do you remember what he said?'

'Come.'

This time she was the one leading. They walked rapidly, almost running, towards the town, along its walls, through its lanes, passing the doors of the slumbering *canchas*.

They arrived at the temple. Villa Oma ordered back the

priests, surprised from their sleep, who had tried to stop Anamaya.

In the room with the nine shrines, they saw the great lord Huayna Capac's desiccated body sitting in its place. Mother Quilla illuminated his gold mask and the cape he wore, made of bat skin and the finest vicuña pelt. There he was, as if he'd never moved. His shining metallic face was turned towards his Sacred Double. Villa Oma would have sworn that it was smiling. The old, wily Sage trembled, aghast. Anamaya whispered:

'He promised me that he would always stay near me . . .'

'We're going to have to look after you, young lady. The great lord Huayna Capac visits you at his pleasure. You walk among the souls of the dead, you not only visit the Under World but return from it . . . you are too valuable to us all!'

Anamaya detected a note of fear in his arrogant voice.

'So you don't want to feed me to the puma after all?'

'Oh yes, more than ever, because now I know that the puma protects you.'

Anamaya remembered the puma's yellow eyes burning in the dark, and the abandon with which she had faced it – surrender stronger than her fear, more powerful than death.

And she repeated over and over the Emperor's words to her, her master's instructions:

'Draw your breath from mine, and trust the puma . . .'

PART 2

CHAPTER 12

Seville, Spain, February 1529

H E HAD BEEN WAITING SINCE DAWN.
It had still been night when they had dragged him brutally from his straw mattress, waking him from a fitful sleep. He had thought, 'Today, I'm going to die.'

But this thought didn't rack his nerves as much as might have been expected. Death was less frightening than torture – and they had been holding the threat of torture over him for months. Death was less terrifying, even, than the mere *threat* of torture, and so he decided to welcome it, preferring to die rather than tolerate this endless waiting.

It was almost noon, and the sun glared into the entrance hall of Triana Castle. But his eyes had grown so accustomed to the darkness of his cell that he had to keep them shut.

And he had to endure this maddening silence.

Since they had brought him here that morning, he hadn't heard a single footfall on the great staircase, not one note of birdsong floating in over the walls. He spread his feet – iron cuffs chafed his ankles and tore what was left of his stockings. The chain linking the cuffs chinked and fell heavily onto the polished floorboards. But the metallic rattling died away instantly, swallowed by the engulfing silence.

Indeed, that was the heart – the essence – of the Holy

Inquisition: silence – the power and the violence of it; its infinite capacity to stifle any noise, whether it was the din of life or the stark sound of death.

Finally, that evening, the Inquisitor arrived, wearing a smile.

A tender smile, harder to bear than a threat.

The grinning Inquisitor motioned with his chubby hand for him to approach.

It was a familiar room. Hanging in front of its tall windows, crimson velvet curtains kept out the day as well as the night. Dancing flames from the chandeliers threw shadows on the painted ceiling panels. A mauve carpet ran across the floorboards from the door. An oak chair stood in the center of the room, a chair with a high, straight back that had been worn and polished by the terrified squirming of the hundreds of accused who had sat in it.

The chair stood in front of a platform. On this platform sat three people behind a long table. One was the Inquisitor himself, his young face round, his cheeks as pale as his forehead. He was wearing a plain black cassock and a four-cornered bonnet covered his prematurely bald head. To his right sat the secretary, also in black, but wearing a tightly buttoned coat rather than a cassock. He was an old man with a sad, watchful face. Finally there was the clerk of the court, a young novice – not long ago a mere boy – with pimples and nervous eyes.

Gabriel had barely seated himself in the chair when he heard the first question:

'Are you Gabriel Montelucar y Flores?'

The Inquisitor's dry and wincing voice belied his face: Its bitterness better suited an old man. Gabriel shrugged his shoulders impatiently:

'You know who I am better than I do. Today is the two hundred and fifty-third day that I have been a guest in your prison, and this is the twelfth time that you have asked me that question . . .'

'Answer His Lordship respectfully!' barked the secretary.

Gabriel felt like smiling, but resigned himself to a sigh.

'Your Eminence is not unaware that my name is what the lady says it is.'

'Just answer the questions, Don Gabriel. Is it true that you entered the seminary of Santa Maria del Jesus in the year of Our Lord 1525?'

'Yes. I was there for four years. It's a pity that I was taken from it, I was learning a lot.'

'Including certain absurd heresies from the North?'

'Absurd heresies, Your Eminence? You call the theological sciences, the laws of nature, the philosophy of—'

'Are you a faithful admirer of Erasmus?'

'No more faithful than half the literate population, Your Eminence.'

The Inquisitor smiled again:

'Half the literate population is not the friend of Doña Francesca Hernandez.'

'Your Eminence is aware that I went but three times to Doña Francesca's house.'

'What does it matter how many times? What did you do there?'

'We talked.'

'Just the two of you?'

'Never.'

'And what did you talk about?'

'Of things pertaining to the soul.'

'And of religion, I suppose?'

'As Your Eminence is no doubt aware, religion occasionally concerns things pertaining to the soul.'

'So you discussed the doctrine of Luther?'

'Rarely! And only to condemn it!'

'Is it true that Doña Francesca willfully encouraged the

pursuit of carnal ecstasy under the pretext that the love of God exists in Man as an urge for joy?'

'Sometimes, yes. You see, it can be a form of communion because—'

'And does she not also believe that merely loving God is enough to keep sin at bay from oneself, and that one should fear neither God nor Hell?'

'But it's infinitely more complicated than that! If your Lordship will allow me to speak, Doña Francesca—'

'Did you or did you not hear her tell that God should not be feared?'

'Only to say that He should be loved with joyful conviction!'

'To the point of committing sins of the flesh, on many occasions, and even in public, under the pretext that it is a 'form of communion', as you put it?'

The Inquisitor's face was as cold and hard as an iron mask. Gabriel stiffened, and lost his wry smile.

'I don't understand the question, Your Eminence.'

'Oh no?'

The young clerk cracked his knuckles as the Inquisitor again slipped on his fake smile. He stretched his sausage-like fingers towards the secretary, who nodded, gathered some papers from the pile in front of him, and passed them to the Inquisitor:

'We found this in a book belonging to you. Erasmus's *Enchiridion*, to be precise . . .'

'Translated by the canons of Palencia, and approved of by the Holy Father, as Your Eminence knows.'

'It is not the book that concerns me, Don Gabriel, but this note found in its pages, written by Doña Francesca . . .'

Gabriel felt his legs weaken, and his heart grew heavy in anticipation of what the Inquisitor was about to say:

'You won't mind it too much, I hope, if I read out only one passage . . . *"My dearest friend, why is it that with you I feel*

*able to attain the grace of God Himself? And with the greatest
confidence? Is it possible to embrace a fire as pure – as divine
– as this, and not be consumed by it? After our tender moment
of privacy yesterday, a moment all too brief, I spent the night
imagining you as the savior, for that is what you are to me. You
are, my cherished friend, a jeweled constellation in the heavens,
marked with the seal of the feline, the wild cats, maybe the
lion . . . or perhaps simply the house cat! But I know that the
animal within you lies peacefully, and I adore his purring . . ."*
We shall spare ourselves the rest.'

The Inquisitor put down the letter. His eyes burned with
hatred and lasciviousness:

'These . . . feline comments – are they a continuation of
a theological conversation?'

'Well, it's to do with a birthmark I have on my shoulder, Your
Lordship, which resembles a fat cat, and Doña Francesca . . .'

'And how did she come to know about this birthmark? Did
she see you naked?'

'No!' Gabriel blushed scarlet. 'We discussed it on one
occasion when—'

'In her note, Doña Francesca makes clear reference to a
"tender moment of privacy". Yet you have just told us that
you were never alone with her. Who am I to believe, Don
Gabriel?'

The clerk's quill stopped scratching. Gabriel returned the
trio's accusing glare. The ensuing silence was as cold as the
cuffs around his ankles. The Inquisitor rubbed his podgy
cheeks with his fingers as he said cordially:

'Don Gabriel, please be reasonable. We merely want you
to tell us the truth! We know that Doña Francesca enticed
you to blasphemy several times. We know that you are not
the only one, and that with her you have spoken favorably
of Luther's doctrine. We know that with her you committed
acts, which—'

Gabriel raised his hand to interrupt:

'Your Eminence!'

He was breathing heavily as he stood up:

'Do with me what you will. I have nothing more to say.'

'Do you think so?'

'If I cannot hold my tongue, then I will die.'

'There are things in this world worse than death, sir, far worse.'

Gabriel stared directly at the Inquisitor, who screwed up his eyes and gave a signal to the guards:

'We shall meet again tomorrow, Don Gabriel, with or without the instruments. It's up to you . . .'

CHAPTER 13

Seville, Spain, 1529

T HAT NIGHT, HIS NERVES FRAYED AND WITH
nausea rising in his throat, Gabriel paced the length
and breadth of his narrow cell for more than an hour.
He knew his cell intimately: four squalid walls with only
a thick wooden door and an air vent through which rats
scurried in and out; a tallow lamp hanging over a stinking
bucket that served as a latrine; dirty straw mattresses heaped
along the walls.

He had, at various times, shared this sordid space with two
cloth merchants, both from Cadiz, and a baker. But for the
past two months he had had as a cellmate a strange monk
by the name of Bartholomew.

The monk seemed still young, yet his head was bald. And
although it was difficult to make them out in the perpetual
darkness of the jail his eyes were of the same pale color as
morning fog, somewhere between blue and gray.

His index and ring fingers were joined together, probably
a birth defect. They were sheathed in the same layer of skin,
forming a single digit, and appeared to be perpetually giving
the sign of the benediction.

He was a man of few words. He never complained, and
never showed his fear.

The guards had come for Bartholomew many times, to take him to interrogations, and had once had to bring him back on a mattress. He had groaned throughout that night, but when Gabriel had questioned him the following morning, Bartholomew had revealed nothing. Gabriel didn't even know why he was in the prison. However, he sensed that it was less a spirit of concealment that kept Bartholomew so taciturn, more an uncommon wisdom.

It was always possible, of course, that the monk was an exceptionally gifted actor, and one of the many spies whom the Holy Inquisition had planted in its gaols to catch out less discreet inmates. Once you had entered its dungeons, anything was possible.

Suddenly, a cantankerous Brother Bartholomew ordered:

'Stop pacing about like that, Don Gabriel! Lie down and calm yourself. You are wasting your energy.'

Gabriel gave a start, and obeyed. He curled up on his mattress and lay quietly for a moment. However, feeling Brother Bartholomew's pale gaze lingering on him, he said:

'I'm scared. Tomorrow they are going to torture me. I can't help it, I'm scared.'

The monk nodded his head wordlessly. Gabriel was grateful, for consolations would only have aggravated his anger and shame.

Oh for the love of God, why hadn't he destroyed Doña Francesca's note the moment he had read it? He had realized its rash and incriminating nature the day he had received it!

Now, despite his mistrustful caution, he felt a burning urge to speak. Who cared if the monk was in fact in league with Gabriel's executioners! He had to speak, to tell the truth. He had to purge himself, and by doing so bury the truth! Bury it deep enough so that tomorrow, when their iron instruments tore his limbs apart, he would have nothing to say, and the courage to stay silent.

'Brother Bartholomew, please hear me. They're wrong

about everything. They imagine things that never occurred. They were only words, you see. Love, ecstasy, divine passion, liberty, softness, delight, possession . . . just words! All just words . . . but they'll never believe me.'

'They never will.'

'I could try to explain to them how—'

'Explain nothing!'

The monk spoke in a low, private voice. Don Gabriel was surprised when the monk addressed him with the Spanish familiar '*tu*' instead of the formal '*usted*' he had used until now.

'Say nothing. Scream in agony if you must, but say nothing!'

Gabriel shivered. He realized his teeth were chattering. He stood up, then sat down again, trying to gather himself together.

'I know that they've already tortured her. She must have confessed to God knows what – to denying the Pope, to apostasy, to Lutheran heresies! That we indulged ourselves in bacchanals—'

'No. She didn't tell them anything, otherwise they wouldn't need you.'

'Do you think so? They want to hear me tell that we were lovers . . . such stupidity!'

'Weren't you?'

'All just words, as I said.'

'Alas, my friend, words are good enough for them . . .'

He fell silent, and for a while they listened to the indistinct sounds of the jail, its ever-present shuffling, scurrying and dripping. Each of them became lost in his own terrible thoughts. And then Gabriel said:

'Tomorrow, when they crush my thumbs, when they stick my feet into the flames, when they pierce the palms of my hands—'

'Don't forget the quartering, and the hot wax poured into your wounds!'

A twinkle in the monk's eye prompted Gabriel to smile. For a fraction of a second he forgot his suffocating terror. Brother Bartholomew returned his smile and laid his hand on Gabriel's sweat-sodden wrist:

'Don't let your imagination run wild, Don Gabriel. There will be enough time to fear the instruments tomorrow.'

'You're familiar with them, aren't you?'

'I am familiar with them, yes.'

'And . . . ?'

Brother Bartholomew lifted his hand from Gabriel's wrist. His eyes drifted away and looked blankly at the wall, and the veins in his neck swelled. Automatically, he massaged his crippled fingers. Eventually he whispered:

'One does not know oneself, I mean really know oneself, until they approach you with their irons white from the burning coals. And then, the self-knowledge you acquire is clearer than anything you've ever known!'

'Did you confess?'

Bartholomew didn't move. A distant smile lit his wise young face. He raised his joined fingers to Gabriel:

'Keep the silence, brother. Now, try to rest.'

Gabriel dreamed, and his cell door suddenly transformed into a shutter. But it was neither liberty nor light that crossed the threshold but a slimy swarm of snakes. A river of reptiles, swamping him, coiling around his neck, tugging at his feet!

He woke with a scream. He wasn't dreaming anymore, and the guards removing his ankle cuffs were real enough.

'Well, finally! You take some waking up!' grumbled a bald guard.

Gabriel watched his irons fall to the ground.

'Is it time?'

'That's why we're here. C'mon, up you get.'

'Where are you taking me?'

'Don't you know?'

Gabriel felt Bartholomew staring at him from the shadows. But neither of them had time to say anything. Gabriel was prodded into the stairway and led through a labyrinth of corridors. To his surprise, he found himself at the jail's gate. No one explained to him why he had been taken there rather than to the torture dungeon. The guards ignored his questions, as if he didn't exist! Then a swarthy guard unlocked the cast-iron door, the metal lock clanging loudly, and it swung open to reveal dawn giving way to full daylight on the square.

It was ridiculous! They prodded him forward. He tripped on the bottom of the door frame, bruising a toe on the corner of a flagstone. He turned in time to see the door close behind him. Here he was, outside, standing in the Plaza del Rosario. His arms and legs were free, uncuffed. The vast sky, an untarnished canvas, spread above him.

He murmured:

'Does this mean . . .'

He couldn't believe it. He couldn't even say it. He was at a loss for words.

A passing dog pissed lazily on the prison gate. Then the animal ambled across the square to the Cuesta del Rosario. Following it with his gaze, Gabriel noticed a double-draught carriage. The coach was painted black and silver, and he recognized the coat-of-arms on its door.

He stood there, open-mouthed.

It was the carriage of the Marquis of Talavera – his father's carriage!

The door opened slightly. From the gap a gloved hand waved in his direction. A footman sat on the driver's bench, watching him.

Gabriel crossed the square, feeling confused. The flagstones, still cold from the night, numbed his bare feet. When he was within hearing distance, a familiar voice blurted from the carriage:

'Get in quickly, you bloody idiot. Do you want the whole town to see you in that state?'

Gabriel obeyed, as he had always obeyed. He had barely sat down when the carriage set off.

The luxuriously appointed coach and the fine Segovia point lace his father wore made Gabriel suddenly self-conscious about his appearance. His breeches, once black, were covered in gray dust, and his shirt was torn. His stockings were full of holes, and he had long since lost his boots, confiscated by his jailers under the pretext that the iron cuffs would 'chafe the leather'.

It was evident from the look in his small black eyes that the Marquis had the same thought. He turned away with a scowl of disgust and pointed his gloved hand at a package on the seat:

'By God, you stink! Here are some clean clothes. You will put them on later. By Christ, what an infectious odor!'

Gabriel gave a little sardonic bow:

'I am most heartily sorry for it, my Lord.'

'I certainly hope so. Your release has cost me three thousand, two hundred ducats! Which is to say the entire revenue of my lands in Almeria! All that for your damned writings, and that wench!'

'My Lord, I—'

The carriage jumped over a bump, and the Marquis's hat wobbled, but his hands clapped sternly:

'No, no, and no! Not a word from you, sir! I do not wish to hear a peep out of you! It is over. Until now I have watched over you to guard the honor of my name. I paid for your college, to guard the honor of my name. And yet from the beginning you have persisted in sullying that name by associating with madmen and heretics! Good God! The Marquis of Talavera suspected of apostasy because his bastard son befriended damned Lutherans! Three thousand, two hundred ducats! The pleading, the humiliating promises,

my knees callused from kneeling, my back aching from
bowing, two months of worry and shady deal-making, all to
have my name removed from the Holy Office's Register! That
is what you have cost me. But now it's over. I promised His
Excellency the Inquisitor-General that you would disappear.
And disappear you shall. I shall erase you from my life as
easily as I brought you into it . . .'

The marquis drew a letter sealed with red wax from his
coat and handed it to his son with a look of disgust.

'Here are the papers for a position with the Dominican
brothers in Naples. A supreme sense of Christian charity
compels me to offer you a final chance. But know that this
is the last thing I shall do for you, and that you are forbidden
from calling on me for anything whatsoever in the future. I
have had a lawyer remove your name from all my registers
and accounts, and—'

'A disavowal, isn't that the name?' said a sullen Gabriel.
'Like one disavows a whore . . .'

His voice was thick with anger and his breathing was short.
He yelled for the driver to stop the coach, and as it slowed
he snatched the letter from his father. He tore it across and
threw the pieces at him, saying bitterly:

'You have never known me, my Lord, and have always seen
me as nothing but an embarrassment. You have given me
nothing, my Lord, and I want nothing from you. Disavowed
by you, *I* disavow *you*. Despised by you, *I* despise and hate
you. That I will no longer bear your name? I couldn't care
less: one day, you will hear mine. Mark my words, my Lord,
my name will be on everyone's lips.'

The Marquis sat there gaping like a fish out of water.
Gabriel jumped from the carriage and slammed the door
shut. With the reins loose in his hands, the coach driver
sat there, unsure what to do, but a blow from the Marquis's
cane upon the window-pane prompted him into action. As
the coach pulled away, the door opened again. A bundle

of new clothes came flying out and landed on the flagstones.

Gabriel laughed derisively, but felt a coldness envelop his
racing heart. And as the rattle of the coach faded into the
distance, a kind of nauseous gasping – melancholic hiccups
– convulsed his chest. He propped himself against a wall
and burst wretchedly into tears. He started trembling from
head to toe, and his legs failed him. Gabriel fell to his
knees – from a distance he looked like a dying man. And
he lay there sobbing disconsolately, indifferent to the curious
glances from people passing by.

CHAPTER 14

Tumebamba, February 1529

'AND THE PUMA SPOKE TO YOU?'

Manco's eyes shone with excited incredulity.

'Lower your voice, Manco.'

Paullu spoke in undertones. The *cancha* was asleep. Anamaya screwed up her eyes:

'I didn't see who was talking to me, Manco. I can't tell you if it was a man or a puma. But it was your father Huayna Capac's voice. I recognized it straight away, although it was stronger and firmer than the one I heard the day he took my hand, and—'

'My father touched you?'

'He was very old and ill – he asked me to look into his eyes.'

'And did you look at him?'

Manco was so stupefied, so wide-eyed that Anamaya smiled. He might have been slightly older than her but she was the one with the greater experience; her heart, her soul, her young life itself was already heavy with existence . . .

'Yes, I looked at the Inca of all the Incas,' she whispered, amused, 'and I lived to tell the tale. Or else I died, but returned from the dead!'

'But where was his desiccated body?'

'I don't know. Perhaps it never left the temple. I'm sorry, I really don't know . . .'

'There are some mysteries that are better left alone,' sighed Paullu.

'And what does it matter, anyhow?' Anamaya smiled. 'The important thing is that your father is back in his rightful seat in the temple, and is once again close to his sons and his ancestors. Isn't that order restored?'

Manco nodded his head in approval, but the two boys remained pensive and silent for a long moment. They seemed to be trying to fathom the significance of the recent prodigious events. Then, in a gentle voice, Paullu announced:

'We're leaving tomorrow.'

'So soon? Why?'

'After what happened,' replied Manco, 'our clan decided to bring forward our return to Cuzco, and join Huascar there as quickly as possible . . .'

'Your brother Huascar seems to me to be in a great hurry. He certainly seems in a hurry to be Emperor!'

Paullu gave a hint of a smile. But Anamaya's touch of sarcasm had slipped past Manco, who stroked the golden skin of her arm.

'When he learns of your powers,' he said quietly, 'he'll want you on his side. He'll go to war over it . . .'

'War? Over me? But that's absurd!'

'No, it isn't. You travel between this world and the other, our father speaks to you from behind the veil, he advises you . . . you afford Atahualpa a very great advantage . . . Huascar won't allow it.'

'It's true,' added Paullu, somberly. 'If he has to, he'll kill you rather than let you continue helping his enemies.'

'Yes, Villa Oma told me as much,' said Anamaya.

An abrupt sound from the courtyard made them jump.

'Someone's listening!' hissed Paullu.

All three looked deep into the black, empty night outside.

Nothing. Manco shrugged his shoulders and threw more wood onto the fire.

'We shouldn't be seen together,' murmured Anamaya. 'In this atmosphere, anything is cause for suspicion. That may have been Guaypar!'

'Forget about that buffoon!' grumbled Manco, his burning eyes reflecting the rising flames, 'Whatever happens, Paullu and I shall always protect you.'

'Anamaya, didn't you promise always to be our friend?' asked Paullu affectionately.

'Yes – I shall always be your friend.'

Anamaya was so moved that her voice became tiny, practically inaudible.

'But you know as well as I do that we belong to different clans. If you're seen with me, the Cuzco people will accuse you of treason.'

By way of reply, Manco took her hand and pressed it to her heart:

'Well, we'll tell them that you're our friend all the same, because you are the one our father Huayna Capac confided in.'

His gaze plunged deep into Anamaya's, and he hesitated for a moment before adding:

'And because you're beautiful, and we love you—'

'Look there!' exclaimed Paullu.

The flames had roared up from the hearth in a huge flickering flower. On the adobe walls, covered in ochre lime, strange shadows were leading a lively dance. In an instant Anamaya realized what Paullu was drawing their attention to: the shadow had taken the form of a bird, a dancing bird. His long neck was clearly discernible, as were his beak, his head, and his pointed, curved wings: a condor! Yes, a condor who would fly to the ceiling of the sky, close to Mama Quilla!

'Watch over us, condor,' murmured Anamaya, opening her hands to him. 'Protect us, and may your wings never fail.'

*   *   *

'Lord Atahualpa!'

Inti Palla's *anaco*, woven from the lightest wool, emphasized the ample curves of her firm breasts. Her black pupils shone excitedly as she entered Atahualpa's room and approached the Inca, bowing her head.

Atahualpa motioned away the servant who tried to stop her from entering. The *yanacona* bowed and shuffled backwards out of the room, into the courtyard where a fountain flowed.

The room was more richly appointed than a temple: gold and silver string-courses, a wall hanging made of blue, purple and bright yellow feathers, an ornate carpet. In narrow, parallel alcoves stood solid gold statuettes, figures of men, women, and llamas; others, in clay, were finely painted and depicted warriors in combat poses, clubs in hand. On a wall to the left-hand side hung a ceremonial robe covered in small, gold squares, and beneath this, on a stool, was a *keros* in the form of a puma's head, its jaws open and filled with *chicha*; its gold fangs glinted ferociously in the torchlight, as if the painted wooden jug could come alive and attack.

Atahualpa lay between two young women on an alpaca pelt, propped up on one elbow. A black-and-white-checkered *unku* loosely covered his strong torso, and in his simple pose, with only a band wrapped around his noble head, he was magnificently handsome. One scarcely noticed his torn ear lobe, the one without a gold earring.

Although it was forbidden, Inti Palla couldn't help herself from admiring his face for a few moments before bowing her head. She couldn't decide whether it was being in the splendid room that excited her like this, or simply being gazed upon by the handsome, noble Atahualpa – being the object of his desire.

'What do you want, Inti Palla?' he asked languidly.

'Only to speak to you, noble Lord.'

'At this hour? Interrupting my rest? I'm very tired: my days are as long as they are difficult. You insolent girl, if you trouble me for nothing, I'll have you whipped.'

Inti Palla's smile was ambiguous:

'My only pleasure is to please you, my Great Lord. And I hope to do so before dawn . . .'

Her husky voice and the exaggerated motion of her hips as she prostrated herself did not go unnoticed. Atahualpa imagined all that she intended him to imagine.

With one hand, he lazily caressed the cheek of the girl to his right, while he let the fingers of his left hand slip from a naked shoulder to rest upon a ripe young breast. He smiled:

'You two return to the matrons, and leave me with the concubine.'

Immediately the two girls left the bed. There was some murmuring as servants appeared with their clothes, but once they had left Atahualpa settled, facing Inti Palla:

'Come closer, woman.'

Feigning shyness, Inti Palla approached him on her hands and knees. When she was in front of him she touched her forehead to the mat, and kissed the sun ring on his left hand. She had coated herself with *cantuta* perfume, and had blanched her cheeks with gardenia cream. Whether deliberately or naturally, she was breathing hard, an anticipatory respiration. She had a predatory look about her, which was not dissimilar to that of the ferocious puma's head resting on the stool.

Atahualpa adroitly untied the sash holding Inti Palla's *cumbi*. The ochre fabric slipped off; she stood there naked, her head bowed.

But the prince stopped there; he contented himself with visually admiring her perfect body, her silky skin. So she straightened herself, and fetched him the *keros*.

He held the jug with his fingers gripping its golden jaws and drew long gulps from it. Then Inti Palla glided onto the matting and wrapped herself around him.

'No doubt you are right, concubine,' sighed Atahualpa after finishing the *chicha*. 'This could not wait until dawn.'

Inti Palla's hands stole under his checkered *unku*, and caressed the prince's smooth, hairless torso.

'My Lord, I am here for your pleasure – but, above all, I am here so that you should know!'

'That I should know? What, exactly?'

'That she betrays you.'

Atahualpa's gaze froze, fixed directly ahead, expressionless. He pointed the puma's gold fangs at Inti Palla's head:

'Who dares betray me, according to you?'

'The blue-eyed girl. I discovered her with Manco and Paullu, your brother Huascar's puppies. I overheard their conversation: she's going to tell Huascar and the Cuzco clans what the Emperor told her on the night of his passing!'

For a brief moment Atahualpa didn't react. He only drew back a little to disentangle himself from the concubine's fingers. Then he threw the *keros* violently across the room. The wooden jug split with a loud crack; the puma's teeth of gold scattered on the ground. The puma's fierceness had passed into Atahualpa's face:

'So that is why you have come to see me?'

Instinctively, Inti Palla retreated, covering herself and bowing low:

'I'm devoted to you, my Lord! I speak the truth!'

With an exaggerated gentleness, Atahualpa seized his concubine by the face, and drew her up: he traced his fingers along her sensual lips, her soft cheekbones, her long, long lashes; he pressed his thumbs gently on her closed eyelids and murmured:

'Do you want to help me, Inti Palla?'

'Anything you desire, my Lord . . .'

'Well, if you ever interfere again with the sacred will of my father Huayna Capac, you'll arrive in the Under World far sooner than the time of my wake. Do you understand me?'

All the blood drained from Inti Palla's face. She trembled uncontrollably. She tried to escape the prince, but he grasped her more firmly, not so gently now.

'My Lord, I only wanted to serve you!'

'There is one way you can serve me, woman, and only one.'

Inti Palla's eyes were wide with terror.

Atahualpa relaxed his grip. His hand slid over his concubine's superb body. As he lifted her vigorously, a sharp edge of his sun ring scratched her dark, hard nipple, and a tiny drop of blood appeared. But Inti Palla kept her mouth shut, and she didn't dare move as Atahualpa leaned forward and licked the wound with his tongue.

The still night filled the *cancha*, barely disturbed by the murmuring fountains.

They were no longer speaking; only their moans floated from the prince's room, occasional little moans.

Atahualpa didn't notice the tears on Inti Palla's cheeks, only the smile she wore for his pleasure.

They were tears of hatred.

CHAPTER 15

Seville, February 1529

THE INN WAS CALLED THE BOTTOMLESS JUG. THE innkeeper, a fat, loutish man with a philosophical bent, brought on perhaps by the proximity of the jail, showed no surprise when Gabriel appeared asking for a room and a tub of hot water to wash in. He replied simply:

'That'll be three *maravedi*.'

And as Gabriel only nodded, he added:

'To be paid in advance.'

Gabriel drew a purse from the remains of his breeches, a very flat purse. He took from it its only coin, a single pathetic *réal*, and carefully counted the thirty-one *maravedi* change from the innkeeper.

Less than an hour later, a different man appeared. Gabriel's new clothes couldn't be described as finery – nothing dandy about them – but they were clean, and they fitted him well. All black, except for the shirt, and his stockings were embroidered. He needed only to visit a barber to complete his transformation. After that, he would brood upon his future.

He was about to leave the inn when an aroma of lard soup wafted towards him: he realized that he was famished.

Sparing him any small talk, the innkeeper showed him to a table in the shade. Gabriel sat on a stool and ordered:

'A plate of *gacha*, a jug of Cadiz wine, and a cob of olive bread.'

'That'll be seven *maravedi*—'

'—Payable in advance, I know.'

In a flash, the plate had been wiped clean with the bread and the last drops shaken from the pitcher of wine. Gabriel thought the soup a culinary marvel, the bread the finest he had tasted, and the wine ambrosia. His head spun a little – from happiness, no doubt. How long had it been since he had had a meal worthy of the name?

Feeling only mildly drunk, he ordered another jug.

And as he emptied this, watching his few *maravedi* migrate to the innkeeper's pocket like flies to honey, he gloomily reflected that liberty, in particular impecunious liberty, was losing some of its gloss.

'Excuse us, Your Grace, but might we importune you with our curiosity?'

The man addressing him was huge. He had the broad, broad shoulders of a stevedore. But his face was refined, his beard trim and cared for. His sharp, hooked nose gave him an artful air that was enhanced by his shining, mischievous eyes. His brow was deeply lined, and his skin tanned by the sun.

Beside him stood a black man, only slightly less enormous than his companion. He had the features of a charmer, confident without being arrogant, his high-set cheekbones accentuating his intelligent, shifting gaze. His lips were thin, his chin smooth, and a big gold ring hung from his right ear, in the seagoing fashion. Here was a kind of black man that one rarely came across in Spain, thought Gabriel.

'Gentlemen?' he replied coolly, on the alert, keeping his guard up.

The white colossus grinned from ear to ear, and pulled up a stool without further ado:

'Your Grace,' he began, tilting his head with feigned deference. 'We were sitting in that corner over there, minding our business, when we saw you arrive earlier wearing them rags and – meaning no disrespect – all scruffy, like. And we couldn't help but notice you when you came back down, as fresh and clean as newly minted coin! And then you ate, nay, devoured, that rancid, ill-smelling soup and that three-day-old bread, and sculled that sour wine as if it came from the table of the King himself! And so I said to my companion here, "Sebastian, here's a fellow who's recently released from a spell inside!"'

The man winked, and smiled at his mate, who was still standing, before adding:

'And not a short spell either, from the looks of things! And I mean no disrespect, on the contrary . . .'

Gabriel sat there silently for a few seconds. Then he went to stand up, raising an arm in an attempt to look menacing. But, as he did so, he was overwhelmed by fatigue and couldn't help but fall back onto his stool, laughing.

'Indeed, it wasn't a short spell! But if you don't mind, I'd rather talk about something else. May I ask whom I have the honor of addressing?'

The colossus waved his massive fist at the innkeeper, called for another jug, and answered:

'My name is Pedro de Candia, but my friends call me "The Greek". And he's Sebastian de la Cruz, sometimes a slave because of his skin, but mostly my companion on many an adventure.'

The black man grinned wryly:

'Your servant, Your Grace.'

Gabriel couldn't help but laugh a little:

'And where do you come from, gentlemen, to be constantly calling me "Your Grace"?'

The Greek cast a sidelong glance at Sebastian. Their surprise was genuine.

'Isn't that how a *caballero* is addressed?'

Gabriel burst into laughter:

'Ten years ago, perhaps!'

He pondered them smilingly: both wore breeches, shirts and jerkins long out of style, their fabric worn and faded.

'It's that we're recently returned from the Indies, only last month.'

'Ah?'

'We discovered a new world there,' added Sebastian.

'I see,' murmured Gabriel, more curious than he intended to be.

The Greek pointed at the sunlit door of the jail on the other side of the small square:

'Our Captain for over ten years now, Don Francisco Pizarro, who led us to the far side of the world and back, is today locked rotting in there for a very old affair, some banal, ugly debt never paid nor forgiven. He was treacherously arrested by the *alguazils* the moment our ship docked. The shame, sir! And he has been wallowing in his cell for three long weeks now, the poor unlucky man. So we decided to wait for him here.'

A shadow of sorrow passed over the conquistadors' faces. Gabriel could not help but feel sympathetic:

'My name is Gabriel Montelu – no. From now on, it will be simply Gabriel. Call me Don Gabriel, and all's well. But you were only half right – I was released from a jail this morning, but not this one . . .'

'Which one?' asked the Greek.

Gabriel smiled as he considered him:

'Why don't you tell me about the Indies?' he asked cheerfully.

The Greek and Sebastian were indefatigable.

'Try to imagine, Don Gabriel! The endless ocean before

you, the sand burning the soles of your feet, the forest as
dense as a wall behind, with savages perched in its trees and
armed with poison arrows. And us, stuck between the devil
and the deep blue sea, as they say, roasting in the sun!'

'Were you there for very long?'

'Why, for months, Don Gabriel! Months and months. We
were reduced to eating spiders, a fat kind that lives over
there, with flesh around its belly. Though you had to be sure
to take out its poison sac, else you inflated into a ball . . .
and also its forelegs, since it's so hairy: they would cling in
your gullet, and make you cough up your guts. Or else some
nice, fat worms, all brown and glistening. We found 'em in
dead trees. Not too bad, when fried . . .'

'But what about your own animals?' Gabriel felt nauseous,
from the wine as much as from the horrors they recounted.
'You could have eaten your own animals, as happens on
occasion during war . . .'

The two conquistadors roared with laughter.

'Ho! We digested them long before! After four weeks on
the beach, the dogs went mad with hunger: we grilled them
first. We had two horses, both more bone than horse. And
those bones we scraped clean. A terrible starvation it was.
I remember when someone took off his belt and boiled it.
After that, we ate our boots! And enjoyed them, too!'

In his soft voice, Sebastian added:

'There were some lizards we found, not too bad-tasting.
But hard to catch. And their bite could kill a man in less
than two hours. We had to choose: die of hunger or die of
lizard poison . . .'

'By all the saints!'

The Greek grabbed Gabriel by his wrist.

'Aye, but the captain, he always believed we'd find the land
of gold, even in the most dire times! Even on that damned
beach when one and all expected to die . . . just like I told
you, huh, Sebastian?'

The black man agreed, smiling as his friend rose to his full height slowly, pushing back his stool. Through his half-closed eyes, the giant surveyed Gabriel from head to toe with the dignity of a *caballero*:

'You should've heard him, the captain, standing tall and proper, his dark eyes shining as he talked to each man in turn, all those on the verge of mutiny: "Patience, I tell you! Have patience, my friends, patience, *compañeros*! Ruiz will return. He will have found the promised land of gold that you all dream of at night, the sea will have parted before him, and the Sacred Virgin will have appeared to show him the way. Trust me! I've seen worse than this in my long life. When you have to fight, then you fight; when there's nothing to do but wait, then you wait. Look at me: I was the first to cross the forest – the forest teeming with wild savages, and infested with lethal, poisonous beasts – to find the Pacific Ocean waiting there for us; and I will be the first to cross that ocean and reach this 'Piru' covered in gold that Holy Mary promises me each night in my dreams! Patience, hombres! I tell you, he will return. And if you don't know what to do with your empty stomachs and your useless balls, then pray! For prayer is another form of combat!"'

The ensuing silence filled the room as the Greek sat back down. Gabriel felt the hairs on his arms stand on end, from fright. His limbs froze and his lungs emptied. In a subdued voice he asked:

'And did this Ruiz return?'

Pedro nodded as he stared into the bottom of his goblet:

'Three weeks later, yes. He brought in the southern ship as easily as if he was sailing on a lake! He's a great navigator.'

'And had he found it?'

'Yes, he'd found it,' said the Greek, smiling.

'Just like Don Francisco said,' contributed Sebastian, wagging his head with respect.

'This . . . Piru?'

'Piru, Peru – it's much of a muchness, Don Gabriel.'

'And covered in gold?'

'Covered everywhere! Gold, gold, and more gold! And Indians we've never seen the likes of before, with marvelous clothes, strange animals, unknown plants . . .'

'You saw it with your own eyes?'

'Absolutely! Ask Sebastian here!'

'Me, I saw it, and I'll swear to it.'

'Don Francisco came to ask the King to name him Governor, as he did for *Capitan* Cortez!'

'Well, he'll have to get out of jail first, or else he'll miss his appointment,' joked Gabriel.

'This is no time for humor,' growled the Greek.

Again, silence fell. Pushing away his wine-filled goblet, Gabriel asked:

'So, if *Capitan* Don Francisco becomes Governor, he'll return to the Indies . . .'

'And how! As fast as possible, as fast as the wind will carry him.'

'To conquer this Peru?'

'Yes.'

'So, no doubt he'll need good men, good-willed men?'

'Ha! It seems our new friend wishes to travel, Sebastian—'

But his friend let out a cry and pointed at the jail:

'Pedro! Look! There he is!'

All three stood simultaneously: there, under the hot sun, an incredibly thin man wearing a garnet-red and gray felt doublet and dated green breeches stepped forward from the jail gate closing behind him. A great big ostrich-feathered hat covered his long gray hair. But from beneath its rim Gabriel thought he saw in the man's eyes a sparkle like he'd never seen before.

The discoverer of Peru stepped forward and adjusted the shoulder belt of his sword. One would never have guessed that he was emerging from three weeks in a damp, dark cell. He seemed capable of anything.

Suddenly, it was no longer Pedro the Greek's voice that echoed in his heart, but that of *Capitan* Don Francisco Pizarro himself. He imagined that he was on a long, bare beach, with all the provisions exhausted, trembling from fever and hunger, but braving the unknown with each new day that God granted, and that that man, armed only with an iron will – an *indomitable* will – had just infected his heart with the recklessness of his dreams.

CHAPTER 16

Tumebamba, February 1529

A LTHOUGH IT WAS VERY LATE, TORCHES CON-
tinued to burn here and there in some of the
canchas. The sounds of preparation disturbed the
stillness of the night air: tomorrow, the procession carrying
Huayna Capac's desiccated body would leave Tumebamba
for Cuzco, and everything had to be ready.

Anamaya slipped unseen from her clan's *cancha*.

She had the ability, when she needed it, to move silently
like a snake through the grass, to blend into the background.

She had heard a call summoning her in the middle of the
night. A wordless call, not one that others could hear, nothing
audible; but she heard it and she instantly understood: she
must go to the temple. She must spend that night with her
husband, the Sacred Double.

From now on, she must take notice of every sign, however
slight. Only her own fear stood between her and the Emperor
Huayna Capac. He could communicate with her in a variety
of ways: the dance of a shadow, or the song of a bird. She must
overcome her fear of the puma's eyes, and not be afraid of his
long fangs . . .

On the eastern hill, the steps to the temple were visible
in the moonlight.

Anamaya padded confidently across the square. The *yanaconas* guarding the entrance recognized her as soon as she entered the circle of torchlight, and let her pass. What's more, they bowed to her, and shuffled backwards respectfully.

Wasn't she, after all, the *Coya Camaquen*? Didn't the most powerful men in the Empire, the most influential members of the court, the great Atahualpa and the Sage, Villa Oma, didn't they all listen avidly when she spoke, hanging on her every word?

Huayna Capac's mummy rested in the room with the nine alcoves. A silver beam sent by the Moon Mother irradiated his golden mask, and he seemed at peace. Strange-smelling herbs burned slowly in the nearby brazier, and their wafting dank odor was so bitter that it stung her nostrils.

Anamaya crouched before the dead Emperor. She bowed her head respectfully and fearfully, perhaps as fearfully as she had that day when, still only a little girl, she had been brought before him for the first time.

Nothing happened for some time.

Then a shimmer of cold air escaped from behind the gold mask and blew over Anamaya's head, the first vibration in a prolonged series. The feathers spread across the mummy's shoulders shivered. Anamaya heard a silent order, and obeyed it: she lifted her head slowly and put her hand on the thick *unku* that covered the sleeping Emperor, asleep for eternity.

Under the fabric, as soft as child's skin, she felt a warmth. She lifted her neck even higher so that the moon lit her face, her black hair shone distinctly, and her eyes and skin paled in the silver light.

She closed her eyes, not from sleepiness but as the outward sign of an inward vigil. Time was suspended, and the boundaries of the past, present and future were undone.

She breathed the humid jungle air, that odor she knew from her happiest days. The heavy clouds hung low over the jungle, and she ran beneath them, light-footed, laughing.

She saw a face and heard a voice: a handsome, gentle face, a voice full of love; but it was too far, it was out of her reach.

Her heart skipped a beat: she heard her mother calling her.

'Anamaya!'

It was a distant, fading echo.

'Anamaya!'

As her mother's voice sang her name, the jungle around her transformed into a liquid world, a blue, crystal lake. Now her mother was everywhere, welcoming and comforting her. The world was her mother's belly, her mother's breast. Her laughter was the wind that lifted the birds, her round shoulders the mountains that carried the world. Her arms were wrapped around Anamaya, her invisible fingers tenderly caressing her head, stroking her hair and the nape of her neck.

Tears streamed down Anamaya's cheeks.

'Don't cry, Anamaya,' said the voice, 'I am here, I am with you . . .'

Anamaya grew calmer. She could feel her mother's warmth, and her hand stroking her hair. Each caress erased all the years of love stolen from her, all Anamaya's fears and terrible memories.

But then a sudden gust of cold wind blew and it carried the tenderness with it into oblivion. Anamaya opened her eyes, and saw her hand resting on the Inca's *unku*.

Mama Quilla's halo, present for the last few nights, had gone. Her silver beams reached the furthest horizons of the sky. She shone so brightly that she seemed to have kissed the sun, an impossible, furtive encounter.

Anamaya's eyes were drawn to her husband, the Sacred Double. The radiant sparkle of his body blinded her. She raised her hands to shade her eyes, and something extraordinary happened.

The ground fell away beneath her feet. She grasped to catch hold of something, but encountered nothing. She screamed, but heard no sound.

She flew high into the night sky.

She saw the temple illuminated beneath her, and she saw herself kneeling next to the Inca.

She saw the sleeping town, the men gathering their strength for tomorrow. She saw Lord Atahualpa alone on his feather-covered mat. He stood up suddenly, and walked to and fro, like a man at war, a caged puma.

Above her the constellations were so close she could touch them. She brushed past *Colca*'s swirl, and saw *Amaro* the snake slip between her feet. Her long, loose hair floated into *Chacana*, the girdled Lord. She plunged her arms into the ever-flowing Milky Way, the celestial twin of the Sacred River.

Finally, she understood.

He needed her.

From beyond the veil, the eleventh Emperor of all the Incas, the Unifier of the Four Cardinal Directions, was reaching out to her.

A ball of fire burst from the south-eastern horizon, the birth of a new star. It was enormous, leaving a sparkling wake in the darkness bigger than any terrestrial mountain, and it tore the night in two as it hurtled towards Anamaya.

As it approached her, it sucked in all the light around it, an unbelievably brilliant blaze, so dense a globe that it seemed bound to explode. All of a sudden it turned abruptly and dived towards the Earth, towards the palace.

And struck Atahualpa's forehead like a stone from a slingshot.

And went out in a flash.

The prince fell to the ground.

And didn't get up.

Anamaya screamed and howled.

She felt a hand shaking her shoulder.

'What's wrong, child?' asked the worried Sage, Villa Oma.

Anamaya trembled.

She had trouble realizing where she was; she looked around the room with the nine alcoves and saw Huayna Capac's desiccated body and his Sacred Double.

The green-lipped sage was asking her questions, a look of extreme concern on his face.

'Not now,' she said simply, 'not now . . .'

She couldn't describe where she had just been. It defied words. No one would understand, not even the Sage.

He took her arm and helped her to her feet. They walked slowly from the temple.

On the road back to the *cancha*, Anamaya's heart raced, panic-stricken. The image of the great Lord falling played over and over in her mind.

Gradually the image dissolved, and a thick fog enveloped her soul. As her lingering fear subsided, she was left with an insufferable sense of loneliness.

CHAPTER 17

Tumebamba, March 1529

'A BALL OF FIRE? AS BIG AS A STAR?'
Colla Topac, the old Law-Elder, repeated Anamaya's words as though she was not to be believed.

Villa Oma had once before called on his help, the time
when the Emperor's desiccated body had disappeared, for
Colla Topac was the one charged with taking the mummy
to Cuzco, and he was the one who effectively controlled the
Law until a new Sun King was accepted by all.

In the scanty light of an oil lamp, he appeared so ancient
that one could hardly believe he was still alive. His back
was humped, his face thinner and more wrinkled than the
mummy's. But his eyes retained an audacious sparkle, and
it seemed as if they were the only form of life in the desert
of his face.

He scrutinized Anamaya's blue gaze by the torchlight.
Then, with a suppleness unexpected in one as old as he,
he turned to Villa Oma:

'Are you sure Atahualpa is in good health?'

Villa Oma nodded:

'I checked on him myself, Your Lordship. At this very
moment, he slumbers amid his concubines. They say he
enjoyed two of them before falling asleep.'

'So what is your opinion of the *Coya Camaquen*'s story? Is it a good omen or not?'

'I don't know, Your Lordship! That is why I wanted you to hear her tell it herself. May I point out that the ball of fire came from the South-East; from the direction of Cuzco . . .'

'But also from the direction of the Lake of Origin,' interrupted the Law-Elder. 'From Titicaca.'

'So, this could mean one of two things. Either a bolt from Illapa the Lightning God will soon destroy Prince Atahualpa. Or else Inti's fire will mark him as Huayna Capac's heir!'

These words were so dangerously loaded that both men fell silent in their wake. Eventually the Law-Elder took Anamaya's arm and squeezed it gently. Anamaya saw an uncommon alertness coupled with gentleness in his burning eyes:

'*Coya Camaquen*, you are as young as I am old. But you know as well as I do the importance of what you saw, don't you?'

Too affected to reply, Anamaya simply nodded her head.

'Then let me ask you one more time: did the ball of fire reach Atahualpa's heart?'

'No, noble Lord. It went out on his brow . . .'

'And then . . . ?'

'I don't know,' stuttered Anamaya. 'I was frightened.'

'Frightened?'

'I thought Lord Atahualpa was going to die.'

'But now you don't?'

Anamaya was terrified of the words that she might say. She lowered her head and kept her mouth shut.

'She is second-sighted, Your Lordship,' intervened Villa Oma. 'But she's still a child. She cannot understand what she sees. Nevertheless, we need to come to a decision. And I take it upon myself to ask you the question, with all the respect that you are due. If the omen bodes ill, should we prevent Huayna Capac's mummy from continuing on its way? Should we keep it here—'

'Absolutely not!' cried the old man. 'The Law states that the mummy must return to Cuzco. None may violate the Law, and I will see to it that none does. Otherwise, the fury of our Father the Sun will fall upon us!'

'Perhaps we are already feeling His fury, Your Lordship!' insisted Villa Oma. 'Perhaps the omen means to tell us that Cuzco, or at least the Cuzco ruled by Huascar the Madman, has become a ball of flames ready to consume us all! Maybe that is what the *Coya Camaquen* saw: Quilla is warning us, and is trying to save us from the road to annihilation!'

'Sure, it could mean that, or the exact opposite!' protested the Law-Elder in a stern voice. 'But there is only one Law, Villa Oma, and you know it! I will go to Cuzco with the Emperor's desiccated body, even if they stone me. And you and the *Coya Camaquen* will come with me, because it is your duty!'

The Sage ran a trembling hand over his bone-weary face.

Anamaya knew what was going through his mind. At least twenty times over the last few days, hoping that Atahualpa would receive a clear, unambiguous sign from his father Huayna Capac, the soothsayers had tried to decipher his will in the embers of coca leaves, from the position of stars and in the entrails of llamas.

And, each time, the omens told of a forthcoming upheaval of the Empire of the Four Cardinal Directions. But not once did they indicate who would be the next Sun King.

'Please allow one concession, Your Lordship,' Villa Oma asked suddenly in a low voice, almost a whisper.

'Name it.'

'Atahualpa should not accompany the desiccated body to Cuzco. He must not meet Huascar face to face, or else there will be war, as you know as well as I do. He should bid his father goodbye here in Tumebamba. But above all, he must never know about what the *Coya Camaquen* saw. Why plant fear in him, when the Cuzco clans are so much trouble as it is? We'll ask him to stay in the North, and to maintain order in the Empire . . .'

The old Law-Elder nodded listlessly as Villa Oma placed his dry hand on Anamaya's shoulder:

'And as for you, *Coya Camaquen*, you won't breathe a word of this to anyone . . .'

Anamaya had no time to sleep.

Before the first light of day, as if forewarned, Atahualpa had her brought to his court. He offered to share his meal with her: maize bread and the jungle fruits that were fetched for him fresh each day.

As best she could, she fought to forget the fear that held her in its vice, and prostrated herself before him with a respectful smile.

In truth, her heart was torn between the relief of seeing the noble prince alive and in his usual good health, and the stinging and incomprehensible memory of the ball of fire.

When they had finished their bowls of carob milk, Atahualpa asked:

'Did my father speak to you?'

Anamaya felt the discomfort of lying squeeze her guts:

'No, noble prince,' she replied in a timorous voice.

Atahualpa considered her for a moment, then looked to the lightening sky with a sigh.

'The Law-Elder doesn't want me to accompany the cortège to Cuzco. I suppose he is right: the oracles are too indefinite, and the Cuzco clans too belligerent. But I shall miss your company, child Anamaya. I like being near you.'

Moved by Atahualpa's tone, Anamaya bowed deeply so as to hide from him her brimming eyes.

'The silence of the mountains is grand and beautiful,'

continued Atahualpa gently. 'But the silence of my father Huayna Capac is dark, and Inti's silence is terrible.'

'He will break the silence soon, my Lord,' ventured Anamaya, emboldened.

'Do you really think so, *Coya Camaquen*?'

Atahualpa's voice was suddenly so full of hope that Anamaya bit her lip to stop herself from talking. Atahualpa laughed raucously, such a rare thing for him that she lifted her head. Their eyes met. Atahualpa's gaze was full of expectation, mixed with affection. It gave him an unusual expression – unusual for him: less potent, heavier, perhaps a little aged.

Anamaya kept her mouth tightly closed, but she couldn't help the tears welling in her eyes. Atahualpa's smile spread across his face. In the first pale light of day, the whites of his eyes were less red than usual, but his eyelids were swollen from his tiring nights.

'No,' he said in a low, low voice. 'No, you're not sure.'

He extended his arm and laid his hand on her shoulder. He caressed her cheek lightly, as if he were scared of finding warm, living flesh.

'But I'm glad that you say so to please me. I'm grateful to you.'

He withdrew his hand and looked at his fingers as if they retained a trace of her. Then he pointed them to the East, now the lightest part of the sky:

'I see war ahead of us, Anamaya. I see Inti bathed in blood. I want to break the silence before that silence becomes blood. I don't want to be the one who brings down the Empire of the Four Cardinal Directions. I don't want to see clan fight against clan. I cannot just wait, doing nothing, while my father is silent.'

Anamaya was absorbing the violence of his words, when Villa Oma's tall, thin shadow appeared from the courtyard door and said:

'It is time, my Lord. You must go to the sacred place. They await you there.'

Atahualpa reinforced his words with a lingering look at Anamaya.

'Come along,' he said, standing up as she prostrated herself. 'Come with me to my father's mummy.'

On the square, under the sun's acute glare, the priests and virgins danced for the noblemen.

At the head of the stairs rising to the *ushnu*, wrapped in a tunic embroidered with two hundred sky blue and bright yellow emblems, each signifying a victory on the battlefield, Huayna Capac's mummy sat upon a palanquin of solid gold. The Sacred Double sat on another, set a little further back. Both peered through their ghostly eyes at the valedictory tears streaming down the dancers' cheeks.

The servants, artisans, peasants and shepherds who lived in bulrush huts in the hills were all crammed together in the square. Each hoped to pay his final respects to the desiccated body of the Emperor Huayna Capac before he began the long journey to Cuzco, the city of his birth and the birthplace of all his ancestors.

Halfway up the stairs to the *ushnu*, Atahualpa stood impassively. His regal dignity came not from his magnificent feather headdress, nor from his breastplate adorned with thousands of red and blue pearls, nor from the gold orbs hanging from his ears. It was marked on his face, on his forehead on which sat the simple band indicating Nobility, and in the unflinching creases of his lips.

Anamaya could still hear his outcry against his father's silence echoing in her heart.

But now, with all the most important noblemen present, he had regained his usual self-assurance. He exuded a force that set him towering above the rest. And when he raised his arms skyward, trumpets thundered and filled the square. The singing slowed, the melodious flutes faded, and the rumbling drums rolled to an end as the dancers came to a standstill.

Silence: by Atahualpa's decree, silence spread across the sacred square and, like a shock wave from an earthquake's epicenter, rolled across the entire city of Tumebamba.

The crowd held its breath.

And then Atahualpa's voice, the voice of the young prince of the North, the voice of the son of the great Emperor Huayna Capac, cut through the crisp mountain air of the Andes:

'I hadn't intended to tell you of my grief, but my grief is overwhelming me. The Emperor is here with us, and watches over us from his seat beside Inti, his father. I am his fatherless son, and I am surrounded by silence. As are you . . .

'The time has come for him to begin his final journey down the road to Cuzco. Cuzco, where Manco Capac and Mama Occlo, our forefathers, first plunged their golden hoes into the fertile land given to us by Viracocha . . .

'The Emperor came to the North, and conquered the North. With Inti's blessing, he expanded the lands Viracocha offered us, he pushed the borders so far that now the Empire of the Four Cardinal Directions is as vast as the dome of the sky. It is so huge that it might fracture as easily as an earthenware bowl.

'The Emperor came here to the North, and he fathered sons here in the North, and he fathered them in the wombs of northern women. My father, the Emperor Huayna Capac, obeyed Inti's will, and he sowed his seed in all the directions of the Empire, and his sons proliferated as easily as maize or quinoa.

'The Emperor's desire was to unify, not to divide. He wants peace and cooperation between his sons. He didn't choose between the Cuzco and the Quito clans because he wanted peace to be like a vicuña carpet stretching from the South to the North . . .

'My brother Huascar, disregarding the oracles, has placed the Royal Band on his own head. He wants me to bow before him. He wants all the North to prostrate itself before him . . .'

Atahualpa fell silent. All eyes were on him. Every face looked at him expectantly, desperately. Only the flies were moving, buzzing through the stillness.

'But it's our Law. Everyone must prostrate themselves before the Emperor. If Huascar is our Emperor, then as soon as Inti – the father of us all – sends me his sign, then I shall go and prostrate myself before Huascar. But for the moment, my grief is too great. I don't want to leave my native land just yet, the land from which my father ruled the Empire, and the land where I hope to live and die . . .'

Noblemen and poor folk alike bowed their heads. They were not crying or showing any sorrow. Their faces remained impassive.

Atahualpa turned to face the Law-Elder. On a signal all the priests raised their arms to the sun, their eyes closed, then lowered them towards the mummy on his palanquin. The horns sounded. The bearers lifted the palanquin and proceeded somberly down the *ushnu*'s steps.

Anamaya stood absolutely still, transfixed by the splendor of the occasion. Villa Oma grabbed her by the arms and whispered hoarsely:

'Go to the Sacred Double, Anamaya! Go to the one whose side you must never leave, and whose wisdom sleeps within you!'

The moment the sun was at its zenith, the long procession finally left Tumebamba. Two dozen servants scurried before it, sweeping its path with brooms of arras feathers.

•

Behind them were the musicians, just in front of the palanquin. The instruments sounded one after the other, first the high-pitched calls of the trumpets, then the deep sustained notes of the conches, and finally the fleeting flute melodies. Before and behind the palanquin were a hundred women bearing thin-necked jars of *chicha* and baskets of maize, fruit, meats, fabrics and weavings, jewels and precious stones: in short, all the clothes and food that the Emperor's desiccated body could not do without.

Then came the Sacred Double on his platform. Its feathered awning — feathers of every dazzling color — waved and fluttered in the light breeze, so that it seemed that the Sacred Double was borne not by men but by birds. Its interior was of an unparalleled luxury. Anamaya sat opposite the gold statue on a rug made entirely of feathers — gold, green, and red feathers plucked entirely from the bellies of tropical birds.

Bringing up the rear were the palanquins of the plutocracy, followed by the lesser lords who walked, and finally the servants — hundreds and hundreds of them. And parallel to this great caravan were soldiers in double file — armed with slingshots and bronze axes — forming a mobile wall to each side of the immense procession, and marching to match its speed.

The only irregularity in this impeccable harmony was the dwarf: he ran around the Emperor's palanquin, his oversized red tunic billowing out, endlessly checking and rechecking whether the bearers walked in time, whether the road had been adequately swept, and remonstrating with those who dared kick up dust. Anamaya watched him covertly, tenderly. He bounded about outside her palanquin, miming a grotesque dance.

'So, princess, do you feel safe under my protection?'

'More likely you're in need of mine, no?'

'No doubt. Did you know that they want to give me to the Cuzco clans, as a gift?'

Anamaya perceived a look of terror in his eyes.

'I'm scared, princess. I haven't been so scared since the Emperor found me in that pile of blankets . . .'

She looked at him, but found nothing to say, and he danced awkwardly away amid jeers and laughter.

When they reached the farmyards at the edge of the town Anamaya heard her name being called. She peered out the side of her palanquin to find Inti Palla beyond the cordon of soldiers.

'Anamaya! Let me in!'

Anamaya gave a signal to the nearest officer, but the cortège advanced the distance of a slingshot throw before Inti Palla finally managed to reach the palanquin's side.

Anamaya saw that her eyes were red from crying and her cheeks were sallow from a sleepless night.

'Are you ill?' she asked, worried.

'No!' laughed Inti Palla, walking quickly. 'No, not sick, only sad to see my friend leave. Who knows, maybe we'll never see each other again.'

'Who knows? Perhaps you'll come to Cuzco.'

'Atahualpa will never want to go to Cuzco!' growled Inti Palla angrily. 'He'll never go.'

And then, with an icy glare:

'What a pity that you were unable to convince him of his ascendancy. And that you let the two Cuzco brothers win the *huarachiku*. And now you're going to join them!'

'Inti Palla!' protested Anamaya.

But the concubine grabbed her hand and said quickly:

'Don't worry, I don't hold it against you. I admit that I was wrong. You have certain abilities, I know very well . . .'

There was a quality in her tone and expression that belied her words. But Anamaya didn't want to dwell on it.

'I'll never forget you, Inti Palla, I'll think of you always.'

Inti Palla smiled. Fresh tears welled in her eyes, although

it was unclear why she cried. She stroked Anamaya's arm and fondled the intertwined snakes of gold on her wrist.

'Never forget that I gave you this, Anamaya. I'm your sister, the one who loves you the most; when you get to Cuzco, see to it that Atahualpa becomes Emperor!'

CHAPTER 18

The road to Toledo, March 1529

THAT MORNING AN UNSEASONABLE HELLFIRE heat beat down on them as they progressed, as it had every morning so far on their trip.

Don Francisco led the caravan, followed by Pedro the Greek, and then – a little further back – Gabriel and Sebastian side by side.

They headed the extraordinary caravan. Two of the six llamas who had survived the Atlantic crossing dawdled along, tethered to Sebastian's saddle. They masticated on nothing in particular, and their large doelike eyes seemed to contemplate the Castilian countryside with a maiden's bewilderment.

Further back still were a dozen Royal Halberdiers – soldiers armed with axes – who nonchalantly guarded three creaking carts that overflowed with extraordinary objects never before seen in Spain.

Sitting in one cart were two Indians from the land of gold, and who themselves resembled precious icons. They wore bright colored tunics, and practiced their Spanish with the mule drivers. They had some trouble with the language, but their earnest attempts to learn it greatly amused the Spaniards, who couldn't help themselves from slipping a few of the more vulgar words into the lessons.

Sebastian had been watching Gabriel scowl for a quarter of a league before he finally asked, with a barely disguised snigger:

'Tell me, Don Gabriel, are all the natives of Spain as proud as you are?'

Gabriel threw him a dark look.

'Are all black slaves of the Indies as impertinent as you?'

'Hola, Your Grace!' guffawed Sebastian, rolling his eyes in false fear. 'I know what I am: black, and a slave, and I never forget it. But I'm also one of the discoverers of the kingdom of gold, Peru!'

'What's your point?'

'Ho, I just want to know why you look so crushed whenever the *Capitan* calls you "schoolboy"!'

Gabriel shrugged his shoulders grudgingly.

'I graduated long ago! That illiterate old fogey doesn't know the difference between a graduate and a novice. But more importantly I would like to know once and for all whether he accepts my application to serve under his command in the Indies. I've been telling him for two weeks that I put my abilities, my life and my hopes at his disposition. But does he have the courtesy to reply? Ha! He behaves as if I were invisible, mute, and dumb!'

'Well, who's been filling your belly since Sevilla? Who paid for your bed at Elcija, Cordoba, Morena and each and every stop we've made since leaving Sevilla? Who's been watching you and taking stock of you along the way? Who asked you to read him a letter from his brother Hernando when the Greek could just as well have done the job, and a sensitive, private job at that, a mark of trust?'

Gabriel's hopes rose, although he gave Sebastian a circumspect look.

'You seriously think so?'

'It's pretty obvious.'

'But by the blood of Christ! Why doesn't he just be done with it and engage me to help him conquer Peru!'

'Because first of all, Don Gabriel, until King Charles officially gives him that task, *Capitan* Pizarro has nothing to engage you to do. For the moment all he has is a dream. And dreams, Don Gabriel, are a commodity of which he has sold many, of late. And they have brought him enough trouble as it is . . .'

Gabriel rode on, meditating silently as the dust rose from the caravan. He had to admit the wisdom of Sebastian's words.

For days he'd been living a dream that *Capitan* Pizarro hadn't needed to sell to him. His dream: to leave Spain and put the oceans between himself and the humiliating sting of the Holy Inquisition. And to get as far away from his unfeeling, boorish father as possible.

There in that distant land, he would become another man.

Yes: there he would bring glory to his name. And then he would return to exact revenge upon all those who had humiliated him.

'In your honest opinion, Sebastian, do you believe that Don Francisco will convince the King to name him governor?'

A big smile spread across the Africian's friendly face.

'In all the time I've known him, I've never seen anything – man, beast, or even roaring ocean – that was his equal. Learn from his patience, Don Gabriel!'

It was almost five o'clock when Pedro the Greek reined in his half-bred. Like an awestruck child, he pointed at the splendid sight that they all beheld, a vision that emerged from a wood of pine and cedars they had passed through.

'Toledo?' he asked, wide-eyed with surprise.

Gabriel laughed as he nodded.

Nestled in a serpentine bend of the River Tagus, overhanging the green water, the city rose from its promontory as if its spires aspired to scratch the sky. Under the burning afternoon sun, its brick buildings blended into one unified construction, a superb, massive crown atop the Alcazar cliffs.

Toledo, the crown jewel of the world!

At a first glance from a distance of two leagues, the city told of the fabulous power of the great Emperor Charles the Fifth, who molded the universe to his liking and expanded it to fit his will.

Gabriel felt the urge to mock the Greek's bewilderment, but he hadn't time to get the words out. Don Francisco Pizarro reined in his mount, which circled abruptly. The old conquistador's determined gaze shimmered with anger. His words flew from his lips hidden in his beard:

'What's this then, Pedro! After all you've seen across the ocean, after all that we've gone through together, you mean to tell me that a town built of mere bricks and mortar can impress you so?'

'Forgive me, Don Pizarro. It's just that—'

But Pizarro cut him off with a wave of the hand.

'Don't waste your breath! From now on, no matter what the circumstances, nothing shall impress you, you shall be bewildered by nothing. Do you understand me, Pedro? You are one of the few who have seen a city whose walls are covered in gold! Gold! Have you forgotten?'

He pivoted towards the red-brick city shimmering in the Castilian light, and shouted:

'We are the ones who shall bewilder all the good people of Toledo!'

Don Francisco turned his hard gaze on each of his followers in turn. Gabriel went red despite himself.

'We are the ones bringing the gold, the wealth and power that Charles so desperately needs!' thundered Don Francisco. 'We are the spectacle that shall astonish them all! And when we enter the town, we shall be the ones whom they will acclaim and adulate! And none of you shall appear surprised!'

The old warrior's gray beard bristled with pride. His horse stamped and sidestepped. He brought it under control with a kick of his spurs. He pointed at the Greek and Sebastian.

'You two especially are not to forget that in the coming weeks! You've endured a thousand deaths and lived to tell the tale. No one has done what you have done, or seen what you have seen. You've walked the streets of Tumbes, where the walls are lined with gold. You've fought savage beasts trained by the Indians. You have, under my command, discovered the richest kingdom in the Indies. And we are here to receive what is due to us: the honor of conquering it! I shall leave this brick-built town as Governor of Peru and the Kingdom of Tumbes . . . By the Sacred Virgin, tell me what could possibly still impress you in this country?'

No one replied. Only the crickets and cicadas chirped.

For the first time since they had left Seville, Gabriel thought he saw a smile crease *Capitan* Pizarro's bearded cheeks.

Don Francisco had predicted well. They were the ones who astonished the town, and all came out to see them.

As soon as their arrival was announced, a crowd of Toledo's bourgeois, its craftsmen, women and servants, its elderly, rich and poor all crowded the San Martin city gate, as well as the length of its walls and the tortuous road that led to its magnificent cathedral. Squealing children scurried about the caravan as it advanced along the road from Piedrabuena.

With one hand on the pommel of his saddle and the other on his sword handle, Don Francisco sat tall as he led the procession, followed three paces back by the equally majestic Greek Candia who seemed larger than the horse he rode. The townsfolk removed their hats to them as they passed, and every ten paces or so they nodded their heads in acknowledgement of some compliment, while at the same time they assumed the severe look that they thought appropriate for veterans such as themselves.

Both Indians were smiling, flabbergasted by all the new things, but not in the least bit anxious; in fact, they seemed rather proud as they urged the strange-looking llamas on. Children bounced around the creatures, trying to touch their wool. And Toledo's women, upon seeing Martinello's handsome, impassive face – his broad cheeks colored somewhere between leather and olive, his eyes half open in a languid expression, his gorgeous, well-defined mouth – covered their own mouths and let out little cries. One grabbed the wrist of her neighbor and whispered:

'Look! They look almost like humans!!'

'But that other one looks like trouble,' yapped her neighbor, pointing at Felipillo, his face being thinner and harsher than his compatriot's and his eyes more searching.

A small troop of lansquenets – foot soldiers – joined them as a much-needed escort about half a league from the town, and surrounded the wagons. In the crisp afternoon light, the Peruvian treasure glittered in all its magnificence.

On a whim Sebastian jumped into a cart and grabbed a gold statue in both hands, an image of a naked man with a fine face and lapis lazuli eyes. The crowd voiced its admiration. Then the African lifted an enormous mask, the shape and color of a blood-red sun and stitched with thin, colorful strips. He put it on and eyed the gaping onlookers while growling ferociously. An apprehensive shudder ran through the crowd, and the womenfolk uttered shrill cries. Sebastian then showed them delicately hammered vases, effigies of strange creatures, llamas of solid gold, chiseled silver plates, pots, goblets, seashell necklaces, feather standards stitched with gold thread . . . and the crowd was amazed, dizzy even, from all the gold.

The caravan refused to stop, although the mob pressing against it grew and grew. Those who had seen it once already ran forward to see it again. They were everywhere, pestering the conquistadors, slipping between the carts and the animals drawing them, harassing the mules and grabbing their bridles until threatened by the exasperated guards.

Overtaken by the excitement of the moment, Gabriel jumped into the second wagon, the one that contained the pottery. He held the objects in the air as if he personally had brought them back from the far side of the world. He showed them jugs in the shape of faces, painted and cast so accurately that they looked as though they might move their lips and speak. He showed them pots made to look like birds, feet, hands, fish with teeth, fish without, double pots, gold-leafed pots, pots painted vermilion or purple, pots in the form of lizards, women, pots shaped into flasks, or in the forms of monsters, or even mating couples . . .

All the beauty of a culture, all the knowledge and science of thousands of years of effort by the artisans of another civilization were paraded before hundreds of flabbergasted eyes. Here was the evidence, brought by the witnesses, that a true new world had been discovered across the ocean.

It took them more than an hour to reach the cathedral square from the city gate. The cathedral, where all these wonders would be blessed and cleansed of their pagan spirit. And Gabriel's heart burned as if his long journey to Peru and its marvels had already begun.

CHAPTER 19

Rimac Tambo, April 1529

T HE ROYAL ROAD WAS WIDE AND WELL PAVED. IT was bordered by two stone walls of medium height, conscientiously looked after. When the builders had run out of suitable stones, they had substituted pikes of the same height. Wide steps had been fashioned into the steeper slopes, and here the cortège proceeded cautiously.

On the approaches to the *tambos*, those imposing strongholds that held quantities of food, weavings, pottery – all the local region's products – for the Inca, messengers scurried to and fro, making sure all was prepared for the cortège's stopover.

The *curacas* – local leaders – of each town approached the palanquin in which Huayna Capac's desiccated body sat enthroned. They bent their spines under the heavy stones they carried on their shoulders, a traditional gesture of subservience.

Everywhere people went to great lengths to show their respect for Huayna Capac.

Meanwhile Anamaya felt oppressed by the dull, repetitive days. She had lost count of how many had passed since they had left Tumebamba. Every stop they made seemed identical to the one before. Many moons ago she had given up remaining all day in the palanquin with the mummy and the statue for company. She preferred to disappear among the womenfolk and elderly who walked with the procession.

Occasionally the Sage, Villa Oma, took leave of the important noblemen to walk beside Anamaya. Nowadays he treated her respectfully, and was occasionally almost fearful of her. But he was a grim and anxious companion. The procession rustled with fresh rumors every day. Faces appeared tense, and the further South the column advanced, the more fearful it became, if for no other reason than that they were always moving closer to Cuzco.

Only the dwarf managed to lighten the gloomy atmosphere. He was often seen at the head of the cortège, where his oversized red tunic would trail from him and sweep the road of dust like the hundred servants whose job it was to do so and who were inexhaustible in their duty.

But these days he more often than not fell back until he was scurrying along beside Anamaya in her palanquin.

'Are you daydreaming again, princess?'

'Only of you, my Lord . . .'

The dwarf grinned. He felt the tenderness behind their teasing. They had sustained their precious, silent friendship since that first night when they had opened their hearts to each other. Both were misfits who stood out from the others who were following the dead Emperor's palanquin. The glances thrown at the two of them were as often laden with envy as with revulsion. The next day was especially full of unknowns for the pair of them.

'What shall become of us, princess?'

'How should I know?'

'I thought you could see into the future!'

'Mock me if you must, my noble Lord! But I only see what you see: messengers coming and going, rumors of villagers in Lord Atahualpa's territories being massacred, and the stories they tell of Huascar's cruel wrath . . .'

The dwarf laughed sardonically:

'It's because he's impatient to see me! Apparently they're giving me to him as a good-luck charm! But they also say that he hates all who are not pure Inca – who haven't pointy heads and long legs.'

'To think that he's waiting for me as well,' murmured Anamaya.

For once their light-hearted banter failed them.

Side by side they moved along, near the seething river. The rainy season had filled it with yellow mud, and the river rumbled as if the earth itself was hurting.

That afternoon the well-kept road led them up a steep slope to the Rimac Tambo plateau. Anamaya saw a mountaintop to the north that resembled an arrow's tip, framed exactly in the center of the valley.

As usual, the villagers ran to meet them, prostrating themselves before the palanquins while the horns and flutes sang to the valley.

The local *tambo* was modestly sized, but the esplanade's retaining wall was perfectly built. The temple had harmonious lines, its polished stones, expertly joined, catching the last rays of the sun before it retired behind the mountain crests.

The *curaca* had black, rheumy eyes, and drank a lot more *chicha* than the ceremonies required. He went to great lengths to show his subservience to the plutocracy, remaining prostrated before the Elders for so long that old Colla Topac, exhausted from the trip, eventually lost his temper.

At last, after the evening offerings, they were shown to a *cancha*, halfway down from the sacred square. The rooms had been carefully cleaned and furnished with pretty mats, fine pots and brand new blankets from the repositories.

That evening, Anamaya stayed late in the courtyard. The

river's rumble could be heard from far below, but from here was only a relaxing murmur. In the sunset the mountains surrounding the village seemed like petals protecting a flower's core. Directly opposite her *cancha* a deep, narrow valley opened to the past. In the falling night, the fog-filled valley seemed strangely translucent and ephemeral.

Villa Oma came looking for her, worried by her absence. She asked him about the valley:

'Where does it lead to?'

The Sage frowned and looked at her defiantly. Anamaya turned to look at him, surprised by his reluctance to speak.

'I don't know,' he finally muttered. But his tone wasn't confident enough to mask the lie. Anamaya felt anger increase her heartbeat.

'Sage! How much more time will it take before you trust me? How many tests must I undergo to prove myself?'

'I know who you are, child,' smiled an embarrassed Villa Oma, 'and I know your nature as well. No, it's nothing to do with that . . .'

'Then why lie to me?' Anamaya was getting annoyed. 'That valley surely has a road. It's only a road, so why not tell me . . .'

'Child!' interrupted Villa Oma, grabbing her by the arm. 'You know much, but you are also still ignorant of many things. And there are some things that you are better off not knowing.'

Anamaya was disarmed by his gentleness. She would have liked to draw out her anger and continue pressing him, almost for the fun of it, but she saw something that stopped her in her tracks. The Sage fell silent also, as if spellbound.

A fireball had appeared in front of them amid the early stars of night on the black horizon, directly over the mysterious valley.

Yes: a ball of pale yellow flames, a sun in the night only slightly smaller than the moon. A long wake trailed behind it, like a train of hair lifted by the wind. It seemed to be both careering through the sky faster than a puma's prey that had taken flight and yet hanging still, suspended in the night. Very slowly, it rose above the dark silhouettes of the mountains.

Anamaya shuddered and let out a fearful cry. She murmured in an unsteady voice:

'Villa Oma! What is it?'

He turned to her to see her trembling mouth and her bright blue eyes wide with fear.

'Is this what you saw the night before we left Tumebamba?' he asked. 'Is this what terrified you?'

Anamaya nodded and folded her arms tightly against her chest. She felt her stomach knot and her knees almost give way.

'Yes . . . yes, that's it. But it was going fast, so fast . . .'

Villa Oma took her hand in his bony fingers.

'Abandon your fears, *Coya Camaquen*,' he said softly. 'Let your spirit guide you. Remember your journey into the ancestors' stone. Abandon your fears . . .'

She stared at the comet so intensely that her eyes hurt. But her fear ebbed and her heart grew quiet, perhaps from the Sage's reassurance. And then suddenly she understood, and uttered a little cry.

The comet and its trailing plume were exactly the same shape as the *curiguingue* feather that topped the Royal Headband. What she had seen strike Atahualpa's forehead was not the mark of death. On the contrary, it was the emblem of an Emperor. What she watched as it streaked across the sky that night was a sign from Inti nominating his son, the Inca Atahualpa!

'What is it?' asked the Sage. 'What do you see?'

Anamaya looked at him. She didn't dare speak. She lowered her head and closed her eyes.

'What do you see?' insisted Villa Oma.

'Nothing.'

CHAPTER 20

Toledo, April 1529

'SO THE OCEAN WAS AS SMOOTH AS A POLISHED stone that day, and there was barely a breath of air, despite the gray sky. I didn't see them arrive over the horizon,' explained Sebastian, 'because I was down in the *San Cristobal*'s glory hole. Ruiz, the pilot, had put me in irons for an unfortunate remark I had made, and I had been ordered to cook the soup . . .'

The Greek uttered a disgusted groan.

'Soup, my arse! You ever made soup in your life? There was doubtless nothing in the storeroom but some fish-heads, some pickled cabbage and old pease-meal, and not too much of that either! If I know you like I think I do, no doubt you thickened it with weevils!'

The big African barely smiled, and continued:

'We'd been heading into the unknown South for three weeks, never once being able to land, the coast being so uncommon inhospitable . . . and whenever anyone complained, Ruiz would reply, "They're nearby, I can sense it."'

The morning sun's beams struck deep into the armory of the house where they were, a house lent to Don Francisco by the Duke of Bejar, one of his recent and most fervent admirers. The dust danced in the sun's rays.

While sweat trickled down his athletic torso under his open shirt, Gabriel listened avidly to his companions' tales. His fist gripped the hilt of his brand new sword. Meanwhile Candia the Greek was scratching his cheek with his glove, and some private, unpleasant memories darkened his expression. Sebastian continued telling his story:

'So there I was stirring the soup, when all of a sudden I heard Niceño, who had the watch, bellow, "Sail! Sail-ho! Sail on the larboard bow! Sail-ho!"'

'Ah!' uttered the Greek, putting his hand on Gabriel's shoulder, deeply moved. 'I'd give the fourteen teeth I have left to have been there. Look, just imagining it gives me goose bumps!'

'And so, was it them?' asked Gabriel.

'Why, of course!' replied Sebastian impatiently. 'They were sailing a large raft, a well-made craft, as big as a giant's hand, with a sail and a rudder. There were twenty of them, more or less, men and women. Most jumped overboard as soon as they saw us! Imagine it, Don Gabriel: from their low perspective on the tide, the *Sun Cristobal* must have seemed like a floating wooden mountain!'

'But the sailors saw immediately that they weren't your usual savages,' insisted the Greek, 'seeing as they all wore the tunics you were waving from the wagon the other day. They say that one of them . . . well, they weren't anything like our interpreters Martinillo and Felipillo—'

'There was in fact one who stood out, who stood as straight as a post,' interrupted an irritated Sebastian. 'I saw him, I did! He stood almost as straight as Don Francisco himself! And he had a strong, unflinching eye, and was wrapped in a big cape, and wore those kind of plugs made of solid gold that they all stick in their ears over there . . .'

His eyes shining with excitement, the Greek was obviously burning to contribute to the story. He waved his enormous open hand in the air, and Sebastian continued:

'Yes, exactly like that! Gold disks as big as that great big hairy palm you see there. And attached to his ear lobe by a tube also made of solid gold. And the hole that it passed through so big I could stick two of my fingers in it, and that's God's truth!'

Candia stayed still, his eyes a little vague.

'But it wasn't just in his ears!' insisted Sebastian. 'When the *San Cristobal* came close enough, Ruiz gave signals for the Indian to come aboard, which he did. And on the deck he opened his cape . . . aye, by the Sacred Virgin! He was covered in gold from his chin to his navel! And more still gleamed from his wrists, isn't that the truth, Pedro?'

'That's how Ruiz and the others tell it,' he murmured.

Gabriel nervously wiped the sweat from his brow and squinted a little. The trio fell silent for an instant. And then Gabriel spoke in a low voice:

'An Indian nobleman.'

The others both nodded their heads.

'One of the kind we'll have to deal with if Don Francisco is to govern Peru!' growled the Greek with a snort.

He sliced through the room's hot air with his hand, causing the dust to whirl.

'But enough of this! It's time to continue the lesson. Stand up and *en garde*! If you wish to entertain the slightest hope of remaining in one piece against those Indians, schoolboy, you'll have to learn to hold your sword better than you do now! God's blazes, it's not a soup ladle! Your strike is bloody awful! Come on, let's get to work!'

The Greek stepped back a little as Gabriel stood up with a sigh.

He set himself in position, his knees slightly bent and his chest forward. But his sword-bearing hand was far less supple or firm than he could have wished. The Greek twirled and flourished and struck his sword against Gabriel's with a most unpedantic brutality.

'Keep your position up, and advance your left calf . . .'

Their swords clashed together. The Greek drew back and dodged to the left. He returned with a slanting strike, which glanced off Gabriel's blade. Shoved back by the Greek's momentum, Gabriel recoiled, and his hand was saved from being sliced only by the protective basket hilt of his sword.

'No, no, and no!' cried Pedro. 'A low lunge to the inside! You'd think your ears were already plugged with the gold of Peru! Raise your arm. Twist your wrist towards the sky and thrust – like that! It's as easy as that, for the love of God!'

But easy was the one thing it wasn't. However, Gabriel committed himself to the fencing lesson courageously, and allowed a little rage to surface too. So seriously did they spar that the swordplay soon became a frantic twirl, a human whirlwind.

Sebastian watched the two of them with a smile on his lips. Gabriel warmed to the game, and soon his parries became more self-assured, his lunges more definite, his movement less awkward. His eyes hardened. The Greek dodged in and out of his range as nimbly as a cat. It was plain that he was an experienced swordsman, and his blade seemed to be everywhere. But then, suddenly, Gabriel let out a cry!

'Oh, forgive me!' exclaimed the Greek, jumping back, a contrite look on his face.

'Don't worry, it's nothing,' muttered Gabriel, his hand on his shoulder.

'There's blood,' said Sebastian, approaching Gabriel.

'Why did you throw yourself on me?'

'I thought I'd slip away from you,' Gabriel said lamely, his face a little pale. 'But don't worry, it's nothing.'

'Well, take off your shirt and show me in any case,' ordered the Greek. 'It's better to be sure.'

What they discovered was a long gash, although fortunately it was not deep.

'Ho ... what's this here?' asked the Greek, furrowing his brow.

'Oh, nothing special, just a birthmark,' explained Gabriel as he mopped his wound with his shirt.

The Greek turned him round brusquely, and slapped his huge paw on Gabriel's back.

'A birthmark ... Sebastian, doesn't it remind you of something?'

'Certainly: it's just like that great big cat that wanted to eat us outside Tumbes!'

Gabriel, irritated by their banter, concealed his shoulder from them. But instead of the mocking he expected, he turned to find them looking at him pensively.

'Well, my friend,' said the Greek, mopping his brow, 'this is a most uncommon coincidence.'

'What on Earth are you carrying on about?'

'We're talking about a large feline that gets around over there in Peru,' smiled the Greek. 'The interpreters tell us that the Indian Lords treat it as something most valuable.'

'Hell's death! It's only a birthmark, and you can give it any shape or name that strikes your fancy!' snapped Gabriel irritably.

The Greek shook his head and considered Gabriel wordlessly.

Gabriel allowed himself to be bandaged and made an effort to maintain his scowl. But inside he felt a sense of anticipation fill his heart like a sail, like a promise.

CHAPTER 21

Toledo, April 1529

I T WAS A BLACK NIGHT. AN END-OF-SUMMER STORM grumbled from the north.

Gabriel was asleep deep in an armchair. The pages covered in the Greek's large handwriting had slipped from his fingers to scatter on the red-tiled floor.

A door hinge creaked in his dream, the same creak he had heard so many times in the darkness of the prison. He awoke with a start and jumped to his feet, his mouth agape, his chest hammering.

He searched the room's heavy shadows wide-eyed, but found nothing.

He remembered his nightmare; he saw himself with arms outstretched before the fat Inquisitor, begging him to spare Doña Francesca, who lay defeated at his feet, her dress ripped to shreds, revealing her shoulders . . .

But it had only been a dream, and now he was awake. At his feet lay only the Greek's papers that he was trampling on with his buckled shoes.

He grumbled against his dread and those stupid hallucinations that haunted his dreams. As he knelt to gather up the papers, he heard a rustling in the room, not a dream this time but a very real presence.

Someone came into the circle of candlelight as he stood up from the floor. Two ink-black eyes shone from a smooth, tigerish face.

'Ho!' gasped, Gabriel, recovering his breath as he recognized the Indian Felipillo. 'What the hell are you doing here?'

The Indian had padded in as quietly as a cat. His much-patched breeches ended above his calves – the hard, defined calves of a long-distance walker – and he had a sort of brown blanket thrown over his shoulders. He smiled, and his well-defined mouth seemed remarkably proud.

Gabriel picked up the papers nonchalantly to mask his fright. Finally, brushing the dust from the sleeves of his doublet, he asked again:

'What do you want?'

Felipillo lost his smile. He announced:

'The Lord *Capitan* wants to see you.'

His Spanish sounded odd, lacking the rasping sing-song of the Castilian accent.

'Now, in the middle of the night?'

'The Lord *Capitan* said: you come now!'

Felipillo's tone was as peremptory as his grammar was simple. It was more his deep, impenetrable gaze, however, that made Gabriel so ill at ease.

'And why does he wish to see me?'

The Indian smiled again.

'He did not sing his thoughts to Felipillo.'

Gabriel couldn't help himself from correcting him.

'No, no, you should say, "Don Francisco did not confide in me his reasons."'

Felipillo nodded, but said nothing. He projected such indifference that Gabriel felt prompted to add haughtily:

'You really must learn to speak correct Castilian, Felipillo. Otherwise what good will you be as an interpreter?'

But still Felipillo said nothing. Gabriel shrugged his

shoulders, rolled up the Greek's manuscript in his hand —
deciding to take it with him in case Don Francisco should
want to see it — and buttoned up his doublet as he walked
towards the door.

'Well, let's go then,' he sighed.

The Indian led him to Don Francisco's door, which he
knocked on once and then pushed open without waiting for
an answer. Gabriel entered, ready to bow respectfully. But
what he saw stopped him in his tracks.

Over fifty candles lit the room more brightly than day. A
massive canopied bed stood behind Don Francisco Pizarro,
who was kneeling with his head bowed before a small
painting of the Blessed Virgin and Child. And to pray, he
had donned his full battle dress!

In the light of the candles his steel-plated cuirass, his
epaulettes, and the tassels on his thighs gleamed lustrously,
despite the patches of rust and all the dents — a map of his
past battles. He had laid his hat and his sword — a fine piece of
craftsmanship with a damask hilt and a clover-shaped guard
— on the ground beside his knees.

Gabriel stood motionless, and heard both the thunder
of the approaching storm and Don Francisco's fervently
murmured prayer:

'Holy Mother of God, you have never forsaken me. Your
hand has always been on my shoulder, guiding my ships
through storms, and sparing my life in the worst ambushes.
O Sacred Virgin, you are my pilot, my guide. And I know
that you want me to do more. I know that you want me to
carry your goodness and your light to the cities of gold in
Peru. O Holy Saint, I know that you will lead me there. I
pray that you will have King Charles grant me an audience.
You are the reason why I get up each morning and why I
continue to do what I do. Holy Mother, do not forsake me
now, and I will bring Peru into the folds of your bosom
like a newborn child. I will do this for you, I who love

you, and think of you at every moment with piety and love . . . Amen.'

Don Francisco Pizarro crossed himself and kissed the icon of the Virgin, although his great beard somewhat hampered this particular devotion. Then he rose to his feet as lithely as a young man. He put on his sword and turned to Gabriel.

Anyone else would have appeared ridiculous wearing full armor in the middle of the night; the conquistador, his cheeks as hollow as bowls, and his waxy complexion, might have been regarded as an old madman by someone who didn't know who he was. Could such an absurd character really conquer a great civilization on the far side of the world?

Nevertheless, Gabriel couldn't help but admire him.

'Do you pray, young man?' asked Don Francisco, narrowing his eyes. 'Do you love the Sacred Virgin?'

'Er . . . I think so – I mean, yes,' stammered Gabriel.

'You think so . . . hmm. For myself, I pray every day. She has saved my life a hundred times. Without Her, the blood would have flowed from me until my veins ran dry long ago. And She wants Peru more than even I do!'

Don Francisco's voice was harsh and his eyes burned like firebrands. He walked across the room and opened a window. As he looked out a lightning bolt streaked across the night and metallic blue light flashed on his cuirass, normally as steely gray as his beard. As the thunder followed, he turned around, eyed Gabriel through a furrowed brow and said:

'Pedro the Greek tells me that you are making some progress with personal weaponry. This is good. Reading and writing are not enough to make a man a conquistador. He also said that you have a mark of fate on your back—'

'Oh, it's only a birthmark, my Lord!'

'Hmm.'

Don Francisco stayed silent long enough for another roll of thunder to follow its lightning bolt.

'My brother Hernando doesn't care for you, schoolboy. He wants me to send you back.'

'But why? We've hardly spoken to each other . . .'

'He's wary of young men just out of prison.'

Gabriel went pale. So this was why Don Francisco had summoned him in the middle of the night. To dismiss him as peremptorily as his father had.

But Don Francisco's face almost betrayed his stern manner by smiling.

'Now don't be so glum, schoolboy! I too am just out of jail! Hernando can say what he likes, but I make the decisions, do you understand me? Who knows, perhaps my brother is scared of being sent to jail himself!'

Don Francisco grimaced awkwardly. Gabriel thought he heard him actually laugh, but he couldn't be sure.

'For the moment, however, you shall stay close to me,' announced the *Capitan* as he closed the window.

'For the moment . . .' Gabriel repeated. 'But what about when you leave for Peru?'

'We shall see. Who knows what tomorrow will bring? I still haven't been given this damned audience . . . What are those documents in your hand?'

He was close enough to Gabriel to grab him roughly by the shoulder.

'Pedro the Greek's account of your discoveries, my Lord.'

'Ah! And does he tell of all of them?'

'Er . . . I think so – there are so many.'

'Ha! There certainly are! No doubt he's forgotten a few . . .'

Don Francisco's face, ravined by wrinkles, ruined by harsh weather and the scars of countless battles, displayed such an extraordinary force of character.

'Schoolboy, the Greek tells me that you've seen the King up close.'

'Yes, it's true.'

'Tell me, what is he like?'

'Well, um . . . he's not very tall. Shorter than Your Grace. But he's not so small either, and—'

'Yes, yes, I know all that! But people mock him. Why?'

'Because of his chin.'

'His chin?'

It's too . . . big. His lower jaw overlaps his front teeth by so much that he can't close his mouth completely.'

'Poor man.'

'Your Lordship should take care to listen to him closely, because it's hard to understand him when he speaks. In addition, Castilian is not his mother tongue, and he stutters and swallows his words . . .'

Don Francisco slapped his breastplate angrily.

'This is important information that no one has told me!'

'You would have been told, my brother, had you asked.'

'Hernando!'

Don Hernando Pizarro had opened the door as quietly as the Indian, and he was looking at Gabriel malevolently from its shadow.

'Why do you pay any attention to this boy's stupidities?' he asked unpleasantly.

He walked into the light, a broad smile on his face. He was as elegant, well-dressed and handsome a man as Don Francisco was not. His purple doublet and his damask breeches smelled of perfume. He had a red nose and small, furtive eyes. While ignoring Gabriel, he burst suddenly into laughter and opened his arms to hug Don Francisco.

'It is done, Francisco! It is done, my brother! I come from dining with the King's counselor Los Cobos. You will have your letter granting you an audience first thing tomorrow morning!'

Don Francisco made the sign of the cross and leaped across the room to the icon of the Virgin, which he brought to his lips and kissed repeatedly. Then he turned around, looking noticeably younger, his face aglow, and waved the icon at Gabriel and Hernando.

'She has willed it! She has willed it, thanks be to God! Come, come and kiss Her image and offer Her a prayer of thanks!'

CHAPTER 22

Rimac Tambo, April 1529

THE COMET SOARED OVER THE MYSTERIOUS VALley every night.

Every night at sundown Anamaya passed the *canchas*, circled around the temple, and descended the steps leading to the esplanade that reached the river's edge.

Every night she saw visions of Atahualpa's coronation. Her heart was agitated and nervous, a private distraction she shared with neither the dwarf nor the Sage.

She worried that sleep would steal away her hope, and so spent long, uneasy vigils sitting on a wall under the stars. Colla Topac, the Law-Elder, often joined her, perhaps because he suffered from the insomnia so common in the old, perhaps because he nurtured a secret affection towards the *Coya Camaquen* and had perceived her anxiety.

He spent their nights together telling her about the past. His manner was that of an old, grizzled soldier who had first-hand knowledge of all the campaigns and rebellions in the North as well as in the South. In Quilla's milky light, his face showed as cracked and parched as the desert.

'After tomorrow, we shall leave Rimac Tambo,' he announced one night. 'The time has come for the Emperor's desiccated body to make his final trip.'

The ancient Law-Elder pointed his rheumatic finger at the steep slope to the south-east of the village. A Royal Road slashed through the bush and passed straight over the summit.

'Soon you'll see the puma,' rasped the Law-Elder.

'The puma?'

'Yes, the city of the puma. Cuzco, where the sun shines its sacred light on Coricancha, our temple. The city that Viracocha ordained Manco Capac and Mama Occlo should found. One day they arrived on the crest of one of the mountains that surround it. From the mountaintop they saw the plain, and in the plain they saw the river, and then a great puma appeared . . .'

And he launched into another tale from the ancient history of the Empire.

Anamaya allowed herself to be nursed by the rhythm of his words, his meandering tales of the gods and great men who created the Empire of The Four Cardinal Directions flowing over her and through her.

When his mouth was dry he would pause for a few moments, and put his leathery old hand on Anamaya's. He would smile and stroke her soft skin, as if drawing energy from her, and then return to his tale.

Huascar's men arrived at dawn, under a heavy rain.

As they did every morning, the priests were sacrificing a white llama, and all the noblemen who were accompanying the mummy were gathered for the offering. The beast's blood flowed over the sacred stone, *chicha* wet the sacred ground, and maize burned at the foot of the Emperor's desiccated body. The funereal wail from the trumpets and conches echoed from the mountain.

Anamaya lifted her eyes to the low, gray sky, and saw them arriving through the northern pass: a dozen soldiers, their bright red rain-soaked *mantas* standing out clearly against the green of the vegetation.

As they approached the village she saw that they were fully armed, carrying slingshots, spears, and the dreaded studded war-clubs. This was no mission of peace. They halted where the esplanade began, as if strangers to their fellow Incas, and held themselves apart, saying nothing, indifferent even to the religious ceremony.

Making an uncharacteristic effort to be polite, Villa Oma approached them and greeted them first:

'Welcome, envoys of our noble Lord Huascar.'

'*Emperor* Huascar, you mean,' corrected the officer. He was an ill-mannered young man with eyes so deeply embedded in his skull that his gaze was shadowed and unfathomable.

'We've come to get them,' he said, pointing rudely at the Elders prostrated before the mummy.

Villa Oma immediately lost his composure.

'What are you talking about, Captain?'

'Our Emperor has ordered the Elders to join him before his father's desiccated body arrives in Cuzco . . .'

'Before? Before? And why? It is against the Law . . .'

'Would they defy the Emperor's will?' replied the officer, a thin smile on his boorish face.

'Well, I just don't know . . .' murmured Villa Oma. 'They must be asked, they know the Law, they *are* the Law. While we wait, however, you must share our meal with us.'

But the soldier declined.

He also declined to wait.

The tension among the members of the cortège had been growing since the soldiers' arrival. The women were whispering among themselves, watching the newcomers. The dwarf said to Anamaya:

'Are they here for us?'

She shook her head.

'No, for the Elders.'

'But . . . are they mad?' he said under his breath.

Colla Topac, embodying impassive dignity, approached the young officer:

'Why does the noble Lord Huascar want to see us now, when the Law dictates that we remain with his father?'

'The Emperor did not tell me his reason. He simply ordered that you are to come with us, along with the rest of the Elders.'

Colla Topac turned to the others. He saw the looks of incomprehension and fear in their eyes.

'I see that you have come armed, officer. Does Huascar fear for our safety?'

'The Emperor wants you beside him immediately!' barked the officer; and then, softening his tone, 'I believe that he is only impatient for news of his father.'

'Ah . . . and would he perchance have seen the comet that crosses the sky these past few nights?'

The officer had no reply, and only lowered his beady eyes.

'Well, Huascar's will contradicts the Law,' continued Colla Topac in a voice loud enough for all to hear. 'But I do not wish to upset him. He knows that we come in peace, but nevertheless I shall prove it to him. If he needs reassuring, then might I beg him to remember the courage displayed by his father Huayna Capac?'

The soldier jerked as if he had been slapped across his face. He scrutinized old Colla Topac closely, but the Elder's voice had remained earnest, despite the irony loaded in his words. The soldier made no direct reply, instead ordering the Elders' palanquins to be prepared.

Rain fell relentlessly upon the immobile gathering. The surrounding mountains were veiled in gray, and fog overflowed from the valleys.

Anamaya felt the fear in everyone around her. Villa Oma chewed his coca leaves with his eyes half shut. When he sensed her blue gaze upon him, he turned away.

So she went to Colla Topac and prostrated herself in front of him before he climbed into his palanquin.

'Law-Elder, I want to thank you for all you've taught me.'

Colla Topac took her hand and lifted her to her feet. He smiled.

'Insomnia is a blessing if one can spend the nights in your company, *Coya Camaquen*.'

Anamaya felt him press her hands ardently.

'Take care of yourself, my Lord,' she said quietly. 'And be careful.'

Colla Topac clicked his tongue and looked at the officer watching them.

'I'm too old to fear. I'm at an age, child Anamaya, when the Other World is the last journey one can hope for.'

She tried to bow again, but he pulled her to him, as if he wanted to lean on her to get into his palanquin.

'Watch the comet tonight, *Coya Camaquen*,' he whispered. 'I know what you've been thinking these past nights and that which you don't dare speak. Watch the comet and support Atahualpa as you have until now. Support him, he needs you. He who carries the Law asks this of you.'

A howling wind ushered in that night, a howl that blasted through all the valleys like horns and returned the echoes of Inti's fury from each and every mountain.

The only peaceful sanctuary was inside the temple. Here, Anamaya placed maize and quinoa at the base of the Sacred Double, keeping her movements deliberately slow in an effort to overcome the dread that had been gnawing at her since the Elders' abrupt departure, after Colla Topac had spoken his last words to her. She poured *chicha* all around the statue.

The air was so damp that the braziers with offerings hardly burned.

She heard a sound behind her, and recognized Villa Oma's discreet step. He too felt the need to lay his soul beneath the Emperor's golden gaze. His tired face betrayed the sleepless nights he had spent with the other soothsayers trying to interpret the comet's significance. His lips were tinted green from coca, as always.

But today, for the first time, Anamaya saw helplessness stamped on his face, and the humiliation of it clearly enraged him.

'What do the oracles say?' she asked.

'That Atahualpa must wear the *Mascapaicha*, the Royal Band,' he replied dryly.

'I knew it!'

'But you didn't tell me . . .'

'I thought no one would believe me.'

Villa Oma shrugged his shoulders, discouraged.

'It doesn't really matter. War is now inevitable between the North and the South. Huascar no longer obeys the Law. He ordered the Elders to him in spite of it. He wants to force them to acknowledge him as his father's successor.'

'Colla Topac won't do it!' protested Anamaya.

'Then Huascar will humiliate him further. And in any case he'll make do without his endorsement.'

'The great Atahualpa must know that the comet ordains him as our Emperor,' insisted Anamaya. 'He must know it, Villa Oma!'

'And that will unleash war!' cried the sage. 'You don't know what war is, *Coya Camaquen*. And I foresee that this one will bring down the Empire.'

'I do know what war is, Sage Villa Oma,' replied Anamaya softly. 'You forget that Captain Sikinchara razed my childhood village. All the ones I loved died that day. And I was holding my mother's hand when the slingshot . . .'

For once, the Sage said nothing.

Anamaya contemplated the faint light of the braziers reflecting on the Sacred Double's golden body. She continued quietly:

'I *do* know what war is. I understand what it is that you dread. But you are the one who taught me that Inti's will is the only one. I am happy, deeply happy in my heart, that He has chosen Atahualpa. And now I must go to him. He must know that his father has spoken to me and has shown me the ball of fire. He must be told that he is no longer bound in silence and that the spirits of the Other World count on him. He must know that all the signs say that he is the rightful Emperor, and that this is Inti's will. Sage Villa Oma, if I must return alone to be at his side, then I shall.'

This time it was surprise that kept Villa Oma from speaking. Eventually he said:

'But you can't go. You must accompany the Sacred Double to Cuzco. It's the Law.'

'Nothing that happens in Cuzco is in accordance with the Law, Sage,' replied Anamaya. 'The Law-Elder himself said so.'

Villa Oma watched her leave the temple as if she were a stranger to him.

Outside, the rain whipped her face. Despite the uncertainty of the future she felt oddly relieved and peaceful, even happy. At last she knew that she spoke the truth.

She shivered as she crossed the deserted esplanade. Her *llicla* was no defense against this cold. Automatically she glanced in the comet's direction, shielding her eyes from the wind and rain with her hand. But the sky was too clouded and she couldn't make it out. It was equally dark in the South, the direction in which the Elders had been taken . . .

She was thinking affectionately of old Colla Topac when

a footfall in the wet grass made her turn around. But she saw nothing.

A large, strong hand covered her mouth before she had time to cry out. Someone picked her up as easily as if she was a doll.

CHAPTER 23

Rimac Tambo, April 1529

NOT ONE WORD.

Old Colla Topac ran his wrinkled hand through his white hair and then over the square, powerful jaw that once would have commanded obedience. Tonight, however, he was overcome by an awful sense of impotence, and, he had to admit it, fear.

Why hadn't the troops said a word to them since they had left the *tambo*? Why did they look away whenever their eyes met, embarrassed despite their impassive façade?

As they started up the high road, he called for the officer leading the escort, the young man with the beady eyes set deep in his head whom he had humiliated this morning. But it was a waste of time. He was aware of the Elders' agitation.

The road followed a fast-running stream, and became narrower and narrower. The overhanging trees grew closer together until they closed over them, shutting out the day. It rained intermittently. Colla Topac was chilled to his bones.

That night they stopped at some miserable clay huts built on a steep, slippery slope. The officer now came to him. And this time he did not turn away his gaze.

It was then that Colla Topac realized that they were all going to die.

Right there.

That very night.

'Couldn't you think of a better way?'

'I didn't want you to cry out!'

Anamaya looked at Manco through the whipping rain. Despite the darkness, she noticed that his features had hardened. They had last seen each other only a few weeks earlier, but now his hawkish nose seemed to protrude even more sharply from his face, a face that had grown as hard as a highland rock.

'I had to hide from some soldiers while I waited for you—'

'You could have waited a long time!'

'I told myself that my father would speak to you.'

'What is happening, Manco?'

'What's happening is that Huascar has gone insane.'

'Insane?'

'I don't know if it's because of the celestial omens or the rumors of Atahualpa's rebellion, but everyone in Cuzco knows that Huascar gets drunk frequently, that he passes out at orgies, that he insults his own mother by calling her Atahualpa's whore. He was found howling between the towers of Sacsayhuaman's temple, convinced that the Chancas were about to attack. He was hurling insults at a bunch of rocks, ordering them to transform into warriors . . .'

'What about you and Paullu?'

'Until now he hasn't paid too much attention to us. But when he does, then who knows what treasons he will suspect us of?'

'Why did he order the Elders to be taken to him?'

Manco looked blank.

'The Elders? I don't understand.'

'Earlier, some troops came and took them away. They said Huascar wanted them to go ahead to prepare for the mummy's arrival.'

Manco leaped to his feet, causing Anamaya to do the same.

'Come on, we must hurry!'

'Wait! First we have to get the Sage, Villa Oma.'

'The green-mouthed Sage? Are you sure?'

They could see the temple in the torchlight ahead of them. The esplanade had transformed into a mudlake in the rain. Anamaya ran as fast as she could, her straw sandals squelching in the mud.

'The Sage will know,' she said confidently.

But as she ran, she thought to herself that Villa Oma might not know at all.

'What are your orders?'

'We have no orders, only one duty: to accompany the mummy of the Inca Huayna Capac to the Temple of Coricancha at Cuzco, where the accession of the next Emperor is to be ratified.'

'What are Atahualpa's orders to you?'

'None whatsoever. But his ambassadors are with the cortège. They bring gifts and assurances of allegiance to the Inca Huascar from his brother.'

'What are Atahualpa's real intentions?'

'If you suspect me of committing the crime of treason, why don't you take me to Cuzco to be tried, and punished if found guilty? Why are you hiding me in this hut lost in the middle of the mountains, as if this crime had to remain secret, unknown to the gods?'

Despite the great weakness that he felt, Colla Topac spoke as confidently as he could. He was tied to a post with agave rope, in an earth-floored hut. His companions had been killed one by one – a sling shot to the forehead, an arrow from close range into the heart – and their blood flowed into the river he could hear nearby.

He was the last of them to remain alive.

The beady-eyed captain had ordered the rest of the soldiers to get out of the hut. Only the two of them remained.

'You are their leader, aren't you?' said the officer slowly.

'No! I am the principal of the Elders.'

'You were sent by the traitor Atahualpa to spy on the Sapay Inca's troops, and to gather information to help the traitor in his rebellion.'

'Don't be absurd. Ten pathetic old men hiding behind the mummy's palanquin to better spy from? Ridiculous!'

The captain's expression betrayed a flash of doubt. He approached Colla Topac and squatted in front of him, gazing deeply into the old man's eyes.

'It's what they say in Cuzco.'

'Look at me, young man. Look at the corpses of my companions whom you tortured and from whom you obtained only looks of terror before they crossed the threshold of death. You didn't manage to get a scrap of information. You have nothing, nothing but blood on your hands.'

'You too shall cross the threshold of death. Tell me what you know if you don't want to be tortured first, and your liver fed to the puma.'

'You'll get nothing from me, my boy. Not even a moan.'

The captain didn't respond to this. He stood up straight, untied the old man and prodded him out of the hut.

It was a beautiful night. The Milky Way, that eternal celestial river, flowed brightly through the sky. It was true that the officer could have been Colla Topac's boy, his son. It was also true that in his younger days as a warrior, the senior Elder had not spared his enemies. But how could this young man fail to realize that the orders behind which he hid in so cowardly a fashion were the fruit of a deranged mind? How could he not see that he was preparing the downfall of the Empire of the Four Cardinal Directions?

But he knew that no words would convince him.

Colla Topac would have to die.

Eight soldiers took hold of him, two men gripping each of his limbs.

He opened his eyes as wide as he could so that the universe could more easily reclaim his soul and reward him with eternal peace. He looked to the night sky and saw the edges of the receding clouds lit by the comet's glow, producing a halo effect.

Dozens of hands were pulling him apart, and he could hear the grunts of the soldiers' efforts. He heard a gruesome tearing sound, and realized in his final moments of consciousness that it came from his own chest.

Colla Topac's last sensation was of his old body splintering like a stone hurled against a rock and exploding into fragments.

The dwarf ran ahead of them.

He had been born in the forest, and he knew how to read its signs: the passage of a man or animal marked by displaced stones, broken branches and ruffled bushes.

Villa Oma, Manco and Anamaya followed with heavy hearts.

In the black, humid night, they could glimpse the stars through breaks in the canopy.

Suddenly they heard a cry.

They found their bodies one after another.

Some had been killed along the path, and their corpses had been left there, looking peaceful.

Others were twisted into grotesque shapes, looking like ghosts who had seen all the evil in the world.

One had been smashed by stones so heavy that his spine had snapped. A bone protruded from his shoulder and pointed to the sky.

They found the grains of a murderously violent type of red pepper in the gaping mouth of another; before being killed he had been tortured with this edible fire that consumed one's stomach and body.

Everywhere they looked they found pools of blood or scraps of torn flesh; and they could hear the silent echoes of the victims' unheeded, agonized cries.

They found Colla Topac last, his body broken, his mouth twisted into an awful rictus.

There was still a little life left in his eyes, a final dignity defying all the outrages he had endured.

Anamaya knelt beside him and took his hand in hers, as she had done that afternoon when the officer was giving his orders under the pouring rain.

'Stay alive, little girl,' said the old man, his life ebbing from him. 'Keep your blue eyes alight . . .'

'Why? Why?'

The old man lifted his gaze with a final effort. He seemed to be directing her to a point high in the night sky – the comet.

She was crying when she stood up. She turned to Manco:

'Where were you? Why did you come so late?'

Manco made no reply. He had no reply to make, she told herself. The only thing to do was to dance like the dwarf in his oversized red tunic, dance until one collapsed from exhaustion.

'I must go,' said Manco at last.

Anamaya turned to Villa Oma.

'What shall we do? Return to the Tambo and wait for another troop to massacre us?'

'You must go as well,' said Manco. 'That is what I had come to tell you.'

Villa Oma suddenly seemed terribly old. His eyes were shadowed with gloom, and his face was long.

'Manco is right. We must do all we can to protect you.'

'Paullu and I must stay in Cuzco, but you must go, Anamaya, and warn Atahualpa.'

'What about the mummy? The Sacred Double?'

'Huascar, in his madness, might destroy them. You must live: you carry the Emperor's words inside you.'

The sky was clear now. It was as if it had never rained, as if no cloud had ever passed through it. The comet was brighter than ever and Anamaya looked directly at it to clear her mind.

Manco and Villa Oma remained silent. Anamaya breathed deeply and recalled the moment when she had become aware of her destiny, and when she had consciously accepted it from the depth of her being.

The dwarf was seated on a stone as large as himself.

'Need I ask you as well, princess?'

She smiled and tousled his hair.

'You know that your word is my command, my Lord.'

'Then let's go,' said Villa Oma. 'We must hurry.'

'Where to?'

'Just follow me.'

Meanwhile, Manco disappeared towards the mountaintop and the plateau that would lead him to Cuzco.

The dwarf, the Sage and the young girl hurried into the night.

CHAPTER 24

Toledo, April 1529

'HERE THEY ARE! HERE THEY ARE! OOOHH, BUT aren't they pretty! Oh, Your Majesty, they're as soft as lambs! And so much bigger! *Mira, mira!* It's real wool, as soft as anything off an ewe. Ooooh, they're so cute, cute, cute!'

The dwarf's voice gushed, squealed and shrieked hilariously. It was astonishingly penetrating for such a tiny person. Dressed up in lace and dolls' clothes, and with an enormous hat upon his head, the dwarf flung his minuscule arms into the air and scurried from one llama to the other, slipping under their middles, stroking them, grabbing at them, hanging from their long necks, and rubbing his cheeks on their fleece before bounding away.

The creatures yanked on their tethers and dragged Martinillo and Felipillo around in circles. Both Indians were awestruck by the ostentatious palace, and they spoke vehemently to each other in their own language as they tried to calm the llamas.

'Ho, but listen how those two cackle on, Your Highness!'

The dwarf took to mimicking the Indians, making ridiculous sounds, pulling on their *mantas* and leaping between their legs with a comic grimace on his face. Suddenly, faking an accident, he lost his balance and fell into Felipillo, and the two landed on the thick carpet. The now unattended llama made the most of the situation, launching into a gallop directly at the throne. Pedro the Greek jumped in just in time to capture the beast, which brayed raucously before spitting at him.

By now the dwarf and the interpreter had disentangled themselves.

'What in the world does he think he's doing?' exclaimed the dwarf, feigning horror at the llama's antics. 'How dare he disrespect a King!'

'When llama angry, *Señor*, always he do this,' attempted Felipillo in Castilian.

'When llama angry . . .' repeated the dwarf comically, spitting at Felipillo.

The crowd responded with laughter, even applause. And so, encouraged in his foolery, the dwarf smacked Felipillo with his hat.

'See, Your Majesty: this one has only two legs, but he doesn't know how to use them! And look: even if he doesn't have wool growing on his calves, he still grazes on the carpet!'

Gabriel was horror-stricken, and saw Don Francisco grow pale from fury at the affront. The conquistador ferociously kneaded the hilt of his sword with his leather-gloved hand. His nostrils flared as he turned to face the royal dais. Although the young Queen wore a hint of a smile, Charles the Fifth looked on impassively. His large, powerful chin gave his face an odd, lumpish look that belied the intelligent light in his eyes. And, if one were paying close attention, one would have noticed the slight – very slight – nod of his head acknowledging the *Capitan*.

Don Francisco's chest immediately swelled. With all the elegance he could muster, he bent his thin form double and brushed the ground with the green feather of his hat.

Pedro the Greek held the llama's tether, and Felipillo was upright again, pacified by a signal from Sebastian. Gabriel allowed himself to relax, and sighed discreetly.

They had been on the warpath for over twenty hours. Don Francisco, unable to restrain himself, had woken them all up in the middle of the night. He had repeated the same recommendations, advice, orders, a hundred times or more; he incessantly asked that his black doublet be dusted, although it was brand new, and he changed the feather in his hat for a yellow one, then white, followed by red, only to decide at dawn on green. He ordered over and over that the five of them – Pedro the Greek, Sebastian, Gabriel, and his brother Hernando – as well as the two Indians should kneel before the icon of the Virgin.

In the very early morning they all found themselves at the Alcazar, hungry and weary, where their leader, his hands clammy, paced blindly up and down the magnificent gardens as the sun warmed the day. At the approach of noon they were ushered into salons, where grand ladies in farthingales and pearls, Bruges lace, and glittering jewels came to examine them as if they were bulls soon to be speared in the arena.

The sun was dipping towards the horizon when they were finally shown into the audience room. All the gold treasures, pottery, and fabrics carried back from Peru were displayed on a long table. But alas, in that huge, resplendent room, already brimming with furniture, tapestries, and paintings, the Peruvian objects appeared small in comparison, despite their exotic splendor.

Everyone who was anyone in Spain was there. Hundreds of notables with high-sounding titles milled about, dressed in silk brocades and covered in the baubles currently in fashion, their beards waxed or cheeks powdered red, depending on their sex. They gazed around haughtily with fixed smiles.

Gabriel was profoundly upset by their gibes at Don Francisco, the discoverer of Peru, whom they scoffed at as if he was a buffoon, lacking as he did their courtly manners.

But the King cut their laughter short with a vague wave of his hand, and called out to the dwarf as one would to a dog.

'Enough, Estabanillo!'

His voice was calm and seemed comprehensible enough, and he added:

'We are ready to hear from you, *Capitan* Pizarro.'

A heavy silence ensued.

Don Francisco seemed to have lost his tongue. His brother Hernando advanced and bowed smilingly, but Don Francisco pulled him back.

'No! I am the one to speak,' he snarled under his breath.

Pushing Hernando aside, he spoke in a harsh voice:

'Your Majesty, I have discovered a land that is a gold mine and that shall fill the coffers of Spain for centuries to come.'

The King didn't stir. But the dwarf, standing next to him, sneered:

'Gold! Gold! Gold! Ho ho, gold everywhere, my King! That's what the man says! But yet I could swear that those great big sheep over there are covered in wool, not gold!'

A snigger from the crowd was cut short by the unexpected sound of the Queen's clear voice:

'*Capitan* Pizarro, we would like to hear you tell the story of this discovery.'

'It's a long tale, Your Majesty. The venture took more than ten years!'

'In that case, please give us a brief account, Don Francisco.'

'A brief account, Your Majesty, would be difficult . . . well, I shall try. It all began when we discovered the Southern Ocean, as we call it, across the Darian. That in itself was tremendously difficult! I am one of those who founded

Panama City with the governor at the time whose name was, um . . .'

'Balboa,' whispered Gabriel, without thinking.

Hernando Pizarro hurled a black look at him. But Don Francisco simply nodded.

'Yes, that's right, Governor Balboa . . .'

Gabriel was relieved to hear Don Francisco's voice relax.

With each sentence he warmed to his task, and gradually he spoke with greater ease and vivacity. And thus, for over an hour, his epic tale gripped his breathless audience: how they had had to dismantle an entire caravel and carry it in pieces across the jungle, from the Atlantic to the Southern Ocean; how they had endured the jungle's insects, snakes, wild beasts and Indians, as well as thirst, hunger and diseases; how only the most single-minded had survived, only those with enough fire and fury to continue each day, spurred on by stories of a land covered entirely in gold that existed beyond the jungle; how they had had to overcome skepticism, incertitude, despair, a lack of funds, and the gangrene of doubt; and how, so often during those ten long, miserable years, they had had to survive the sea itself, and all the horrors that the adversity of the unknown could inflict upon the children of God.

'And then one day, Your Majesty, there it was! From our ship we saw a town on the coast, an enormous town. The jungle had retreated all around it and exuded smells that can only be found over there. And you must believe me when I tell you that in this town were at least two thousand houses! And the entire town glittered – like a celestial city, Your Majesty! Only when we got closer did we realize that it was the light reflecting off gold, gold as bright as the sun itself! I swear by the Grace of the Sacred Virgin, its walls were of solid gold! This is the glory of Tumbes, as the town is known.'

Carried away by his own passionate words, Don Francisco dropped to his knees and crossed himself. And all his companions did the same without thinking twice, so moved were they by his fervor: Sebastian, Hernando, the Indians, the Greek and Gabriel, all of them were on their knees, making the sign of the cross!

A murmur of admiration rose from the audience. The crowd had been won over by the conquistador's passion. But once again it was the Queen's limpid voice that interrupted:

'Don Francisco, it's a fine tale that you've just told. But I have heard tell that a great many men perished during these terrible adventures . . .'

Overwrought as he was, Don Francisco jumped to his feet. He completely disregarded the Queen and directed his burning gaze at the King instead. He ignored the courtesies due to royalty and launched into a passionate defence.

'May Your Majesty forgive me, but this criticism is pure idiocy! If it were easy to discover a land covered in gold such as Peru, then Your Majesty would now be at your dinner table rather than listening to me!'

'Well said!' cried the dwarf, clapping.

'Is it not true nevertheless, *Capitan* Pizarro?' asked the King in his clumsy Castilian.

'Certainly men died. They die more often than not in the Indies, if I may say so. But to reproach me for this! I've never stopped any man who wished to from turning back—'

'They say, *Señor* Pizarro, that you confined a hundred men on an island for over a year, and that half of them died . . .'

'Not at all! Not at all, Your Majesty! I confined myself as well because some tried to stop me from going on. And only twenty passed away, no more. And do you know what I did when a ship finally arrived to rescue us? We were on a beach, the launches were waiting, and each man had to decide whether to continue south or return to Panama . . .'

Don Francisco paused, took a step forward, drew his sword and waved it above his head, causing the crowd to gasp and the dwarf to scurry behind the throne.

'This is what I did, Your Majesty: I raised my sword thus – and then I plunged it into the sand . . .'

Acting out his words, Don Francisco pointed his blade at the thick carpet. With a furious grunt he slashed a line in it . . .

'Lord Don Francisco!' exclaimed the young Queen, waving her hands. 'I beg of you, please be careful with the carpet. It was taken from the Ottomans!'

Don Francisco jumped back, then contemplated her from beneath a furrowed brow. He made a vague gesture of apology and then, without worrying about it any further, said to the King:

'On the beach of Gallo Island, I traced a line just like this one, Your Majesty, although perhaps a little deeper . . . in any case, I said to them: "Companions and friends! I shall not return to Panama. I shall continue south into the unknown. Those who wish to follow me should cross this line. By doing so, you may reasonably expect to suffer hunger, thirst, disease, perhaps death! Those of you who do not so wish will return to your safe, normal lives in Panama. Yet I will thank you, because until now you have shared with us tribulations never before suffered by anyone, a martyrdom that dictates that I should love you as much as the others. But to those others, I promise you Peru and its rivers of gold. I shall not force anyone to go. But one day the courageous among you shall enjoy the fruit of your efforts! I am sure of it!" That is what I said, Your Majesty. And the truth of it is that many returned to Panama, and I didn't lift even my little finger to prevent them! But thirteen joined me across the line I had traced: those thirteen, Your Majesty, are the heroes of a legend that will be told for centuries to come!'

The women in the perfumed crowd began to clap, and the severe faces of the dukes, marquises, chamberlains and royal advisers nodded and grunted approvingly.

At that moment Gabriel – who had been holding his breath

– saw King Charles, the fifth Emperor of Europe, and her richest sovereign, rise to his feet. The monarch smiled widely, opening his large, odd-looking mouth. He left his throne and came down from the dais. Looking almost like an ordinary man, he pointed at the two Indians and the llamas:

'Tell me about these strange creatures, *Capitan* Pizarro.'

CHAPTER 25

Salcantay, 1529

'WHERE ARE WE GOING?' ASKED ANAMAYA.
They had now penetrated deep into the night,
the lights of Rimac Tambo far behind them, and
Anamaya had been asking the same question over and over.
But Villa Oma hadn't replied, remaining instead absorbed
in an almost hostile silence. He had taken with them only
two servants, two guards, and, at Anamaya's insistence, the
dwarf, who promised to make himself useful as a porter, or a
guard, or indeed to perform any task that they asked of him.
Villa Oma had yielded grudgingly to his pleas.

Soon the lights on the *tambo* receded from their view
altogether. The only thing that remained of the valley that
they had left behind was the rumble of its river. This hadn't
diminished at all, despite the altitude they had already
reached on their climb up the steep, narrow path that was
overgrown with vegetation.

The noise of the running water conjured the image of
blood flowing from the body, and the image of the dying
Colla Topac remained fixed in Anamaya's mind's eye: She
remembered how his white hair had been plastered to his
head with sweat, how his vacant eyes had rolled back
into their sockets, and how his old and parched hand had

clung to hers. She clenched her teeth to stop herself from crying.

Despite the dark she could tell that they were passing through layers of fog that hid from them the night shadows. Those sounds of animals she recognized – squirrels and forest deer – reassured her. But a rustle from the dark would cause her ears to prick; it could be a weasel just as easily as the advance guard of troops sent to torture them as they had the Elders.

The path grew steeper, and she searched its loose surface with her feet to find solid rock so as not to lose her balance. She sensed that they were approaching a summit. The vegetation around the path thinned as they finally came out onto a large rock platform. Villa Oma led her around the back of a sparse *tocacho* grove where there stood the ruins of an adobe house, its straw roof pierced with holes. It was surrounded by a roughly hewn stone wall, around which a serpentine drain carried water before disappearing between two rocks. For the first time in many hours, Anamaya felt a little peace in this other-worldly place.

After the offering ceremony, the Sage spoke his first words since their departure.

'We shall rest here a while.'

'Will you tell me where we are going?'

'Its name doesn't matter, girl. I am taking you there. It's my decision, and perhaps my mistake.'

One of the servants made to light a fire, but Villa Oma gestured for him to stop. It was cold, but they were safer in the darkness.

They walked into the room where their sleeping mats had been laid out, and Anamaya felt a wave of exhaustion hit her. She lay down, wrapped up in her *manta*.

'Princess?'

She opened her heavy eyelids. The dwarf had slid his mat

next to hers. And, as he reached out for her hand, she took it and fell asleep.

The sky was deep blue, and the sun had already climbed high above the horizon. In a few minutes it would come out to the right of the peak and chase the shadows from the dale. Anamaya watched the flight of the snow torn from the mountain top by the violent, blustering wind.

A patch of copper light had filtered down the mountain behind her, and she could feel its heat lick her ankles.

'A day of beauty after one of death.'

Anamaya didn't move. She knew that it was Villa Oma behind her.

'If that's not where we're going,' she said, pointing at the mountain top, 'then are you allowed to tell me what it's called?'

'You know things that we don't, yet that is not enough for you . . .'

'What do you mean?'

'Nothing, my child, nothing at all! That Mountain is called Salcantay.'

Anamaya turned and faced Villa Oma. His eyes had an almost savage glint to them.

'Come,' he said. 'We must move on.'

For three whole days they crossed the range, with Salcantay and its eternal ice always above them. Each night they stayed in a tumbledown hut as decrepit as the first. They saw the glacier change with each permutation of the light, each caprice of the sun, every shadow from every cloud. They had almost circled Salcantay entirely when Anamaya turned around to see the white ice-lake, almost gray, scarred with blue lines and the dark daggers of crevasses.

Villa Oma was right; this was no place for human beings. Beyond the last peak, the landscape opened up. Deep valleys plunged into the forest's blue-tinged haze. As they descended, the sparse grass along the path gradually gave way to shrubs. Anamaya felt as if they were entering a different world.

They reached a wide, elevated road built of carefully joined rocks. Its flagstones were flat, and Anamaya could daydream without fear of falling into the void. As they journeyed on, shadows and sunlight alternated. The shadows fell in the tunnels carved through the massive rock, the sound of water dripping nearby.

They kept up an unflagging pace. By sunset they were thoroughly exhausted.

It was still night when Villa Oma put his hand on her shoulder to wake her. He motioned for her to follow him.

They climbed a steep track. The sugar-loaf peak had been cleared and only one rock remained.

'To go where we want to go, we have to ask the *Apu*'s permission,' murmured Villa Oma.

Anamaya said nothing. She had given up trying to find out where they were, and moreover felt ill at ease about it. The stars were fading in the shy dawn, and a massive mountain, terrible and majestic, slowly emerged from the night.

'Salcantay is one of the most powerful *Apus* around. He doesn't allow anyone near his llamas. Very occasionally the oblivious have returned from his heights, raving about a red woman before sinking into utter madness. But if you show him respect, child, he will protect you.'

Still Anamaya said nothing, so impressed was she by the sheer spectacle of the mountain. Its peak had suddenly lit up into a brilliant white flame fired by the wind. A moment later, the entire glacier flared into a red-orange whirlwind.

'Look, Villa Oma: Inti embraces Apu Salcantay.'

Fingers of fog had slowly risen from the forest, run along

the length of the slopes and gathered into a thick bank at the foot of the mountain.

Villa Oma was crouched in front of the rock on which he had placed six clay flasks that he had filled with clear water. He spread a small square rug on the ground. Anamaya barely noticed him carrying out his unchanging ritual. She was still uneasy and fearful, but a joy was growing in her.

The Sage held his coca-filled *chuspa* in front of his lips and blew on it, his eyes closed in concentration. While murmuring to himself he took out three of the best leaves in the pouch, full and evenly green ones, and placed them delicately on one corner of the rug, then repeated this for the next corner. He placed llama figurines, skeins of dyed wool, and white, violet, and black maize kernels in its center.

The thick cloudbank had begun to creep imperceptibly up the mountain, shutting out the ice pinnacles at the bottom of the glacier one by one. The *Apu* shone like gold. Light glinted off its lines, some sharp, some soft.

The priest gave her a look, and Anamaya sat facing the rock. From where she sat, she saw that the rock was a perfect smaller-scale version of Salcantay.

Floating on the surface of the water in the flasks, grains and powders slowly disappeared in colorful rising froths – fermentation was under way: The *Apu* had accepted their offerings.

Villa Oma took each of the flasks and held them over her head one after another, all the while murmuring words she didn't recognize, apart from her own name and that of the mountain. He poured the contents of each flask over the rock.

'Now you.'

Anamaya folded each corner of the rug, careful not to upset the order of the offerings, held the wrap towards the mountain, and blew upon it three times.

Villa Oma took it from her and placed his hand on

her hair. She felt his warmth. He began chanting softly:

'Hamp'u Apu Salcantay, Hamp'u! Hamp'u Apu Salcantay, Hamp'u! Hamp'u Apu Salcantay, Hamp'u!'

His chant gradually swelled in volume. And when the sage's voice was loud enough it echoed back from the space around them. It seemed like all the mountains were clamoring for the coming of the *Apu*.

The final echo fled to the bottom of the valley and died there. Salcantay's radiant peak disappeared behind the cloud's chaste veil.

Anamaya felt at one with the mountain. A deep peace came over her.

The dwarf was waiting for them at the foot of the peak. Along with the guardians of the *Apu*'s sanctuary, he looked on silently as the servants secured the baggage on the backs of the llamas. A wide stone stairway plunged from the small plateau into the sea of white below them. Apart from a few other mountain tops – other islands – nothing was visible through the clouds.

'Here we are on the roof of the world,' said the dwarf, his eyes shining with pleasure.

Villa Oma didn't give Anamaya time to reply:

'Let's go. Time is short.'

And drawing a fistful of *chuño* from the *manta* held out for him by a servant, he started on the long descent.

The stones were slippery from the moisture. The small group was very soon lost in the thick fog. A humid heat oppressed them as the forest grew dense with ferns and brightly colored flowers. The tree trunks were covered in thick carpets of green moss. Water trickled down the mossy rocks, between the creepers and bamboo shoots. There was an abundance of life and growth.

Anamaya hadn't seen the jungle since the violent death of her mother. Her nostrils absorbed all the once-familiar smells, and she saw in the jungle's large, languid leaves, in the blooming corollas of red, pink and yellow flowers, and on the wet squelch of the ground with its swarming insects, all the teeming of life. It was as if her body, deadened by struggle and exile, had been reborn.

Even the horror of Colla Topac's murder seemed to rest in a faraway place and time.

She looked at the dwarf: he was jumping from step to step, flitting like a butterfly. Like Anamaya, he was from the forest, and he was part of its life, a life foreign to those who lived in the mountain valleys and on the platcaux.

The vegetation was so thick in parts that they felt they were walking through shadowy tunnels built by Mother Nature to keep out the sun. Sweat streamed down the napes of the servants' necks. One of them sang quietly to himself in a mournful voice that saddened their hearts.

At last the seemingly interminable steps came to an end. The stepping stones of the path were no less slippery and were covered in a colorful moss. The path narrowed in some places, just wide enough for one person. With each step Anamaya breathed gently to resist the temptation to let herself go, and slip. One false step and she would be flying with the birds.

When at last they came out under the cloud cover, they saw the unfathomable depth of the abyss. They were walking along a steep ridge, with almost vertical cliffs falling away to each side, their walls covered in vegetation.

The dwarf was at the head of the file. He was not dancing now: he made sure of each step, his movements stiff with apprehension, and was short of breath. Suddenly he cried out, his voice sounding from up ahead, round a corner in the path.

The file halted.

Anamaya glanced up to see what was happening.

Their way forward was interrupted by a breach in the path. The rock wall disappeared into the depths.

As easily and calmly as a mountain goat, Villa Oma made his way to the front and pulled the dwarf back. The dwarf moaned fearfully, saying that he couldn't move because he was about to die. He eventually made it back to Anamaya.

'I saw my death in that awful mountain, Princess, and that mad, sneering Sage forced me back!'

There was a movement across the gap. Anamaya made out the shape of a structure behind a large grove of ferns. Two warriors were approaching slowly.

Villa Oma gave his name and title. Then he turned to the escort and said:

'Only her.'

The dwarf let out a touching if comic cry:

'Princess! Don't abandon me!'

Anamaya, her heart constricted, couldn't help but smile.

'If you don't want me to personally throw you into the abyss, you'll go back to Rimac Tambo with the *yanacona* and the guards,' continued Villa Oma impatiently. 'Only the *Coya Camaquen* is authorized to continue from here!'

The two warriors had bridged the gap in the path with dozens of long branches, each one as thick as a human arm.

The dwarf gave Anamaya a desperate glance, but he didn't dare disobey the Sage. She touched his shoulder affectionately before he disappeared with the servants and the guards around the corner, back the way they had come.

Anamaya's heart beat heavily. She was alone with Villa Oma.

After crossing the gap, she found that the path widened to become a proper road and they continued up a gentle slope under the jungle canopy until they came to another halt, this time at the foot of the mountain itself. To her left Anamaya saw a stone stairway rising directly into the mountain, each of its steps high and wide. By leaning back she could make out two massive pillars that marked the end of the stairway, like a doorway into the sky. Despite her fear, she was gripped by a fresh exaltation.

'This is it, isn't it?'

'Always asking questions, always wanting to know everything . . .'

'Answer me, Villa Oma.'

'We are entering the territory of the gods, a place where very few humans are allowed to go . . .'

Anamaya remained absolutely still, staring at the sky.

'. . . And you must take an oath never to pass through that door with a stranger, and never to speak its name, which I shall now tell you.'

'I am bound to the secret, and it to me.'

'This place is called Picchu.'

Anamaya stepped into the light.

CHAPTER 26

Toledo, 1529

'Ho! Ho!'
Don Francisco appeared from behind a thick grove of holly oaks and junipers. He raised his hand and, spurring his mount, cut off Gabriel and growled:

'Just where are you going at such a pace, my boy?'

Gabriel's horse, already trotting quickly, shied violently at the sudden apparition. He almost threw his rider before leaping down a narrow path and taking off in a panicked gallop, the thorns on the juniper trees clawing at his hocks.

Lying low along his horse's neck, Gabriel allowed the beast to run off its panic. He spoke to it in a low, soothing tone, all the while patting it, making sure he slowed its gallop only gradually.

When he finally made it back to Don Francisco, the old *Capitan*'s half-blooded Andalusian hadn't moved an inch. As straight-backed as ever and wearing his faded old velvet doublet, the one he had been wearing when he came out of the Seville jail, Don Francisco observed Gabriel wryly.

'Well, here's a lad who can ride a horse properly, who's not just a pen-pusher!'

'I've been in the saddle since my earliest years. But you *did* almost have me out of my stirrups, Don Francisco . . .'

'Why were you following me? You've been on my tail ever since I left town!'

'Forgive me, Don Francisco, it's just that — well, every morning, I've seen you heading off on a ride . . .'

'A *ride*? Nonsense! I've been reflecting at the *gallop* for thirty years now! A day without a gallop is like a day without a prayer!'

With a bad-humored grumble, Pizarro smacked his horse's flank. He headed off at a moderate trot towards the river.

It was an overcast day. The clouds hung low, and the humidity created arabesques of fog along the Tagus. Here and there in the recently ploughed fields, women and children gathered turnips. The red roofs of Toledo had disappeared behind a patchwork of hills and woods.

Gabriel followed Pizarro and spurred his horse on. When he had caught up again with Don Francisco, he said, a little rudely:

'My Lord, please! Allow me a moment of your time.'

'What for?'

'I need to know. Are you going to take me with you on your conquest of the land of gold? Soon you will receive the letter nominating you Governor of Peru and then . . .'

'What would you know?'

'You will be Governor, I'm sure of it! I saw the look in the King's eye when you were speaking of the conquest.'

'The look in the King's eye? Is that it, then? Ha! My boy, don't you know that kings become virtuoso actors the moment they come into the world?'

'No, my Lord, you pleased him, and shall leave Spain as Governor of Peru, I'm certain of it.'

Gabriel cracked his reins. This time it was he who put himself and his horse across Don Francisco's path, obliging him to stop.

'My Lord, I implore you not to let me languish without purpose! Yesterday your brother Hernando was absolutely adamant that you had no use for me, and that there was not the slightest chance that I would come aboard your Indies-bound squadron. And then a little later, Pedro the Greek assured me of the opposite! He says that you might not mind me so much . . . Don Francisco! I am in a difficult position . . .'

But Gabriel didn't dare finish his sentence. Don Francisco kicked his half-blood to go around him and carry on. While passing, he said tersely:

'Yes, you *are* in a most uncomfortable position, my dear boy, son of the Marquis of Talavera!'

'I am nobody's son, my Lord!'

Gabriel had shouted this loudly enough for Don Francisco to turn around, a look of intense curiosity in the gaze he fixed on Gabriel.

'That is not what I am told.'

'In that case, my Lord, you are being trifled with! I am no longer the son of any man, and if you are being told otherwise, then it is only to do me injury. I am but myself, body and soul. My heredity goes no further than the tips of my boots!'

It was an odd and most unusual smile that twisted the old conquistador's thin lips:

'Now there's something I might have said of myself, in my younger days!'

He looked at Gabriel as if seeing him for the first time, as if he was witnessing a grown man finally emerging from the outgrown chrysalis of a schoolboy.

'Was it a serious offence that got you in trouble with the Inquisition?'

'Serious only if one suspects even the leaves of a tree of thinking bad thoughts! But laughable if one cares for reality.'

'And are you absolved?'

'Better than that, my Lord. I no longer officially exist. I am a confirmed shadow!'

Again, Don Francisco smiled faintly. But his gaze sharpened:

'Are you able to swear your fidelity to me? *Absolute* fidelity, I mean. An abnegation of yourself that will commit you to obey me and only me under any circumstance? It may cost you, perhaps a lot . . .'

'Yes, my Lord.'

'For some reason of which I am not aware, my brother Hernando hates you. You will have to suffer him. And no doubt you will have to surrender occasionally to his arrogance, of which he has plenty . . .'

'I will force myself to, my Lord. My only wish is that you trust me as I trust you! Don Francisco, I have no father. But I admire you as I would have wished to admire my father! I swear to you by the Sacred Virgin who is your holy patron: I will be loyal to you if it costs me my blood!'

Don Francisco nodded his proud head gently. But his mouth was trembling. He was grinding his teeth and running his clenched hand over his beard. Then his hand plunged suddenly into his doublet and withdrew a thick envelope sealed with an emblem that Gabriel recognized immediately.

'My Lord! It's the royal letter!'

'Yes, it came yesterday. Delivered by two pages with all the required pomp. Luckily, Hernando wasn't there. I wanted to pray a little before we read it and at last knew for sure. It may be that it is a refusal . . . Read it to me, Don Gabriel.'

Frantically, Gabriel broke the seal with his thumb and unfolded the letter. Very soon he burst into a happy, relieved laughter.

'What did I tell you, my Lord! You are named Governor of Peru and Commodore of New Castille, called "Peru" in the Indies . . . and – and you are entitled to a royal pension of seven hundred and twenty-five thousand *maravedi*. It is a long letter, my Lord, but it is signed by the Queen's own hand, and dates from last July.'

'Is there any mention of my companions in Panama? What title is given to Almagro?'

'One moment – ah, here we are: "*Don Diego Almagro, who did participate with his own person in the efforts to discover New Castille, and in the financing of which he did employ his own funds, and—*"'

'The title, the title!'

'"*Alguacil Mayor of Tumbes,*" my Lord! The rank and accompanying privileges of Captain of the Tumbes fortress and three hundred thousand *maravedi* a year.'

'Mmmh . . . Now read everything to me in detail, Don Gabriel, and omit nothing . . . and not too fast, either.'

So Gabriel read aloud as Pizarro had asked him, slowly enunciating each syllable. And he felt as if each word entered into his blood and warmed the cockles of his soul – as if he were already crossing those faraway jungles, and clambering up precipitous slopes to find those cities built entirely of gold!

When he had finished, he kept his eyes fixed on the letter for a moment before allowing himself to look at the *Capitan*.

Pizarro was crying, and he obviously wasn't timid or ashamed of it like a man scared of appearing effeminate. He wept openly, with joyful warm tears streaming down his cheeks and soaking into his beard.

Gabriel said nothing. Pizarro eventually turned his shining eyes upon him:

'The world is ours, my son. It's all ours!'

Gabriel no longer thought with wonder that he had found a country. No, he was overwhelmed now by the astonishing thought that he had found a father.

CHAPTER 27

Machu Picchu, January 1530

I N ONE SUSTAINED ASCENT THEY CLIMBED THE steep steps and reached the two stone columns that framed all the light in the sky.

Villa Oma went ahead. There was a sort of tenderness in the air, as if the sky's limpidity, the blue of the Other World Above, and all the varieties of greenery that carpeted the slopes possessed within themselves a unique life, a contained and peaceful breath.

But when they arrived between the columns, Anamaya found only a wide thoroughfare, paved so well that no grass could find enough space between the flagstones to grow through. This road led about two hundred paces up another slight slope and was bordered by bamboo groves, purple azaleas, and large orchids. Then it gave once more onto the gaping void.

Anamaya's heart beat so strongly that she had trouble breathing. Her nape and hands were clammy with sweat. It wasn't from exertion. The walk that day hadn't been as long as some she had made or as difficult.

As far-off mountains came into view, Villa Oma, walking ahead of her, suddenly stopped and stood with his arms spread, his fingers pointing to the ground. Anamaya caught up with him.

Below them was the Forbidden City.

Her eyes had never looked upon such splendor. Her heart had never known such beauty.

The city had been erected on the adjacent peaks and in the valleys between like a huge, immaculate sculpture. Its innumerable terraces fell vertiginously away from its center towards a river pounding far, far below.

Houses, streets, temples, courtyards and squares, walls and sacred crops composed a marvelous weave of brown, ochre, and soft or sharp greens, as fine and subtle as a royal *unku*.

The surrounding mountains soared into the blue sky, now weighed with clouds, like sentries guarding Picchu, and the peaks stretched over the horizon, deep into that world unknown to man. The dizzy slopes clambered over one another in the evening light, as sharply contrasted against one another as a *cumbi*'s weave, each covered in a green velvet. Much further away, the night fog was already condensing over a yellow river flowing through a steep-sided valley like the celestial snake.

'Picchu,' murmured Villa Oma, 'Picchu!'

Anamaya shivered, her throat dry.

Smoke rose here and there from bright yellow or gray *ichu* roofs, laid out in a methodical grid. A group of men and women were crossing the long central court, which was carpeted with grass cropped painstakingly short. The group's brightly colored tunics and capes shimmered in the sun's flat light, their gold ornaments throwing off occasional flashes. The evening shadows had already grown long in the valleys.

'Stay five paces behind me,' ordered Villa Oma as he set off again.

But Anamaya, realizing what lay before her, stayed rooted to the spot. In the shadow play of the gloaming, the shape of the peak, which overlooked the Sacred City from the West, became clear: it was the Puma.

Like a predator wearied by a long, rewarding hunt, the mountain was lying down, resting. It held its head up proudly, and gripped between its powerful paws the temples, streets, houses and terraces of Picchu, the terraces overlapping one another like folds of fur.

'The mountain is alive,' whispered Anamaya without realizing that she was speaking to herself. 'The mountain is alive!'

Ahead of her, Villa Oma turned around and motioned curtly for her to come along, to stop dawdling.

When they were within a slingshot's range of the city's outer walls, he stopped again. He pointed at a little house with large doors. It stood on a raised terrace.

'Wait for me there,' he ordered. 'Wait as long as is necessary. Above all, don't go anywhere.'

Questions stumbled over one another in Anamaya's head, but the sternness in the Sage's eyes prevented her from asking any. He had spoken dryly, as if forbidden by that sacred place from showing affection, and he marched away without a word.

Anamaya watched him as he walked down a long stone staircase, which turned abruptly and then continued steeply down beside a high wall. In the turn there was a door covered in thick bamboo. Villa Oma stopped in front of it. Anamaya heard him shout something that she could not make out.

Nothing happened for a while, and it seemed as if the Sage had been refused entry.

Then, suddenly, the door lifted slowly to reveal a narrow street between low houses. Three men appeared, carrying spears in their hands but with capes thrown over their left shoulders, the way priests wore theirs. The greetings took a long time. Villa Oma spoke a lot and bowed frequently. At last he passed through the door, disappearing with the priests as the bamboo panel came back down.

*   *   *

Anamaya remained seated in front of the empty little house overlooking Picchu until after nightfall.

She had seen below her hundreds of peasants working the terraces until there was no more light to work by. Some hoed the young shoots of maize that would eventually become ceremonial *chicha*, others planted sacred broad beans, while those on the lowest terraces picked coca leaves that were carried up to the city in enormous bundles by young men. The bundles were so large that Anamaya could make out only the men's feet beneath them as they climbed the steep stairs.

The peasants made little noise, and never raised their voices. There were also priests on the terraces, recognizable by their silk *unkus* and the gold plugs they wore in their ears. They oversaw the flow of the water in the irrigation canals and the new plantings, occasionally chanting prayers over the furrows or else simply taking stock of the coca bundles.

Not once did anyone approach her. A gang of children herding a flock of llamas to a far-off terrace climbed the steps and passed her by. Not one of them even looked in her direction.

It was as is if she didn't exist. As if she were but a shadow from the Other World!

Suddenly the banks of fog lifted off the river and rose rapidly between the slopes like flights of mad birds. The humidity freshened into a breeze, bending the maize shoots and rustling the branches of the azalea trees.

The sound of women singing echoed from the city. Anamaya saw them swarming from one of its districts. They crossed the esplanade and headed towards a collection of small houses nestled against the outer wall. There were a great many of them, all dressed in white, red or yellow, and all wearing gold headpieces. In rows of three they marched in step and climbed the stone stairs.

And then the singing stopped, abruptly replaced by a horn's

long wail. It came from the highest point of the city, where a great stone anchored Inti, the Sun God.

Men appeared on the esplanade. They were not in ranks and files as the women were, but instead were spreading out in four opposite directions. Anamaya recognized Villa Oma heading towards a wide flight of steps with a priest wearing a headpiece full of feathers, their color indistinguishable in the failing light. After they had slowly climbed the stairs, they rushed into a large rectangular building.

A few minutes later it was completely dark.

The mountains were now only indistinct masses that heaved in the night like sleeping monsters. The moonless, starless sky was thick with clouds.

A light rain quickly moistened everything.

Anamaya took cover in the house. There was nothing in it but the beaten earth floor, not a single bench, whether stone, *ichu* or adobe.

She squatted against a wall, facing one of the doors. She listened to the rain. She smelled the smoke from the city's hearths carried in the damp air. Occasionally she caught the odor of soup.

She was hungry. But she realized that she wouldn't be eating that night.

For as long as possible, she kept her eyes open in the dark, expecting a torch to appear, or Villa Oma to call for her.

But there was only the mountain's silence.

She fell asleep despite herself, emotionally exhausted.

She woke with a start, thinking she had heard an ocelot yap. She thought she had slept for only a brief moment. But, in fact, the rain had stopped, and through the wide doorway she could see that stars shone brightly in the sky.

She stood up and went out of the house. Yes, the sky had cleared, and now the air was warm and clammy, almost solid enough to squeeze between her palms. The Sacred City slept in the dark between the puma's paws. Under the twinkling stars, along the flight of stone steps where she had seen a succession of fountains the previous night, stood gold statues as tall as children.

Anamaya moved away from the house to better see the stars and the shadows of the Sacred City. She was wide awake now. She sat on a step and wrapped her *manta* ineffectively around herself against the dampness. She watched over the valleys as if she was alone in the world.

Completely alone.

She would have liked to have heard Huayna Capac, the old Inca. She would have liked to have heard his mysterious, comforting voice. But there was only silence.

Without knowing why, she was scared of entering the Sacred City. The wonder of her first sighting of it had waned, and now she felt as she had when she had been a child, a powerless little girl. She felt like she had when she had known nothing of the invisible world; like she had when she hadn't seen pumas disguised as mountains.

At the first light of dawn, when her entire body was sodden from the dew, the city's door opened.

The three priests who had received Villa Oma the day before climbed up to her and ordered her, with gestures rather than with words, to follow them.

'Vow to Mama Quilla that you will keep the secret for ever, that you will never tell anyone how to get here or about anything you see here.'

Standing between two waist-high walls, Anamaya stood on the edge of a platform atop a cliff so high that the crease of the valley far, far below seemed tiny enough to hold in the palm of her hand.

The High Priest, Huilloc Topac, barked his order from behind her. His lips were as thin as Villa Oma's, and tinged green with coca like the Sage's. But his eyes were oddly gray.

According to Villa Oma, it was the hundreds and hundreds of nights spent observing the stars that had so bleached his irises.

'Look at Mama Quilla, and give her your oath!' snarled the High Priest once again.

Anamaya fixed her gaze on the jagged crests of the highest mountain, which loomed over the western horizon. The clouds tore themselves on it, revealing its slopes covered in a green fleece of vegetation. As if cued by Huilloc Topac, the sky, wind, and rain conspired to reveal a long band of blue sky. The waxing gibbous moon, pure and white, hung in its center.

'I vow to you, Mama Quilla,' began Anamaya in a strong voice, 'I vow never to reveal the secret of the Sacred City. I shall never tell of the roads that lead to it, and will bury deep in my heart all that I see here. May my lips and tongue be torn from my mouth should I ever break this promise . . .'

She had barely finished when she felt Huilloc Topac's hard hand close on her shoulder. He made her lean over the stone wall, pressing her stomach into it, forcing her to hold herself back with her hands.

'Take a good look at the void beneath you, child. Commit it to memory, for that is where you will be thrown if you ever break your promise. No one must ever learn of Picchu! No one must ever learn of its existence! And even if your Lord Atahualpa should question you, your only reply must be silence. Do you understand me?'

Huilloc Topac released his grip, allowing Anamaya to turn around and look into his eyes as she answered:

'Yes, O Powerful Priest.'

Villa Oma had kept back throughout the oath, his eyes downturned. His whole posture told of his humility in this sacred place.

'Now follow me, prodigal girl.'

Huilloc Topac's words carried disdain as well as irony.

He turned on his heels and proceeded down the paved path along the cliff's lip, then turned right and climbed the first flight of steps, which led to the sacred observation area. Anamaya followed. She could hear Villa Oma's sandals shuffling behind her.

She had been on Picchu's outskirts for four days now. For four days she had been kept in a tiny room with walls colored ochre but with no decorations of any sort, and no alcoves containing effigies. For four days no one had spoken to her, not a man, woman, or child. Not even Villa Oma, whom she had glimpsed only once, drinking sacred *chicha* with other priests around the *Intihuatana*, the stone that anchored the sun.

From time to time Anamaya had tried to approach the city, whether it was the temple district, or one of its gold fountains, or the Condor's *huaca*. But each time people would raise their hands and shout angrily at her, and so she would retreat. She had spent an entire afternoon crouched at the threshold of the jewelers' workshops, watching them hammer llamas out of gold and fashion ear ornaments and set emeralds and feathers in headpieces and breastplates. But not one goldsmith had even looked at her.

Running children bumped into her as if she were invisible, and women seated in dozens before their looms averted their eyes whenever she approached, as if she were able to soil their marvelous weavings with a mere glance. And when at last she returned to her lonely room, she would find a bowl of *chuno* mixed with broad beans placed on the ground. But she never saw who had put it there.

'You had to be able to vow to Mama Quilla,' whispered Villa Oma, beside her at the top of the steps. 'And the sky has been hidden behind clouds these last few days.'

'But why haven't you come to see me?' exclaimed Anamaya, surprised to hear from him after such a long time.

'Lower your voice! In the High Priest's presence, we may

only whisper! I couldn't come and see you earlier because no one was permitted to see you or speak to you until you had taken your vow. It was as if your body had not yet arrived in Picchu.'

Huilloc Topac was walking rapidly in front of them, taking them through a street that opened onto the esplanade. But he turned sharply to his left and headed down a very narrow alley, one that she had been forbidden to enter previously. She hesitated a moment, and Villa Oma urged her on gently.

'You are allowed to enter. Huilloc Topac is a certainly a severe and taciturn man, but he is fair. He knows the Truth of the sky like no one else. He has been living here for twenty years, and spends most nights communing with the stars. What's more, he is Colla Topac's brother. If anyone still has the power and the will to re-establish peace and order, it is he.'

Anamaya followed the High Priest into a very odd room. Its evenly grained stone walls were perfectly joined, and graded so that the smallest stones were at the top. It was the sign of a very important place. Two trapezoid windows opened onto Wilcamayo valley, and she could see the western peaks and the yellow snake of the turbulent river. But there was no roof. Two massive, shallow granite fountains held crystal-clear water. Sitting in one corner were some young priests busily counting the knots in a number of *quipus*, a sort of spider's web of ropes. Occasionally they added a knot, or else undid a whole string. They worked the ropes quickly and dexterously. This was how the history of the Incas and their Empire had been recorded over the eras.

Huilloc Topac ordered the priests to leave the room. When they had he turned to Anamaya and said dryly:

'So, you saw the comet, and imagined it to be an omen. Atahualpa is to be the Inca?'

Anamaya was taken aback by the directness of the question, and failed to reply immediately.

'Huayna Capac spoke to her throughout his last night in this world,' whispered an embarrassed Villa Oma. 'And she met with the puma in the—'

'I know all that!' interrupted Huilloc Topac, 'My questions are for her. Answer me, blue-eyed child!'

'Yes, O Powerful Priest. I saw the comet, and I am sure that my Lord Atahualpa must be crowned Inca.'

'You are sure, are you?'

'Yes.'

'You know what happened to the mighty Colla Topac?'

'I was holding his hand when he died. He also knew. That's why he was tortured and murdered so barbarously.'

'Ah!'

With an expression of grief, Huilloc Topac turned away and bowed before the granite basins. Clouds were passing in the reflections.

'I have seen shadows in the night,' he murmured. 'I have seen the darkness in the dark. Stars have failed to shine, and holes have appeared in the sky. I have never seen the like before.'

His contemplative and anxious tone encouraged Villa Oma to speak more forcefully:

'If we don't do something, then the Empire of the Four Cardinal Directions will collapse! A war between Atahualpa and the Cuzco clans would lay waste to the country. And if the two sides are evenly matched, then the Empire is doomed.'

'You are asking me to take sides, Villa Oma. I am a priest, a star-reader. I serve neither Atahualpa nor the Cuzco clans. I serve only Inti, Quilla, and all our forefathers who watch over us.'

'But that's exactly my point, Huilloc Topac! I'm not asking you to side with any clan, but to save us all, all the Children of the Sun. The order has been unbalanced. We take energy from our ancestors without offering anything in return. I have come with this girl because the Ancients in the Other World trust her. Invest her with the energy and purity to hear their voice. May Huayna Capac speak his will through her before it is too late! It is only here that she may receive this gift! And we also pray here. There is no more sacred place than this.'

'The purity and the energy,' growled Huilloc Topac, looking at Anamaya. 'Well, if she's capable of receiving it, then we shall perform an investiture after tomorrow morning. In the meantime, she is to bathe in the Twenty Fountains. Tell the women to prepare her.'

CHAPTER 28

Cadiz, January 1530

ALL DAY, SHOUTING AND NOISE ROSE FROM THE Cadiz docks.

For three days, beginning at dawn, a constant procession of wagons and heavily laden mules drew up alongside the *San Antonio*. Two or three dozen men, in what looked like a very determined choreographed ballet, unloaded sacks of flour, chickpeas, dried meats, heating wood, jars of oil and wine, cases of grease and crates of oranges . . .

Despite the coolness of January, most went shirtless, and their shoulders glistened with sweat. Gabriel oversaw their comings and goings from where he stood on the poop.

He had had a writing desk set up on the side of the deck nearest the dock. In a leather-bound register he noted the type and volume of cargo being loaded. From time to time he saw Sebastian leap fluidly from the ship to the dock, there to lift a bundle, open a sack, evaluating and even counting everything that was to be shipped, much to the irritation of the ship's captain. When he had satisfied himself that all was well, Sebastian would wave his large, open hand at Gabriel, who duly added the cargo in question to the ship's register.

Twice, however, Sebastian showed Gabriel his closed fist,

with his thumb pointing to the ground. Each time the
stevedores halted their ballet. A hundredweight of flour
was found to have been cut with rye. Then some barrels
of gunpowder for the culverins were discovered to have been
so damaged by humidity that the powder had coagulated.

'A wet powder is a dead powder,' said Sebastian, smiling.
'And a dead powder puts a lot of men at the wrong end of a
culverin!'

The *San Antonio*'s captain, a gaunt, gray man with skin
as dark as a Moor's, became irritated and sided with the
merchants. He bellowed:

'Hey, coal-face! Who do you think you are? It's not some
black Moor who's going to waste my time with his whims!
I'm the ship's master here!'

'My apologies, Captain,' retorted Sebastian, further irrita-
ting the sailor by remaining absolutely calm in the face of his
slurs. 'You're master aboard, aye, but down here on the dock,
nay, you're not the master, he is!'

He pointed at Gabriel, who had joined them from the
deck, having foreseen the disagreement. Gabriel gave them
both a dry look before turning to examine the flour and the
powder.

Their gazes burned holes in his back, gazes blacker than
Sebastian's skin. With an icy reserve, Gabriel confirmed
Sebastian's diagnosis.

'*Señor* Sebastian is absolutely in the right of it, gentlemen.
Do you delude yourselves that I will accept these scraps?
This powder wouldn't even explode in an oven. As for this
flour, perhaps the weevils might find it edible!'

The merchants protested, the captain took offence. Gabriel
caught Sebastian's glance – the African's sly smile had widened even further – and said in a tone designed to cut glass:

'I said no, gentlemen, and I mean no. We are wasting time.
Take away your sacks and barrels before Sebastian throws
them into the bay.'

After this, the provisioning continued without incident. But an hour before nightfall, the dock suddenly emptied, leaving the *San Antonio* alone.

The last wagon had gone. Silence returned, punctuated by the creaking of the hulls and masts, the squawking gulls, and the laughter of the sailors repairing sails.

Gabriel was blotting his writing with a little sand when a powerful voice surprised him:

'I suppose you are pleased with yourself, Your Honor the Counselor to the Governor! The hold is full and to your liking . . .'

The ship's captain had padded onto the stern castle as quietly as a cat. Pointing at the open register and the quill still in Gabriel's hand he added:

'No one has ever overseen my provisioning in such a manner! If you would like to know what I really think, sir, those are the methods of the Holy Inquisition!'

Gabriel couldn't help but laugh.

'What you really think, sir, is as imaginative as it is wrong. The truth is that Governor Pizarro entrusted me with a task, and I shall accomplish it as best I can. So! Don't look so sour. Sure, you won't be seeing your private commission on the flour and gunpowder. But the purseful of ducats – the incentive for our speedy provisioning that you coerced me into offering – should amply make up for it.'

The captain's cheeks reddened with indignation. His tone became as bitter as salting brine:

'You are still young, sir, to allow yourself to speak thus. What's more, I understand that this will be your first crossing. I tell you this: I've seen many a greenhorn such as yourself, young puppies swollen with pride, set sail for the Indies. But far, far fewer have I seen make the return journey! Now, good day to you, sir. We weigh anchor an hour before sunrise, as planned.'

After he had disappeared in a huff into the stern deck-house, Gabriel heard Sebastian's easy laugh.

'Now there's one fellow who won't be laughing at your jokes over the next two months!'

'As long as he gets us across the ocean, and not to the bottom of it, then I can get along without his cordiality.'

Gabriel shut his register and put away his quills. When he looked up, the big black man's usual smile had given way to an uncharacteristic look of embarrassment.

'I want to thank you, Don Gabriel . . .'

'Me? Why?'

'Because whenever I get "nigger" or "coal-face" or "blacka-moor", or any other endearment thrown at me, I've not too many friends who come back with "*Señor* Sebastian". Except the Greek, of course . . .'

Gabriel hesitated for a moment under Sebastian's intense gaze before laughing out loud.

'By the Faith, *Señor* Sebastian, I don't think it so out of the ordinary. We're off to conquer Peru together, and the boundaries of the world grow closer. It's only natural that at least two of us should appreciate your company!'

They laughed together at this, but a mutual self-consciousness prompted them to direct their gazes at the forest of masts and rigging swaying gently in the reddening sun.

In a few more minutes, reflected Gabriel, *that fiery disk will sink into the ocean, an ocean that pretends to be flat. While night covers us here, it will shine on all the gold of Peru! Peru, where we shall soon be and where I can at last be myself, unfettered . . . and, who knows, perhaps the Greek is right, perhaps the mark on my shoulder is indeed a stain of fate . . .*

'It's hard to know what we'll find there, Don Gabriel,' said Sebastian in a low voice, as if he had read the other man's thoughts. 'Sometimes I dream that we'll find so much gold in Peru that I'll be able to buy my freedom, be as free as if my skin were white . . . But for the moment it's all fairy tales. Don Francisco may be the Governor of Peru in name, but until we conquer it he's just the governor of a dream. This Peru is on the far side of the world, and what's more its masters are these Incas that Felipillo keeps telling us about. They won't give it up without a fight. And Don Francisco hasn't enough men, no, not by any measure . . .'

'I know,' interrupted Gabriel, 'and the ship's captain knows too. He stung me for fifty ducats to slip out of port in the middle of the night, to avoid having to wait for permission from the Office of the Council of the Indies. But we'll find some reinforcements in Panama.'

'If there are any there mad enough to want to follow us. I tell you as a friend, Don Gabriel: you've done everything possible to show that you're truly on our side.'

'Some days I wonder if they really think of me as being on their side . . .'

'You mean Hernando?'

'Yes, and the *Capitan*'s younger brothers are not much better, from what I've seen. Juan and Gonzalo are certainly hot-blooded, and I hope that they fight proudly, but still . . . However, tonight nothing can vex me. Don Francisco is not the only one with faith in his dream. Tonight is the first night of my new life. I can feel it! Aye, it's as if that red sky ahead of us is calling me on – as if the sun, now ducking under the horizon, is pulling me to him!'

CHAPTER 29

Machu Picchu, January 1530

THROUGHOUT THE NIGHT ANAMAYA FELT THE cold dampness penetrate her skin, despite the protection of the walls and blankets. Before going to bed she had spent some time leaning out of a window watching the sun set on the valley, and listening to the turbulent waters of the Wilcamayo far, far below. From her high vantage point she had felt so close to that vast open space, and had imagined launching herself into it, like a bird.

The words of Villa Oma and the priests flitted around in her head like moths: war seemed so remote from this sacred place, a place where man had been received by the gods on the condition that they kept it secret. Yet, as Villa Oma had said over and over again, they were on the verge of a terrible war.

'Tomorrow morning – at dawn . . .' he had murmured vaguely before leaving her for the night.

So all night, already drained by her difficult, emotionally charged days, she shivered and waited for the dawn. Tomorrow, at dawn? She listened to a muted singing that floated through the night from some invisible source, a song evoking grief rather than celebration. The voices circled around her, and invited her to join them. Tomorrow, at dawn? Whenever she opened her eyes, she sought to clear her mind by looking to the pure, open space through her window. She called out silently to Huayna Capac. But there was no light, no flash, no voice to comfort and direct her.

When at last the dawn shone on the snow-capped peaks of a distant cordillera, Anamaya, finally exhausted by her involuntary vigil, was sleeping so deeply that Villa Oma had to shake her awake. She opened her eyes and gave a start: her heart was beating hard and fast. Only a feeble gray light found its way into her tiny, cell-like room. She sat up and adjusted her *tupu*, the pin that held her *manta*.

'It's time,' was all Villa Oma said.

They made their way through the city's narrow alleys. She could see the dome of the Temple of the Sun where they were headed. Her gaze was time and again drawn towards the mountains, towards the valley and its river, despite herself. When she turned, she saw the light of the rising sun reach the ochre rock of Huayna Picchu, and the mountain gleamed like gold.

The priest Huilloc Topac was waiting for them in front of the temple. He wore a white tunic of fine vicuña wool, and he had again donned his ceremonial headdress. A golden sun symbol hung on his forehead.

Villa Oma bowed to him.

Anamaya saw a small group of *yanaconas* coming out of the temple. They carried a *rampa*, a far less elaborate palanquin than the mummy's although covered in a very finely woven *cumbi*.

Although the sun had risen, the air still held moisture. A few clouds had gathered above the Door of the Sun.

The small group climbed silently slowly towards the keeper's house, making their way along the spectacular terraces of sacred crops, terraces of mauve quinoa stepped above an explosion of golden maize, one after another all the way up the slopes.

The High Priest and the Sage walked ahead, followed by the *yanaconas* bearing the palanquin, and another group of servants leading six white llamas. Anamaya was the last in line.

As they increased the distance between themselves and the buildings of the city, she realized that they were taking the road to the Door of the Sun, the *Inti Punku* from which she had first looked breathlessly upon Picchu. The road was excellently paved, and the climb was easy despite the steep slope. They were soon above the maize terraces. She lifted her eyes towards the summit that stood out above them like a giant bird's wing against the still pale sky.

Machu Picchu. The old mountain. Whispering these words to herself, Anamaya felt knots of disquiet in her stomach.

Suddenly the priest left the road to the *Inti Punku* in favor of another that led to the right, heading up some steps leading directly to the mountain, to *Machu Picchu.* Anamaya hurried to join Villa Oma and the priest at the front. On her way she tried in vain to peek into the *rampa.*

'Where are we going?'

Villa Oma gestured vaguely towards the peak.

'What are we going to do there?'

Her badgering tone annoyed the High Priest, and he looked severely at her, then at Villa Oma.

'How is it that this child dares to speak to us so impertinently?'

'I only want to know what we're going to do on the summit.'

'An offering to Inti,' said Villa Oma wearily.

'The llamas?'

Villa Oma made no reply. Anamaya turned her gaze upon the palanquin. Villa Oma looked away.

*   *   *

The path grew steeper and narrower. They were passing under a thick ceiling of leaves and branches that shut out the sky. Bunches of yellow, red, and pink blooming orchids punctuated the verdant canopy. Little streams were everywhere – alongside the path, between rocks – and everything dripped with moisture.

When they emerged from the forest, Anamaya turned around and was deeply stirred by the heady sight of the city below her. It was as if she was a bird and had risen up with a single flap of her wings to this great height: only now could she see the perfection in the symmetry of terraces, houses, and temples, with the green strip of the central esplanade the center of an immaculate balance.

She looked up once again at *Machu Picchu*, contrasted black against deepening blue sky.

'Did I not teach you from your very first day? Did I not lead you to knowledge?'

Villa Oma's voice surprised her with its almost doleful tone.

'Didn't I instruct you about our long road to the light, and about the terrible war that already burns us with its flames?'

'You wanted to feed me to the puma. Only Huayna Capac saved me.'

'I taught you everything. I brought you here to our most secret, sacred place, and now . . .'

'I don't understand, Villa Oma.'

Two bare walls bordered the path. Anamaya's heart beat faster and faster: here, the mountain would reveal its mystery.

The *yanaconas* put down the palanquin. The thin fabric of the *cumpi* fluttered lightly in the breeze. A child stepped from behind it. She was around ten years old, certainly no older. A green stream of coca juice dribbled from between her lips. She wore a simple white *anaco*, with a band of red about her waist. She looked directly at Anamaya with her intense black eyes. Anamaya sensed neither fear nor joy in her gaze. Nothing at all.

Anamaya understood, and her heart rebelled.

'Is this what you wanted to teach me? That you are going to sacrifice a child?'

'Shut up!'

Villa Oma's imperious character was present once more in the tone of his voice. All the servants bowed their heads, and the llamas tugged nervously on their tethers.

'The universe is undone, war is already upon us, Viracocha shakes the ocean, a great disturbance is in the making – and you worry about the life of one small child? *Capacocha* – such sacrifices were the way of our fathers, and of their fathers before them, and they are what have made the Incas masters of this world. And you, a blue-eyed girl, would wish to see the natural order of the universe disrupted, and prevent blood from returning to the earth?'

Every word he spoke jolted Anamaya's heart, Yes, she had followed his teachings, and what she had learned while in the sacred city had led her to understand the deepest truths of the Inca. Yes, she had learned that life had to be given for life to continue, and blood shed for life to renew itself. Yes, she despaired at the troubles ahead. Yet still, the little girl's expressionless gaze had woken some deep, deep part of Anamaya's being, some elemental truth that had lain dormant within her for many, many moons.

She closed her eyes to shut out the light.

Villa Oma said nothing. He knew Anamaya wouldn't rebel.

'Let us go,' Villa Oma commanded.

Anamaya walked up to the little girl. She stroked her hair, and took her hand.

'Come,' she said gently. 'I'm going to stay with you.'

And as they made their way along the path, Anamaya felt the girl's small hand in hers. It reminded her of the warm, soft fur of a small animal entrusting itself to her.

CHAPTER 30

Machu Picchu, January 1530

THE PATH WAS BORDERED BY A ROCK BOUNDARY as high as the wall of a fortress.

As they walked along it, Anamaya tried with all her might not to tremble for fear of alarming the little girl holding her hand.

When they came to a gap in the rock Anamaya didn't stop. Instead, she went through it with the child gathered in her arms. She turned around only when they were on the other side, on a path running along the lip of a cliff. They were a step away from the immense, terrifying emptiness, the city a tiny stain on the landscape far below.

The mountain peak itself, just above their heads, was a feather separated from its bird, buffeted by the wind.

Emptiness above, emptiness below – it was as if the Earth were no longer, as if there were only air and sky, and nothing more solid anchored Anamaya to the world than the tiny hand wrapped in hers.

Just below the summit, on a narrow strip of ground that seemed to be suspended from the sky, a sacrificial altar was cut into the *huaca*. In the distance, Salcantay rose, with its everlasting snow, through the clouds. A spire of fog formed and re-formed, like threads of fine vicuña wool led a dance by the wind. In the blink of an eye light would give way to shadow as a cloud passed across the sun.

Anamaya sat down and put the child on her lap. She took both her hands in hers and began rocking back and forth, as if drunk. Anamaya had also chewed coca and drunk *chicha*, and she felt as indifferent as the child to the idea of being sacrificed. Occasionally she felt the little girl's tiny fingers hook under one of the snakes' heads on her bracelet.

They only had to get up and take a couple of steps to fly like the condor before plunging to the river whose raging waters, surging far below, could barely be heard.

In front of the *huaca*, the servants prepared a fire for the first offerings of maize, quinoa, and coca . . .

Next would be the llamas.

Then the child.

Anamaya wasn't scared. Her heart no longer resisted.

She hadn't yielded only to Villa Oma, but to the entire universe, to the mountains, the clouds, the sun, and the shadows.

Her gaze drifted across the landscape, rising to the thunderclouds that charged the air, then swooping like a bird down to the houses of the secret city that from this height looked as small as pebbles, even grains of sand. She crooned softly into the child's ear. She lulled her.

The fog grew increasingly thick as it rolled down the valley, gradually engulfing the city. The sky became a fainter shade of pale blue. The bird in her had wandered away, and the only sound remaining was the moaning of the mournful wind.

She saw the puma.

It cast its enormous shadow over Huayna Picchu, the mountain that loomed over the city and protected it with all its power. Its eyes were two rocks, and its mouth the shadow of a crevasse; its ears were pricked as if it were

coiled to spring, and its paws dangled in the ocean of
fog.

Anamaya smiled: the puma was an old friend.

'Don't be frightened,' she whispered to the girl and the
wind. 'Don't be frightened, and look at the puma . . .'

The llamas' blood had been collected in gold jugs. The
priest and the Sage turned to the two girls.

They rose to their feet, and Anamaya put her hands on
the child's shoulders, their bodies linked as one.

'Now,' said Villa Oma.

As Anamaya opened her arms, a great crack of thunder
rolled in from the horizon.

The condor. The bird of power and death filled the entire
sky with its noise and cast its shadow over them.

The sky turned black.

The priest held up his shining silver *tumi*.

'I am Huayna Capac,' said Anamaya in a strong voice that
cut through the wind and the first drops of rain. 'I am the
Inca whose reign oversaw the height of the Empire of the
Four Cardinal Directions.

'I see all that is ahead of you but that you don't see. I see
the sun hide, and the moon set; I see the whirlwinds that
disturb the sky and the quakes that shudder the earth.

'I see chaos. I see blood shed in vain, I see the universe
shatter, I see armies marching besides rivers like floods, I
see brother against brother, I see sons killing sons. I hear
the cries of women being raped and murdered.

'I am shedding real tears.'

Anamaya's chest rose and fell gently, and her breathing
was shallow. She didn't dare lift her eyes to the condor, her
eyes were clouded, and she saw the priest, the Sage and the
little girl only as shadows. It was her voice, but it was not
her speaking.

'I see men tearing themselves apart over greed. I see hunger devouring their bodies and spirits. I see the wells and fountains drying up. I see the paths of shadows and light, by which we know the universe, closing.

'I see only grief descending the steps to the heart of the earth.

'I see my Sacred Double, my Sun Brother, having to flee, having to hide in the shadows before re-emerging into the light many, many moons from now, to pronounce the dawn of the next *pachacuti*.'

Anamaya stopped.

She didn't see the priest drop his knife. She didn't see the blackness in Villa Oma's eyes or the terror of the servants.

She didn't hear the condor fly away.

Only when she felt the heat of the sun return and strike her nape did she wake from her dream with a shake of the head.

'Anamaya,' said the Sage, 'girl with the sacred lake in her eyes, I don't know what it is that you tell us, but I believe you.'

'I don't know myself.'

'That's why I believe you. Do you understand, now, why your rebellion was useless?'

Anamaya acquiesced, but couldn't resist murmuring:

'Yet you haven't sacrificed the child.'

'Don't be impertinent. Don't imagine that it's because of you. No, it's because the omen was sent—'

'That I do know, Villa Oma.'

The servants had slung the llamas' still-warm carcasses over their shoulders. The fog was slowly dispersing and Anamaya could see the town below sparkling in the middle of its emerald-lined jewel case.

She slowly made her way down the length of the narrow ridge, back to the steep steps . . .

The city was always within her view, and with each step

that she took its walls and straw roofs became clearer and clearer.

All during her descent she thought about how the universe was going to be torn by war. Everything Villa Oma and Huayna Capac had said and all her own visions pointed to the same things: blood, death, and destruction.

She asked herself over and over what the puma in the mountain across from her was trying to tell her.

And all the time she felt the little girl's hand in hers. She felt, too, a silent serenity beating in her chest like a second heart – happiness impossible to share, or even to describe.

PART 3

CHAPTER 31

Puná Island, March 1532

'YOU SENT FOR ME, MY LORD?'
Gabriel instinctively spoke quietly, despite the crashing breakers.

The night was almost completely black, and only occasionally did a sliver of moon peek through the clouds, its slight reflection scattering in the cross-swell. All the ship's lanterns squeaked and swung erratically, as though a whimsical devil was shaking them. The masts creaked, and the wind whistled through the clewed-up yards. The entire ship strained at its anchor chains, the watch-bell clanging incessantly.

Although it was within crossbow range, Puná Island could not be seen.

With his hands firmly gripping the bow cathead, his feet apart and his sword hanging like a rigid tail, Don Francisco Pizarro gazed directly into the night. Through the darkness his beard was as eerily white as the foaming ocean. He didn't look at Gabriel when he said:

'Twelve leagues! Twelve leagues, three days sailing, that's all there is between us and Peru, Gabriel! Tumbes is right there in front of us – the first town we landed at, five years ago now. Tumbes, where the promise of the Kingdom of Gold was made . . .'

He fell silent for a moment, narrowing his eyes as if straining to see the temples shimmering gold.

'It all begins tomorrow, my boy,' he whispered suddenly, so low that Gabriel had to move close to hear. 'Whatever the traps, we shall conquer this land, with the Sacred Virgin's blessing.'

'I have not doubted it, sir,' said Gabriel in an equally faint voice, 'since we left Cadiz. We shall prevail, even if months stretch into years – though our progress until now has been deadly difficult, and we had to wait an eternity in Panama, with its intrigues and its unbelievers . . .'

'I've handed out more promises than gold or emeralds,' said Pizarro with uncharacteristic irony.

Don Francisco hooked his worn fingers under his shoulder belt, and allowed the crash of the surf to fill the pause in their conversation. Then he asked suddenly:

'What is your opinion of Captain de Soto?'

Gabriel chose his words carefully:

'Well, he seems to me a very brave captain, and well experienced in warfare . . .'

Pizarro yanked on his beard nervously and grumbled:

'All of what you say is true. And yet . . .'

A cross-wave returning on the ebb made the ship pitch violently, interrupting Pizarro. Gabriel grabbed the rail to prevent himself sliding across the wet deck. Once he had righted himself, he said to Pizarro:

'If I may speak openly, Your Excellency, I am most gratified that he joined us from Nicaragua. I am thinking mostly of his two vessels, one hundred men, and twenty-five horses. That doubles our force.'

'Benalcazar also joined us. But I have no doubts about Benalcazar.'

'But Benalcazar has only thirty men.'

Pizarro dismissed the argument with an irritated wave of his hand:

'It's not with mere numbers that we'll conquer this land, my boy.'

Gabriel privately reflected for a moment how exasperating Pizarro could be, with his faith in the Virgin's protection under any and every circumstance.

'As I said,' continued Gabriel calmly, 'I have never doubted, and I still don't. However, I've aged two years since we left Spain, and so far have done nothing but wait and scrape between bad-tempered brawls and diseases.'

'And in that you've done well, my boy!'

'At long last, we have sighted the coast of your Peru,' Gabriel went on, ignoring the interruption. 'But the weather has kept us on this island for six months now. And the Indians, who were most hospitable upon our arrival, now seem determined to slay us whenever they get the chance. Yesterday I saw some blackguards whom you mistook for soldiers when you recruited them raping some Indian girls, and thinking nothing of it. Today, a mere glimpse of an Indian face sends them running for their weapons. Your brother Hernando, who behaved no better than the other ruffians, will not be able to ride for two weeks because of the arrow sticking from his thigh. And both your younger brothers, Juan and Gonzalo, think only of enjoying themselves and of pillaging, without having conquered the smallest reed hut . . . please forgive my frankness, Don Francisco, but without Captain de Soto you shall never be Governor of Peru.'

Oddly, instead of taking offence at Gabriel's outburst, Pizarro emitted a sound somewhere between a cough and a laugh:

'No matter. I am already Governor. The Sacred Virgin wills it, the King wills it, and I will it. But de Soto wants a whole territory for himself, and I'm worried that he'll abandon us as soon as it suits him . . .'

'He may, Don Francisco,' grumbled Gabriel, 'he very well may. But for the present the danger lies elsewhere. The men are exhausted and they haven't even set foot in the land of gold. Its proximity is driving them mad. They are hungry and diseased. And since a rumor has spread that this disease of revolting verruca warts – which claims more hands every day – is spread while sleeping, they no longer dare sleep! Others say it is caught from the fish and crabs, and so they no longer eat them, although there is precious little else by way of food.'

'You are new to this game, my boy!' said Don Francisco, amused. 'It's your first campaign, and you're still learning the tune. Myself, I've been hearing it for forty years now!'

His eyes as expressionless as his beard, Pizarro fell silent for a moment, and stood straight despite the pitching of the deck underfoot. But suddenly he grabbed Gabriel tightly by the wrist, and adopted a formal tone:

'Do you recall, Don Gabriel, that day when you followed me into the countryside outside Toledo and begged me to take you along to conquer Peru?'

'That moment shall remain engraved in my memory for the rest of my days, my Lord.'

'And what did I tell you then?'

'You asked from me "an abnegation of myself that will commit me to obey you and only you under any circumstance and that might cost me, perhaps a lot".'

'Well, the time has come for you to fulfill at least part of your promise. Tomorrow at dawn our boats shall leave for Tumbes. But their holds are not big enough to carry all the men and horses. I've made a deal with the Indian chief of Tumbes, and he is going to send us some of their rafts, constructed in their fashion—'

'I saw their rafts earlier,' confirmed Gabriel enthusiastically. 'They're very well built, much bigger and sturdier than I had expected. Your sea-chests, along with your brother Hernando's, are already loaded onto them . . .'

'It is not the sturdiness of the rafts that is in question, but my trust in de Soto,' interrupted Don Francisco, irritated. 'Pretending that those *balsas* sail faster than our ships, de Soto has proposed to go ahead with the Indians to prepare our arrival. Certainly, I would appreciate an easy landing. But I would hate to have half my troops disappear . . .'

Another strong wave rocked the boat, and they were separated for a moment as they staggered apart, trying to keep their footing. They heard shouting and neighing from the far side of the island. Pizarro grabbed Gabriel by the elbow and held him so close that the hilt of his sword dug into the young Andalusian's side.

'I want you to keep an eye on Captain de Soto's meddling with the Tumbes Indians.'

'They say that those *balsas* capsize easily—'

'Well, swim then, my boy!' growled Don Francisco, returning to his usual boorish familiarity. 'But, above all, make use of your eyes and your brain. And try to hold your tongue, for once!'

'I need a companion I can trust. Let Sebastian go with me.'

'Ho! If you're going to place your trust in a black slave, that's your affair . . .'

The *balsas* were certainly sturdy.

They resembled enormous hands with bollards acting as masts in their centers, and they were rigged similarly to the feluccas of the Mediterranean. They positively raced over the water, so much so that with each uncommonly large wave they were swamped by the sea. The rafts' logs, each as big as a bull's thigh, slid and flexed within their lashings of agave rope. Barely off the water, Don Hernando Pizarro's sea-chests were already soaked through, although they were only an hour out of Puná Island.

'By all the Saints,' whined Bocanegra. 'If this keeps up, all

Don Hernando's doublets will rot! And his fine linen shirts! And his spare boots! Another day like this, and those chests'll be as soft as firewood! He's going to be ill with rage!'

'If I were you, I wouldn't worry too much about His Excellency the Brother's malingering,' sniggered Sebastian. 'You've got enough disease to cope with yourself . . .'

Andrés de Bocanegra turned away his grimacing, deformed face, and doubled up with pain. The poor man was one of those afflicted with verruca. A horrible and grotesque appendage hung from his left cheek, about the size of a fig. Another, only slightly smaller and of a sinister purple color, was balanced on the tip of his nose, while a dozen smaller warts, each the size of a chickpea, covered his neck and shoulders like newly hatched maggots seething on a piece of meat.

That same morning, no longer able to stand the pain, Bocanegra had sliced a verruca hanging from his chin with his own stiletto. He had done this gruesome self-surgery about an hour before they had left the island. Blood had flowed freely from it, and so he had wrapped his face in fabric. But new, disgusting buboes had popped up on his right temple, somehow dilating his pupils, and transforming Bocanegra for the rest of his life into something resembling one of those stone gargoyles that stood guard over Christendom's cathedrals.

He was so repulsive, in fact, that Gabriel could barely bring himself to look at him. But in any case the greater part of the young man's mind was occupied elsewhere.

He was standing on the chests, holding on to the *balsa*'s mast, and had been looking out to sea for a long while.

'Nothing,' he cried out to Sebastian. 'Nothing at all.'

He stepped down from his perch and seated himself carefully at the stern of the *balsa*.

'Just one sail,' he said, furrowing his brow. 'Yet there were eight rafts this morning . . .'

'It's the currents,' murmured Bocanegra, without turning

around. 'I've seen it before. These things have no keels, they give a lot of leeway . . .'

'Perhaps the currents – or else the doing of Captain de Soto!' replied Gabriel. 'The interpreter is with him. He might have ordered the Indian sailors, through Martinillo, to lose us. Don Francisco was right to be wary of him . . .'

'Myself,' muttered Sebastian, 'I'm worried it was neither the one nor the other.'

He pointed his chin discreetly at the four Indians who were manning the big oars that acted as rudders.

'I don't like them. They smile strangely whenever I look at them.'

'So?'

'One thing you've still to learn, Don Gabriel, is that when an Indian smiles at you, then it means he's planning to do you some harm.'

Gabriel was on the point of replying when one of the Indians cried out something in his own language, incomprehensible to his passengers, and pointed at something ahead of them. They all turned to look.

An island appeared over the crests of the waves, not far ahead of them at all. It was a strip of land covered in trees that were entangled in a deep green, almost black, vegetation.

'The island!' exclaimed Sebastian, already on his feet.

'Well then,' said a smiling Gabriel, 'our companions haven't such bad intentions towards us after all. At least they know where they're going, and we'll have a dry place to sleep tonight. And tomorrow evening we should arrive at Tumbes, as planned.'

'Well, I'm not getting off the raft,' whimpered Bocanegra. 'I vowed never to sleep under another tree or on sand again in my life.'

*   *   *

At sunset, Sebastian and Gabriel sat in silence on the island's beach, their eyes fixed on the gilt peaks of the mainland across the water. The sound of the Indians' chattering – blended with the susurration of the breaking waves – was like a soothing whisper.

Gabriel had removed his shirt and was examining his torso and arms. His skin was dry and cracked from malnourishment and privation.

Sebastian was drawing in the sand.

'What are you drawing?' asked Gabriel.

'Look carefully . . . It was over there, on the beach in front of Tumbes, that the Greek and I saw him for the first time . . .'

Gabriel started laughing.

'The big cat! The one I've got on my shoulder, right?'

'Don't you think it's time you met him?'

Sebastian finished his drawing with a simple line that brought alive all the savage power of the animal.

Gabriel's gaze slid over the big cat in the sand, across the ocean, towards that distant, out-of-sight shore, the forest, and the mountains; he was intoxicated by the proximity of his dream.

It was perhaps midnight when Gabriel heard the first cry.

He was wide awake when he heard the second, and he quickly threw aside his blanket and sat up, sensing Sebastian already standing beside him.

'Bocanegra!' exclaimed Gabriel. 'How the poor man suffers. Perhaps he's carving off another wart . . .'

Another shout, much more violent, ripped through the night and carried above the sound of the crashing surf.

'No,' said Sebastian. 'Bocanegra doesn't shout for a wart, not even for thirty of the filthy things. It's something else.'

Both simultaneously had the same thought.

They took off running, leaving behind the twisted trees that they had taken shelter under, and raced across the sand.

The night was as black as the inside of an oven, but Bocanegra's repeated yelling directed them as clearly as a beacon. When he felt the sand beneath his feet become wet and hard, Gabriel drew his sword so quickly that the movement made its blade whistle through the air.

Bocanegra's cries were becoming clearer and clearer:

'Help, companions! To me, to me! They rob us! Help, they kill, they kill!'

Gabriel made out a shadow in the darkness – the sail filled by the breeze. The *balsa* was already standing off from the beach, rising as a roller passed under it. More shouting could be heard:

'Fucking Indian traitors!' bawled Sebastian. 'They're abandoning us . . .'

Driven by a blind fury, Gabriel leaped into the waves. The whiteness of the breakers striped the darkness. He lunged towards the raft, waving his sword above his head, and for a moment he thought that his momentum would carry him all the way to its stern. He could now distinctly make out Bocanegra being held down against the logs by two Indians, and he watched as a third knocked him out with a single blow of his club. The shouting stopped, leaving only the sound of the ocean. Then Sebastian yelled again:

'Don't be stupid, Don Gabriel! Come back, come back! You're going to drown . . .'

But Gabriel's rage was too strong. It was driving him forward more than the tide was pushing him back. He breached a wave, his sword slashing through the wall of water. Now the rear of the raft was only a sword's length away, and the Indian who had the rudder was frozen with fear!

But then a wave reared before Gabriel like a roaring beast, and he suddenly felt as heavy as a lead weight. His boots, breeches and shirt filled with water as the surface around him dropped, sucked into the towering wave.

It came crashing down on top of him, tumbling him relentlessly, kneading him like a lump of dough.

His blade slapped his face, he was head over heels, he had no idea which way was up, his limbs were trying to split from his trunk, there was nothing but water everywhere, and a terrifying, rumbling sound, which he thought would be the last thing he would ever hear, filled his ears.

Gabriel's head slammed against the sandy sea bottom, and he swallowed sea water. Asphyxiation crushed his chest. For a fraction of a second, he was lucid enough to lament the irony of drowning on the shore of the new world.

Then his feet found the bottom, and with a desperate effort he thrust to the surface. Half drowned, his guts full of salt water, he splashed furiously to the edge of the raft. The Indians could have easily kicked him back, or else clubbed him as they had the unfortunate Bocanegra. But they just stood there unmoving, as if stupefied to see him emerge from the deep, like a ghost.

'Hold tight, Don Gabriel!' shouted Sebastian, his voice reassuringly close.

The arrival of the black man was too much for the three Indians, who jumped into the water and tried to swim away. Gabriel, completely out of breath, had just enough energy left to climb, gasping, onto the raft. But Sebastian dived in after the slowest of the three natives caught him by the ankle, and threw him onto the *balsa* as he would a sack, before getting back on himself, coughing and spitting.

'If you even try to escape,' said Sebastian, holding the Indian by the neck, 'I'm going to eat you.'

The young man, a mere adolescent, trembled with fear. Gabriel and Sebastian recovered their breaths.

'What shall we do with him, Don Gabriel?'

'If you want to eat him, don't let me stop you.'

'To tell you the truth, my sodden head thought we might instead encourage him somehow to guide us to Tumbes. But only if you have no objection, naturally.'

'Sebastian?'

'Don Gabriel?'

'I thought you couldn't swim.'

'Alas, I can only confirm it – unless the disorganized thrashing of limbs that I adopt to survive that monster is called swimming,' he said as he pointed to the dark, heaving ocean.

The swell lessened a little. Sebastian pointed at the rudder-oar, and after a moment's hesitation the young Indian took it. Gabriel allowed the joy of still being alive to flood through him.

'Sebastian?'

'Don Gabriel?'

'I owe you a life. And what's more, I want to ask you another favor. Would you do me the kindness of simply calling me Gabriel?'

Sebastian didn't reply. He was staring at the sea, lost in reflection. He turned around and took Gabriel's hand. Gabriel pulled him to him, and the two men hugged like brothers.

CHAPTER 32

Huamachuco, March 1532

A LIGHT RAIN FELL EVENLY ACROSS THE HUAM-
achuco plain. Banks of fog streamed around
the surrounding mountains and veiled their peaks.
Smoke rising from the houses lingered over the roofs, spreading the spicy odor of burning carob tree through the air.

Atahualpa's cortège had arrived the evening before. Now,
the *tambo* was filled with shouting and laughter, with flutes
singing to dancers, disrupting the quiet regularity of country
life.

'I love this plain,' murmured Anamaya dreamily. 'Wouldn't
it be wonderful if we settled in a village like this for the
dry season! We could at last stop traveling roads, crossing
bridges and mountain ranges ... I'm beginning to hate
palanquins ...'

Both girls were having their hair washed with a fine, gray
mud. They were luxuriating under the nimble fingers of some
servant girls, and Anamaya heard Inti Palla utter a reproving
'Tut' from somewhere behind her:

'You shouldn't say such things out loud! You who can
see the future, can't you tell that Huascar is losing the
war?'

'You know very well that I haven't heard or seen anything

for months,' sighed Anamaya. She closed her eyes to better enjoy relaxing under the servant girl's caresses.

'Oh, I know that!' exclaimed Inti Palla. 'My Almost-Husband is seething because of it ... I've never seen Atahualpa so worried and tormented. It's amazing that he's so angry even though he's so close to total victory.'

'What shall I do, if I no longer have the power?' murmured Anamaya, almost inaudibly.

They fell silent as the servant girls rinsed their hair with crystal-clear water. Some other young girls, spinning from a great bale of alpaca wool in the corner of the *cancha*, watched them in awe.

Across the yard, a dozen young women were weaving beneath a canopy. They were crouched amid dozens of brightly colored balls that looked like lush flowers. They were bent over their looms, which were supported at the bottom by belts around their waists while at the top they were fixed to a post. The women's hands darted to and fro with expert dexterity, weaving and undoing threads of all colors, and they were absorbed in the serene rhythm of the shuttles moving back and forth. Some fabrics were almost finished. Anamaya saw their splendid quality, and knew that this was the cloth that only the Emperor would wear.

As the servant girls dried her hair with an unguent mixed with gold dust, Anamaya felt moved by these 'Virgin Weavers', who found such serenity in their work. She would never be one of them. She would never know their sense of satisfaction, their calm ...

So much had happened since her short stay in the secret city!

Nowadays, Anamaya was as close as a woman could be to the Emperor Atahualpa without being either his wife or his concubine. She was surrounded by servants, and everyone respected her. Even if she had been a more demanding girl, she would have wanted for nothing. The old, weary generals, who at one time would have thought of her only to condemn her to the flames, now listened respectfully whenever she spoke! Inti Palla, who had at last achieved her ambition to be named Favorite Concubine, had become Anamaya's closest friend and confidante.

And yet, Anamaya found court life terribly heavy and constricting.

'You've changed a lot these last moons, it's true,' said Inti Palla, as if she had been following Anamaya's thoughts.

Inti Palla haughtily shooed away the servant girls laboring over her superb hair, and moved closer to Anamaya.

'Only your eyes haven't changed,' she continued.

'You think so?' giggled Anamaya. 'My cheeks are pudgier, and I've become as serious as an old shrew – that's what you really mean, isn't it?'

Inti Palla laughed and sat up beside her, taking her hands tenderly in hers.

'That's all true, but above all your ass has grown bigger! And those, too . . .'

Inti Palla brushed her hands across Anamaya's breasts, stroking them through her thin *anaco*, but Anamaya pushed them away.

'Almost real breasts!' continued Inti Palla, squeezing Anamaya's thighs. 'When I first met you, you were only a weird, arrogant child, I didn't like you at all.'

'That's because you were jealous.'

'True. But I understood who you were. Like everyone else. And it's now that I should be jealous. You've turned into a real woman! Almost as beautiful as me . . .'

'Almost?' laughed Anamaya.

'Almost. Certainly not *more* beautiful,' Inti Palla assured her seriously. 'You're still missing something . . .'

'Oh?'

Inti Palla stepped back, pouting provocatively, and arched her back. She pulled the *tocapu* wrapped around her slim waist tighter, to better push up her breasts. All the servant girls bubbled with mirth, their hands covering their mouths.

'Mine are better, aren't they?'

'Maybe,' admitted Anamaya, blushing.

'Not "maybe". *Definitely*. And do you know why?'

'Because Mama Quilla gave you more breasts than brains,' teased Anamaya.

The servant girls burst into laughter, but fell silent again when Inti Palla threw them a black look.

'Mama Quilla gave me something else: our Emperor between my thighs. That's what makes a woman really bloom . . .'

'Idiot!'

But Anamaya said nothing more, and relapsed into her usual serious mood. Someone had entered on the far side of the *cancha*, escorted by four soldiers. Inti Palla followed Anamaya's gaze, then let out a greedy cry:

'Oh! Isn't that the handsome Captain Guaypar? The hero of the battle of Angoyacu himself! Well, there's at least one person who would like to initiate you into the pleasures of the night, virgin Wife of the Sacred Double!'

Guaypar said a few words to one of the eunuch guards, who then hurried towards them through the rain. The weavers and spinners under the canopy in the corner of the *cancha* were frozen with curiosity.

'Bid him come!' said Inti Palla, smiling.

They had barely enough time to wrap themselves in *mantas* and cover their still-wet hair before Guaypar arrived at the doorway. The warrior spread his hands, his palms to the sky, a very deferential greeting. But he avoided Anamaya's eyes.

'Princesses!'

'May Inti protect you, Captain Guaypar,' replied Inti Palla in a honeyed voice. 'I am so happy to see you walking. You must be recovered from your wounds.'

Narrowing his eyes with pride, Guaypar pressed his finger-tips against his left shoulder.

'Yes. I shall be able to fight again, as soon as our Emperor decides when the next battle will be . . .'

'You're so very brave,' continued Inti Palla, a touch of teasing in her voice.

But the young captain seemed not to hear. He looked to Anamaya.

'Wife of the Sacred Double, the Inca calls for you.'

'Now?'

'Yes. He is waiting for you, and I am to escort you to him.'

He had barely finished speaking when Inti Palla was on her feet, frantically chivvying the servant girls to prepare Anamaya.

With Guaypar and his soldiers around her, and with servants holding an awning over her head against the rain, Anamaya made her way from the *cancha* of the Wives along the outer wall of the *curaca*'s palace where Atahualpa was staying. Heads turned to look at her as she passed.

Once they had crossed the threshold, the soldiers dispersed in the outer court, and the servant girls returned the way they had come. Guaypar moved to hold Anamaya back, but she stepped sharply away from him, causing the silver and gold decorations in her hair to click against each other.

'Please, give me a moment of your time!' exclaimed Guaypar in a shaky voice. 'Please don't be frightened of me, Anamaya!'

Anamaya was on the verge of a sharp reply, but she saw the fear and confusion in Guaypar's eyes.

'What do you want from me?'

'Your forgiveness!'

'Guaypar, I—'

'No, let me do the talking. The words have been stuck in my throat for years – I'm suffocating on them! Anamaya, I was a young fool, vain and proud—'

'I have forgotten all about it, and the Emperor waits . . .'

'Just listen to me, Anamaya! I know that you remember that night in Tumebamba, the night of the *Huarachicu*. I was humiliated in defeat, drunk on *chicha*. I was possessed by evil devils. The demons were gorging themselves on my blood, but . . . but that was long ago, very long ago. Already four winter solstices have passed! The seasons have done four full cycles since that night! I was a child, and so were you. But today I am a warrior, and our Emperor promoted me to the rank of Captain after the battle of Angoyacu bridge . . .'

'Look, I know that you were very brave at the battle. It is said that you captured two of Huascar's generals!' said Anamaya with gentle approval.

'Yes!' exclaimed Guaypar, lifting his hand to his wound, his eyes burning with pride. 'Yes! I'm no longer the vain weakling whom Manco, our Emperor's false brother, humiliated in front of you!'

Anamaya let this arrogant outburst pass. Guaypar continued, only slightly lowering his voice, still full of ardor:

'You've changed too. You are the most beautiful woman in any corner of the Empire of the Four Cardinal Directions. No other woman has even half your beauty. No other woman can equal the power of your eyes, none can claim to share the strength and tenderness of your mouth—'

'Please, Guaypar . . .'

'Anamaya, listen! Ever since that awful night, not one moon has passed when I haven't thought of you. Even at the height of the battle of Angoyacu, I held you in my heart! I was the first to see your beauty, Anamaya, the very first . . . and ever since, I've kept my mouth shut. I avoided you. Now, however, I'm close to our Emperor, and I organized it so that it would be me who—'

'What do you want from me, Guaypar?'

'That you become my wife!'

'You're mad! You know very well that I belong to the Sacred Double!'

Guaypar shouted in anger:

'That means nothing! It's only a title Atahualpa gave you when he wasn't even Emperor! He *is* Emperor today, largely thanks to you! He can undo what he has done . . .'

Anamaya felt suffocated as she frantically racked her mind to find the words that might make Guaypar see reason. But she was bowled over by the deep and sincere look of distress in the young officer's eyes. Certainly, he was no longer the young adolescent drunk on *chicha* whom she remembered from Tumebamba. But the type of intoxication that gripped him today was no less violent. And she was the cause of it.

'My soul lives only for you, Anamaya!' Guaypar cried out. 'Your husband, the Sacred Double, is made of solid gold – he doesn't suffer from love. But me, I bleed from it. Just thinking of you makes me burn up inside. Let me tell you: the worst torture that criminal Huascar can dream up is nothing in comparison . . .'

His distress was confirmed by his trembling lips, by the shivers that traveled visibly up his body and put a tremor into his voice.

Anamaya retreated a few steps, overwhelmed.

No one had ever made such a declaration to her. She could feel the young man's pain as clearly as if she were touching an open wound. But still, every bone in her body, every thread of her instincts told her that she must reject his passionate plea.

As gently as possible, she said:

'I've forgotten all about that night in Tumebamba, Guaypar. And I will forget this moment also. I cannot and will not hear your words. But I thank you for your . . . for your courage. And I hope that Inti will make you the greatest and happiest of Atahualpa's generals. And now I ask that you take me to him, before he grows too impatient.'

And with that Anamaya turned and walked across the courtyard. She never saw the grimace of pain and impotent rage that twisted Guaypar's face.

Of late, Anamaya had been repeatedly struck by the change in Atahualpa's physical appearance.

He was no longer the lithe, lively man who once had encouraged and impressed her with one look.

He hadn't lost any of his power – quite the opposite. Ever since the elaborate ceremony in Quito when he had placed the royal *borla* on his forehead, ever since he had become the Inca of all the Incas, everything about him expressed power and domination. What was more, he had grown heavier, due to the innumerable jars of *chicha* he had to drink at official ceremonies. During these he frequently entered into a state of sacred intoxication, desperately hoping to find some sign or hint from his ancestors.

Now his cheeks were swollen, and his chin had grown thick and heavy. He was fleshier around the waist. The whites of his eyes were redder than ever before, as if his heart was pumping an overflow of energy. His complexion had turned an odd black-and-purple color. It was difficult to read what he was thinking or feeling, although he looked imbued with a bottomless sadness.

As Anamaya prostrated herself before him, with her hands and knees on the ground and her neck bowed, he asked impatiently:

'Has my father Huayna Capac spoken to you yet?'

'No, my Lord.'

'Why not?'

'Perhaps because he has no reason to—'

'No reason! Are you mad?'

His voice quivered with bitterness and fury. Still prostrated, Anamaya asked:

'May I speak freely, my Lord?'

'You always have, I don't see why you wouldn't today!'

'My beloved Lord, I cannot understand your fear and impatience. You have fought nine battles against your brother, the Madman of Cuzco. Huascar has won only two. You went to Quito and, in accordance with the wishes of Inti, and the wishes of the northern nobles, and of all the priests, the sages and the Ancestors, you placed the *Mascapaicha* and the *curiqingue* feather on your forehead. You are our Inca, the only Emperor of the Empire of the Four Cardinal Directions. You shall enter triumphantly into the sacred city of Cuzco. Tomorrow you will fight one last battle against Huascar's men. Then you shall rule over a peaceful land, with war fading in everyone's memory. And there will not be a person in the whole Empire who won't owe you their life, their livelihood, the food that they eat and the *chicha* that they drink . . .'

Anamaya paused. Atahualpa said nothing, so she continued even more emphatically:

'My Lord, you have no reason to doubt, and nothing to fear. It's true that your father Huayna Capac hasn't spoken to me for a long time. But it's because you are now so strong and powerful. Inti and Mama Quilla are at your side. You fight with the puma's rage, and you walk under the condor's shadow. That should be enough.'

Atahualpa commanded in a muffled tone:

'Stand, *Coya Camaquen*, and look at me . . .'

Anamaya saw a ghost of a smile on Atahualpa's lips, something she hadn't seen for a long time.

'I know you think I've changed,' he said. 'But you too have changed. You've become as serious as a priest! Yes, Villa Oma has taught you well. You're at an age when other girls are looking for husbands, but you're as serious and argumentative as their mothers!'

'Only with you, my Lord, because I owe you my life.'

'As for that, I don't know who owes more to whom, blue-eyed girl. After your time in the secret city, you came to me. I was at the time humiliated in battle. I was a prisoner in a hole in the ground, and you worked out how to get me out – by making me pretend to be a snake!'

Atahualpa couldn't help but laugh.

'I remember seeing you put snake sloughings on top of the wall as the guards slept. It was one of the funniest things I've ever seen!'

But his good humor faded almost instantly. He stood up brusquely from his seat, and came so close to Anamaya that she could feel his breath.

'Yes, you assured me that I could defeat Huascar's generals and go to Quito. But then, my father had visited you: first in Tumibamba when his desiccated body had disappeared, then as a ball of fire, then in the secret city. At each crossroads, he showed you the way. The Other World opened itself to you. But now there is only silence. Why?'

'Perhaps the silence will be broken when I find my husband, the Sacred Double, in the sacred city?'

'We still have to get there!'

'You will defeat Huascar, my Lord. I am sure of it.'

'No!' exploded Atahualpa, his bloodshot eyes shining ferociously, 'It's not Huascar or his men that I fear. They're exhausted, they're almost finished. It's Cuzco itself. It's the Cuzco clans that loom before me like a black hole. They have never accepted me, they have always treated me as the offspring of a mere northern woman, although my father's blood also ran in my mother's veins. But they don't care that I too am the son of their Inca, through my mother. We are so many sons! They say that I'm impure, they consider me a bastard. Anamaya, there's only one who could lift my suffering, and that's my father! If only he would come to you . . . If only he would speak to me through you, and tell me that he's with me against the Cuzco people. But he says nothing . . . If only you could at least remember what he told you on his night of dying. If at least that came back to you . . .'

Anamaya prostrated herself, shaking her head desolately, finally seeing what had been eating away at the Inca for so many moons:

'No, my Lord. It's never come back to me.'

Atahualpa looked at her for a moment. He made as if to touch her, but changed his mind and went instead to stand in the doorway. Outside, the guards instantly bowed to him.

He stood and thought for a while with his back to her, and then, pointing to the fog wrapped around the summits above Huamachuco, he said:

'There is a powerful oracle there. Catéquil can tell the future. We shall go there tomorrow.'

CHAPTER 33

Tumbes, March 1532

'GO LEFT! MOTHER OF GOD! GO LEFT, OR ELSE we'll drown the horses!'

Don Francisco's cries rose above the booming surf.

Despite the weight of two panicked horses and half a dozen men, the raft tilted up the slope of the wave. Its sail had been dropped, and the horses' bridles tied tightly to the mast. From where he stood on the beach where they had landed earlier (with some difficulty), Gabriel could make out Pedro the Greek's large frame and red cotton hat.

The Greek leaned all of his considerable bulk on the heavy oar that acted as a rudder. But alas, no matter in what direction he tried to urge it, the raft continued to be sucked askew up the wave. Now it was being drawn towards the fiercest breakers as if by an invisible force.

For a moment the raft was moving so fast that it seemed to be floating above the surface of the water, as if, despite its size and weight, it was a plaything in the hands of the devil.

Now the wall of water roared under its logs. The men aboard screamed simultaneously. The horses sensed their fear, yanking on their bridles, kicking out with their hind legs, and their jaws gaping like those of neighing dragons.

Everything happened so quickly that time seemed to freeze. Gabriel was speechless with worry. He heard Sebastian let out a startled cry.

As the raft tilted in the thundering spray, the panicked horses huddled together on the port side while the men slid across the foam-covered logs. The wave bloomed into a gigantic, fan-shaped body of water beneath them, and for a heart-stopping instant the *balsa* rose balanced atop its peak . . .

And then, the white, foaming fury crashed onto them, swallowing the men up to their waists. The *balsa*'s mast tilted over almost into the water, and its stern lifted as easily as a leaf in a breeze. But now those on the beach saw Don Francisco's sword thrust high in the air. He sliced through the horses' bridles just as the sea closed its waters around him and the force of the wave snapped the agave ropes and scattered the thick logs of the broken raft as easily as twigs.

'They're dead!' screamed Gabriel despite himself.

'Not yet!' yelled Sebastian.

The wave ran itself out, washing up in a slow swathe of green water onto the beach, and one after the other the horses emerged from the billows. And now bearded faces popped up here and there in the swirling stretch between the beach and the breakers roaring behind them, open-mouthed and with startled looks in their eyes.

'Ho! Over there, it's Pedro!' shouted Sebastian, pointing at a head still wearing its red cap.

Not far from the Greek, the white-haired Don Francisco could be seen commanding everyone to swim ashore.

Limping badly, Gabriel tried to follow Sebastian who rushed into the water to meet them. But he turned back after the first wave hit his thighs.

'Well, at least that will be the last trip for this evening: the sea has grown too strong,' he murmured to himself.

The memory of his near-drowning was still fresh in Gabriel's mind, and his throat still burned from the volume of salt water he had coughed up while in Sebastian's arms.

In any case, they didn't need him: each man had managed to grab hold of one of the horses, who instinctively made their way quickly to the beach, eager to have solid ground under their hooves again.

Don Francisco made a point of emerging from the ocean upright in his saddle, with the horse's reins in his hand and water streaming from him, looking like Neptune creating continents under his earth-shaking step!

'I knew that I couldn't count on him!'

Half lying on a sandbank, Hernando Pizarro foamed with as much rage as the surf, and pointed menacingly at Gabriel.

Earlier that afternoon, the ships had at last anchored a few cable lengths from the coast. But ferrying men, horses and supplies from the ships to the land had become too dangerous. Only a handful of men and horses had made it ashore, and now they were isolated from the boats and rafts.

Despite his many concerns, Don Francisco hadn't left his saddle since his heroic emergence from the sea. His tireless eyes searched for an opening in the thick wall of mangroves beyond the beach, for some passage to Tumbes.

'It was only some personal effects, brother,' he said. 'We'll have them bring you more . . .'

'Twelve linen shirts, a pair of boots, three doublets worth the price of a horse, and a spare suit of armor . . . that's what you dismiss so lightly as personal effects, brother!'

'They almost died bringing it, brother. And I need every man I have.'

'Even them!' breathed a bitter Hernando.

Don Francisco pursed his lips. He was irritated and still soaked, and he dug his heels into his horse's ribs, urging it away from his brother's bad mood.

At that moment Sebastian appeared, hurrying up the beach towards them, waving towards a river mouth that cut through the mangroves and spewed yellow mud into the Southern Ocean.

'Other rafts! Five or six, heading towards us . . .'

'Indians?' asked Don Francisco.

'They're too far off yet. I can't tell.'

But the uncertainty didn't last. The Greek, who had left earlier on a reconnaissance mission to the river mouth, came galloping back, his horse kicking up dark sand and scattering the little red crabs that swarmed over the beach.

'De Soto, Governor! It's de Soto, back at last!' he yelled as soon as he was within earshot.

'He heard us! He understood! With these other rafts we'll unload more quickly tomorrow!' exclaimed Gabriel.

'And what did de Soto, understand, exactly?' grumbled Hernando, massaging his injured thigh. 'Having an arrowhead in my leg doesn't make me deaf, as far as I know. I too would like to understand whatever it is . . .'

Gabriel searched Don Francisco's expression. The governor only nodded his approval before riding his horse towards a group of *hidalgos* trying to dry themselves.

'We managed to warn Captain de Soto of the Indians' treachery just in time,' said Gabriel simply, pointing at Sebastian.

Hernando raised a bushy eyebrow, not understanding, and waited for more. After an unpleasant silence, he uttered a hostile 'Ah?' and said no more.

The Greek jumped from his horse and tenderly stroked its mane, his wet breeches and shirt clinging to his skin. He turned to Gabriel:

'Tell us about your night! It seems to me to have been a

lot of fun, and I too haven't quite grasped yet, what sort of shithole we've landed in . . .'

In a few brief sentences, Gabriel told him of Bocanegra's sorry end, of how he had been kidnapped and murdered by the Indians in the middle of the night.

'As for myself,' he concluded, pointing towards the ocean, 'without Sebastian here, the crabs would be feasting on my innards at this very moment.'

As the Greek looked fondly upon his black companion, Don Hernando gave the three of them the same impatient look that he leveled at the stubborn crabs, now emerging from their holes in the sand and heading provocatively close to his boots.

'And that is how you sent my things to the bottom,' he growled.

'With all due respect, Don Hernando, I was too preoccupied with staying alive to worry about your precious things. I am aware that you wouldn't mind sending me after them, twenty leagues down. But with your permission, that will be for another time . . .'

A few *hidalgos* laughed to themselves.

'Not bad, schoolboy,' whispered the Greek.

'All that panic over a few monkeys . . .' grumbled Hernando, piqued.

'Those monkeys, as you call them, killed Bocanegra and tried to leave the two of us to die on three feet of sand. And they intended to massacre Captain de Soto and his men as soon as they landed near that river mouth over there, near the mangroves . . .'

'And you defeated their devilish trap all by yourself?' asked Hernando sarcastically. 'Pray tell, how did you do it?'

Gabriel kept his mouth closed as Hernando looked him over, but Sebastian let out a laugh as he turned towards the Greek.

'We had to use some pretty methods to convince our guide to bring us here . . .'

He pointed to the northern side of the river, where de Soto's sails could be seen, filled by the breeze.

'The beach there is narrower, and the mangroves thicker. And what did we see there? Dozens of Indians! Dozens of smiling faces! 'May the Sacred Virgin protect us,' said I to Gabriel. 'They look like they're going to boil us up, and not even bother with the spices!' To which he replied "All we have to do is send them a clear message."'

'We slit our guide's throat,' said Gabriel, his face impassive.

'Those on the beach got the message!' laughed Sebastian, 'and what with the wind and the blessing we managed to sail to here. The breakers turned us ass-over-tip just like they did you, but in the end spat us out safely. Out of range of the Indians, since they were cut off by the fast-flowing river – and as for our raft, it was intact until your delicate landing . . .'

'We hid in the mangroves while we waited for the captains' *balsas*,' continued Gabriel. 'And as soon as we saw them near, we shouted so loudly and waved so wildly that he initially moved further off the coast . . .'

Gabriel was about to say more, but Hernando Pizarro, no longer listening, stood up and limped lamely away.

'Brother!' he shouted. 'Night will fall in less than an hour. What is your decision?'

Don Francisco came towards him unhurriedly, his horse walking slowly along. He drew his sword from his scabbard, and its blade gleamed under Hernando's eyes. Each man could see the drops of water on it gather and stream down its length before dripping off its point.

'It seems to me,' Don Francisco said as his gaze wandered over his men circled around him, 'that we are in no state to make a dignified entry into the city of gold. Especially if the Indians are inclined to betray us. Our difficult landing exhausted the horses as much as ourselves. It would not be prudent to cross the mangrove swamp now . . .'

He looked out to the gray ocean, where the *balsas* were now near the edge of the flood:

'And de Soto is yet to join us. It would be better to wait for him – we won't have the time to unload many more horses. I suggest that we spend the night here. And that we spend it in the saddle, as a precaution . . .'

'You don't imagine that I'm going to spend the night on that sorry screw? Why, I can't even ride half a league, with my leg!' exclaimed Hernando.

'Not you, Hernando,' replied Don Francisco gently, a twinkle in his eye. 'You can sleep on the sand . . . I've seen our friend here hold his own in the saddle. You can trust him with your screw. And you can sleep soundly while he keeps guard. After all, he's proved himself well: he sacrificed our personal effects to save our lives!'

Gabriel felt himself blush with pride as the Governor pointed at him.

Captain Hernando de Soto could not live without his horse. Instead of joining the small group on the beach, he steered straight for the *Santiago* anchored three cable lengths from the shore, and managed to get his beloved gray Andalusian onto his raft. He too enjoyed a wetting in the tropical waters, but now he rode up the beach, dripping but proud.

He saluted the Governor and nodded his head at Gabriel.

'Good to see you, *amigos*,' he said simply, being a man of few words.

Throughout the night the men had gripped their exhausted horses' ribcages between their numbed legs.

Occasionally they had fallen asleep, only to be startled awake by the faint sounds of a crab scurrying across the sand. They had had hallucinatory visions of screaming hordes of Indians charging at them from the mangroves. But the only sounds had been the cackling of coots and the crash of the blue-white surf.

At sunset, the surf was still so heavy that only six *hidalgos* had managed to land with their horses. Now there were few more than a dozen ashore, including foot soldiers, isolated from the ships and *balsas*. They formed a defensive formation in the shape of a flower, each hairy petal facing out towards the night, testing his own will. Some had unsheathed their swords and laid them across their saddles, and the stars could be seen reflected in their metal.

Each man thought about the nearby town and its walls of gold that stood hidden behind the thick, seething mangroves. Each recalled what the governor and the Greek had told them about it, of its huge palaces and the fortunes to be found there.

Their eyelids felt heavy, wearied by the struggle against sleep and the constant fear of savages. They fantasized about piles of riches waiting for them, and the sky seemed spangled with gold. In their exhaustion, each shadow of the night would magically change into a shining gold shape!

When dawn shone its pale light on the fog to the east, they could hold back no longer.

Led by Governor Pizarro, they crossed a stretch of black, stinking mud left bare by the retreating tide, and finally entered the mangroves.

A dry, narrow path, with stones conveniently placed across difficult places, weaved its way through the entangled trees. Unidentifiable creatures moved about in the foliage high above their heads. Twice the horses shied and neighed when snakes as thick as a man's arm appeared on the path. And then they almost stepped on one of those scaly monsters that looked so similar to rotten tree trunks but had teeth deadly enough to slice a calf in two with one giant bite.

At the thickest point of the oppressive jungle, they could hardly see the sky through the canopy of vegetation, so low that it seemed like a giant had lopped off the treetops with his sword.

They didn't see a single Indian.

Nor did they see one when they came out of the mangroves into the fields, and could see the highest walls of Tumbes in the distance.

They were feverish with anticipation, and pushed their horses to a trot.

When they were within crossbow range, the Greek furrowed his brow and looked at Don Francisco, who looked back at him impassively.

Gabriel was expecting to see gold glinting in the sun, which had at last risen above the distant eastern hills. But he saw nothing of the kind.

Nor did they see any Indians, whether pleading fearfully or shouting belligerently.

Before they even entered the town they could see that it had been sacked. the roofless, disemboweled houses, the fire-blackened walls, the empty streets full of debris, the adobe bricks reduced to mud . . .

The silence around them was one of war, of pillage, of desolation.

The entire devastated town had been abandoned.

This was the Tumbes that they found.

'Mother of God!' burst out de Soto as he turned his horse to face Francisco Pizarro. 'Where in hell have you brought us? *This* is your city of marvels?'

Gabriel looked at Pizarro, expecting to see anger, or even doubt, on his proud face. But he saw only a vague expression of irritation.

CHAPTER 34

Tumbes, April 1532

THE FIRST STONE BRUSHED PAST GABRIEL'S shoulder, chipping the corner of a wall just behind him. The second hit Pedro the Greek's thigh with a dull thud. He jumped and swore like a bargee.

But Gabriel didn't have time to ask questions. Around twenty ragged men wearing morions, their cotton coats undone and their beards unkempt, swarmed from all sides over the path and yelled:

'Thief, thief! Liar! Greek pederast!'

Their hands held more stones. Three landed between Gabriel and Pedro, albeit thrown with a certain lack of vigor and precision.

'I think those vermin have it in for me,' muttered the Greek, whose large body made an easy target.

As he spoke another stone, smaller but thrown with greater skill, hit him on the head.

If it hadn't been for his ever-present red cap, his skull would have split. He swayed nonetheless. Gabriel held out an arm to help him, but the hail of stones fell as thick and fast now as the insults hurled at them. Pedro was hit on the ear, and he reddened as much from fury as from pain. Blood flowed and trickled all over his beard.

Gabriel felt a rip of pain in his back. He had already unsheathed his sword, and he jumped aside to avoid the latest salvo as Pedro lifted his arms to protect his face.

'To the fortress!' yelled Gabriel. 'Quickly, go! I'll take care of them.'

'They're going to tear out your guts!' said the Greek.

'Not mine, but they'll have yours if you don't hurry!'

Hobbling under the volley of stones, the Greek retreated ignominiously back through the door of the fortress that they had just come out of.

'Have you all lost your wits? Have you gone mad?' shouted Gabriel, pointing his blade at a dozen faces intoxicated with rage.

'Mad? Yes, we're mad to have listened to that devil's lies!'

'There's nothing here! There never was any gold!'

'They said the walls were covered in it! But there's not even anything to eat, not even an Indian's shit!'

'Pedro didn't lie: he came here and he saw it!'

'Oh yes? I'd like to see you find gold in this dust here!'

Gabriel attempted to reason with them:

'The town was sacked during the war that the Indians are waging amongst themselves! How could the Governor have known about that?'

'He doesn't know anything! Not even where we're going!'

'And what do you know, kid? You don't even know if he's even really been here!'

'Yes! I saw the precious objects that he carried to the King. I saw them with my own eyes! There were wagonloads—'

'Bullshit! Why should we believe you?'

'You're like the rest of them, kid! You lick their boots and kiss their asses with each new day that the Lord brings!'

'You're not the one with anything to lose, you bastard! You have no family or home! You're just another lunatic like the so-called Governor!'

'The King is not a lunatic!' shouted Gabriel, beside himself. 'The Council of the Office of the Indies are not lunatics! They're the ones who gave him the title, and with good reason! *You're* the only lunatics here! You've as many holes in your brains as you have in your shirts! It's the Indians' war, I tell you—'

'And so?'

'And so we must be patient! You think you can conquer a country in just one day, by taking just one town?'

'Patience, hah! You sound like Pizarro, kid, and your words are as worthless as his . . .'

'Would you rather get back on the rafts?'

The men said nothing, but Gabriel knew that their grumblings and angry eyes promised no good.

'They can't go on like this,' declared de Soto dryly. He turned his eyes away from the Greek's blood-covered face to look directly at Don Francisco:

'They can't keep on putting up with so much for so little. Weeks without food, diseases, treacherous Indians – all that for the ruins of a town and a few promises. Governor, they are right. I insist on knowing what you plan to do. What are we waiting for?'

Don Francisco didn't offer a reply immediately. His beard quivered as rage made his blood boil but he managed to control himself.

'Look around you, Captain de Soto,' he said eventually, his voice strained.

In fact, they were surrounded by splendor. They were in what looked like a fortress protected by five high walls, a space a hundred paces across. The walls were so well built that they hadn't been damaged during the attack that had destroyed the rest of the town. A palace had been built near where they stood in the fortress's center. Its walls had been expertly plastered and brightly painted with intertwining motifs of animals, stars, and geometrical patterns that satisfied the mind's natural sense of balance . . .

'Isn't this the work of a great and powerful nation?' continued Don Francisco.

'I don't see any gold.'

'Gold, gold – Captain de Soto, I know that you would like to be in my place. But conquering this land for our Church and King is foremost in my mind. After we have done that, only then shall we cover ourselves in gold. The Virgin herself will see to it!'

De Soto still cut an elegant figure, despite having lost all his personal possessions. He had managed to shave close that day, and the intelligent gleam in his eye indicated someone who was master of himself and knew how to lead others. He laughed derisively and said:

'Don't try that one on me, Pizarro! Save your talk of the Sacred Virgin for the credulous, thank you very much!'

'De Soto,' roared Hernando, stepping forward with his hand wrapped around the grip of his sword. 'You will speak respectfully to the Governor, or else you will answer to me.'

De Soto calmly looked him over. He smiled disdainfully, and gazed at Gabriel and Pedro before looking again at Hernando.

'The Pizarro brothers! And I hear that you have a nephew with you as well. All sons of one father, but as for the rest—'

Now Hernando brandished his sword, but de Soto immediately unsheathed his own.

'Easy, Hernando . . .' said Don Francisco in an appeasing tone.

'Take heed of the Governor, Hernando. Try and take a moment to think it through, if you can. If I leave with my men, you'll lose the gold that you've already given me, and

you'll lose Peru as well! How many will you be without me?
Fifty? Sixty? And no more than twenty half-dead horses.'

'We're hardly more with you,' growled Hernando.

'There's not many of us, true, but it will still double your
overall force. And as Don Francisco wishes to conquer the
country before sacking its gold, the more men the better,
no? Oh yes, you need me—'

'Your Excellency! Your Excellency!'

Friar Vicente Valverde, one of the two Dominicans who
had come from Panama, froze in the doorway upon seeing
the unsheathed swords. He instinctively spread his hands
in supplication:

'My Lords! Have you lost your senses? Doesn't our
situation merit greater wisdom?'

'Happily, you have put a stop to our idiocy, Friar Vicente,'
laughed de Soto as he returned his sword to its scabbard.
'But not to our blue devils . . .'

'What news do you bring?'

Friar Vicente turned towards Don Francisco, crossed
himself, and whispered conspiratorially:

'An old Indian arrived this morning. He has told Martinillo
some amazing things. You must hear him, Your Excellency.
And you too, *señores* . . .'

He was quite a small man, with a serious, honest air
about him. Oddly enough, the old Indian seemed to be
full of admiration for the strangers from the sea. He
touched their clothes and their beards, and ran a respectful
finger along the metal of their swords and scabbards.
He smiled contentedly, as if they were the fulfillment of
his hope.

He wore only a simple cotton tunic, red and bright yellow.
His skin was tanned and weather-beaten, but his hands
moved animatedly, and his voice was light. He spoke easily

in a fluid and sibilant language that seemed to Gabriel closer
to song than to speech.

Martinillo, dressed in the Spanish manner, interpreted
conscientiously, his Castilian now much improved:

'He says that he fought here for the Emperor of this
country, the Inca Son of the Sun. He says that he alone
waited here for the Great Lords from the sea, because he
likes their way of making war. He says that before Tumbes
was burned by enemies, it consisted of around a thousand
household. But many of the inhabitants were killed, and the
rest fled when the bearded men and their beasts emerged
from the sea. He himself did not flee, because he knows
what war can be like. He says that he has been to Cuzco,
the Emperor's sacred city. It's a city like no other. Its streets
and houses are made of gold, and even its animals and plants
are gold. He says that the bearded men and their creatures
are strong warriors. He thinks that they will conquer all. That
is why he didn't flee, and he asks that his house should not
be pillaged . . .'

The Indian fell silent, as did Martinillo when he'd finished
interpreting. Everyone wanted to hear more, and even Captain de Soto had lost his haughty smile.

Suddenly, Don Francisco fell to his knees in front of the
Indian and crossed himself, reminding Gabriel of that night
in Toledo, now so long ago. He stood up, a proud, full smile
across his face:

'Captain de Soto,' he murmured, pointing at the Indian,
'here is a man who has more faith in us than do you and
your men! Did I not say, just a little bit of patience—'

'You actually believe him?' chuckled de Soto. 'Walls of
gold? Animals and plants of gold?'

'Here in this strange land, I believe a lot of things, Captain,
especially in counting my blessings. In any case, we're going
to find out for ourselves . . .'

He turned to Martinillo and ordered:

'Tell him that we shan't pillage his home: we shall mark it out with a cross. Now ask him to tell us more about this city, Cuzco, and the road there. Is it far away?'

CHAPTER 35

Huamachuco, March 1532

THE THREE ROCKS PERCHED ATOP PORCON MOUN-
tain were still just shadows against the black sky,
the only light being an almost imperceptible blue
rising like a halo from the east.

Anamaya looked at Villa Oma.

The terrible pressures of war had hardened and etched his
features. His eyes, deep in their hollows, shone like the black
stones of the braziers. Ever since the war had begun, he had
been to every battlefield, interpreting the omens along with
the other soothsayers, encouraging the soldiers and invoking
curses against the enemy. It was whispered at court that his
thin, dry body did without food, living only on the juice of
the coca leaf.

The first rays of dawn had not yet dispelled the dark,
yet Villa Oma led the small group confidently through the
night along the path to the summit. Anamaya walked silently
behind him alongside Guaypar, lost in her thoughts. They
preceded the escort of servants who bore jugs of *chicha*, jars
of gold and silver, and other offerings wrapped in cloth. Two
young boys led the ten llamas to be sacrificed at the *huaca*.

Guaypar's presence bothered Anamaya. She couldn't forget
his awkward, confused request. She didn't know how to make

it clear to him that she wasn't his enemy, that she bore him no ill will. She would have liked to reassure him, but every time that she glanced towards him he ignored her and kept his eyes fixed on the slowly brightening sky.

The village's few houses hugged the foot of the mountain. Its inhabitants' only job was to take care of the *huaca*. They had all heard the rumor that the Sapay Inca Atahualpa was to send two of his lords to consult it. They stood in front of their doorways and watched in silence as Villa Oma, Guaypar and the rest passed through. Anamaya could make out nothing in their black, almost expressionless eyes.

The first rays of the sun at last lit the peak. They could now make out the black walls that sheltered the idol atop the highest of the three rocks.

As they started up the slope, Anamaya turned to Villa Oma:

'What does our Emperor Atahualpa want?'

'To hear what his father won't tell you,' replied Villa Oma in a distant voice.

'You still think that it's my fault . . .'

'I think nothing of the kind, little girl,' murmured the Sage. 'I don't need an oracle to tell me that a hero gripped by fear is an ill omen.'

Anamaya said no more. She knew in her heart that the Sage was right.

The ancient priest guarding the *huaca* was frighteningly thin: his neck was no wider than three fingers held together. His eyes looked as if they had been bled of all color. He could barely stand upright and leaned on a stick, its pommel carved into the form of a coiled snake. His bare feet were repulsive, encrusted with dirt, and he wore a long tunic that reached his ankles. His tunic was made of a long-haired pelt – no doubt that of a *guanaco* – and many tiny pink shells hung from it.

Behind him stood a group of priests hardly younger or less filthy than their leader.

When Villa Oma was in front of him, the Guardian-Priest opened his mouth, causing Anamaya to jump back: he was completely toothless, and the sound he made was as deep as a horn − it was the voice of the gods channeled through a shell.

'I know why you are here.'

As the sun made its lazy way towards its zenith, Villa Oma oversaw the distribution of the offerings to the idol − a life-sized stone statue of a man. The temple in which it stood was a single, roofless room, its window open to the sunrise and its door to the sunset. The alcoves in its walls held many golden objects behind rich tapestries.

First, the priests spread coca leaves at the base of the idol. Then Villa Oma and Guaypar each plucked an eyelash and blew it towards the statue. Then they poured the jugs of *chicha* on the ground while invoking the spirit of the idol.

They gave the Guardian-Priest the rest of the offerings. He blew on each one before wrapping them in a wool fabric: coca, maize, colorful feathers. Then the fabrics were knotted and burned in a fire just outside the *huaca*.

When the fire had burned itself out, Villa Oma placed two jars of gold and two of silver in front of the idol. He motioned to the young boys who watched over the llamas. Each animal had been tied to a heavy stone, and each was now led around the statue, one following another. When a llama had completed four or five circles, the Guardian-Priest plunged his knife into the beast's chest, cut out its heart, and placed it to his lips as the other priests collected the streaming blood.

The servants made a low murmuring sound.

Anamaya looked away. She had been initiated into the secret rites and was bound by her oath taken in the secret city, yet she still felt nauseous during the unavoidable sacrifices.

Blood trickled from the Guardian-Priest's lips, down his neck and onto his tunic, drying on its long hairs between the shells. He left the temple without a word, and only Villa Oma followed him.

Anamaya stayed with Guaypar, the servants, the shepherds, and the *huaca*'s priests. A breeze briefly picked up and blew cool against the napes of their necks. Yet the sky remained hidden behind thick black clouds, and the air still hung heavy.

The Guardian-Priest's emaciated form had disappeared behind the idol. Through the doorway observers could make out only Villa Oma's back, bent in supplication, and the terrible face of the idol of Catequil, god of war.

'Ask your question,' said the idol.

'My Lord the Sapay Inca Atahualpa would like to know his destiny.'

Without hesitating the idol boomed like thunder:

'Atahualpa has spilled too much blood, and has angered the gods. His ill-omened end is near.'

Villa Oma didn't flinch, and the onlookers held their breath. Anamaya could hear her heart beating.

'His ill-omened end is near,' thundered the voice again as the black clouds burst and the first drops of rain fell upon them.

Villa Oma stood up, turned around and left the *huaca*, his face ashen.

They descended the mountain without saying a word, and the rain now fell in heavy, thick drops. Below, the village was deserted, as if all the *huaca*'s servants had heard the awful prediction and were now hiding in their homes.

When they saw the walls of the *tambo* of Huamachuco, Villa Oma stopped and grabbed Guaypar's arm.

'Don't come with me.'

'Why not?'

'We were two when Atahualpa was hoping for a favorable

prediction from the oracle. But now I must be alone to tell him that it is not so.'

Guaypar trembled with impatience and frustration. Anamaya gently put her hand on his. Then she pointed at the symmetrical stones of the *curaca*'s palace where Atahualpa was waiting for them:

'We know that you aren't scared,' she said.

Guaypar turned his black eyes on her:

'I alone know what I fear.'

'That's enough, Guaypar,' said the Sage. 'Return to your *cancha* and wait there for your Emperor's orders.'

Guaypar was still staring at Anamaya; his gaze burned intensely, and Anamaya discerned such repressed violence that she was fearful of delving into his black soul. Her words of consolation and friendship remained imprisoned at the bottom of her throat.

'I'm coming with you,' said Guaypar at last.

'Have you heard, Villa Oma?'

Atahualpa's eyes sparked with an odd mixture of fury and joy.

'Huascar is defeated!'

'So I hear.'

'Tell him, Sikinchara, repeat to him what you have just told me, word for word.'

Anamaya recognized Captain Sikinchara, the same man who had taken her from the forest all those years ago. Each time that she saw him, she felt the same fearful reaction that she had had when she was a child, that same little girl that she still was in her heart.

'Our troops crushed Huascar's in a victory that still echoes throughout the mountains. His army is in disarray, its soldiers either fleeing, slaughtered or changing sides to join us.'

In the *cancha*'s courtyard on the other side of the thick walls, cries of joy could be heard.

'You seem taciturn, Villa Oma: does our victory not please you?'

'You sent me to consult Cataquil's oracle, my Lord.'

'No doubt he told you of my triumph.'

'Not exactly.'

'Not exactly?'

Villa Oma gathered his breath.

'The oracle said. "Atahualpa has spilled too much blood, and has angered the gods. His ill-omened end is near."'

Silence stole into the room. Atahualpa was seated on a stool on top of a dais. He wore the royal *borla*, a crown of feathers, and held the *sunturpaukar*, the scepter of might. Sikinchara stood at his side, Villa Oma and Guaypar facing him, their heads bowed, while Anamaya stood slightly behind them. Each time that she was in Atahualpa's presence, Anamaya felt the power that emanated from the Inca of all the Incas, the carrier of thunder and lightning. But he spoke with surprising calm:

'Tell me about this oracle . . .'

Villa Oma obeyed: he told of their walk through the night, the village, the offerings, and the old priest in the tunic covered with pink shells. Then he repeated the words: 'His ill-omened end is near.'

Atahualpa burst out laughing.

'And you believe this prophecy?'

Villa Oma said nothing.

'Answer me, you who are called Sage, and who speaks sagely: do you really believe it?'

'I am loath to answer you, my Lord.'

'Hmm. And what about you, Anamaya?'

She was silent.

'You are scared,' said Atahualpa. 'Scared of this *huaca* who is my enemy as much as is my brother Huascar.'

He made an effort to keep his voice measured. But Anamaya sensed a tone of deep concern and knew that he had been disturbed by the prophecy.

'And you, Guaypar,' he asked. 'What do you say?'

'I say that whoever opposes you must be destroyed, my Lord.'

'Here is a loyal brother!' exclaimed Atahualpa.

CHAPTER 36

Porcon, June 1532

A TAHUALPA'S ARMY ENTERED THE VILLAGE OF Cataquil at sunset. Guaypar and the other captains wore leather corselets and metal breastplates over their *unkus*. They wore helmets of woven reeds that were so solid that no slingshot or fighting stick could damage them, still less crack them. The *unanchunas* – brightly colored standards – fluttered at the front of the column. Behind them were the spear-carriers ranked closely together, then the archers.

There was not a man or woman on the well-paved road that passed through the village. Only one little boy and his short-haired black dog remained, frozen with terror.

Guaypar went up to him.

'Do you know who we are?'

The child nodded his head, unable to say a word. Guaypar pushed him gently aside.

At that moment the blaring of trumpets and the beating of drums echoed against the sides of the mountains.

Arriving from the east, with the sun above it, Atahualpa's palanquin approached at the slow pace of its bearers. The *rampa* was extravagantly appointed with silver and gold, and its multicolored feathers fluttered in the wind so that the palanquin seemed not to advance on the shoulders of men but rather to be carried by a flock of birds.

The procession came to a halt. The fine *cumbi* covers over the palanquin shook slightly in the breeze.

'Are you ready?' the Inca of all the Incas was heard to ask.

'Yes, my Lord,' replied Guaypar. 'We await your command.'

'Then deploy the troops in a circle around the mountain so that my enemy, that damned idol, cannot escape.'

And after a few curt orders the troops were on their way.

At dawn Atahualpa went to the summit, accompanied only by the two lords whom he had sent to consult the oracle: Villa Oma and Guaypar.

The Guardian-Priest was waiting for them in his pink-shelled tunic, as filthy and repulsive as ever.

Atahualpa stepped from his palanquin carrying a bronze ax with gold. The Guardian-Priest did not even lower his eyes, much less bow before the Inca of all the Incas. He stayed upright, leaning slightly askew on his snake's-head stick.

'You know who I am,' said Atahualpa.

He nodded.

'I know you. You are Lord Atahualpa.'

'If you recognized me, then why didn't you prostrate yourself before me?'

'Because others came to consult Cataquil's oracle, and He told them by my voice that there is only one Sapay Inca, and his name is Huascar.'

'You lie.'

'I have neither the power of lies nor of truth. I am the voice of the god Cataquil. He existed before me, and shall exist after me.'

'You lie. Repeat all your lies about me, so that I may hear them from your own foul mouth.'

'You are Lord Atahualpa. You have spilled too much blood. Your ill-omened end is near.'

'You lie. You are the friend of my enemy, and so you too are my enemy. Know that I am not one to be trifled with – not by any man, *huaca*, or idol . . .'

'You are not the Inca. You were not named in the orthodox manner. You are the son of the great Huayna Capac, but your mother was of low birth . . .'

The ax whistled through the air so quickly that no one saw it coming before it had cut clean through the neck of the Guardian-Priest. His head fell free, and blood gushed. For a few moments his old, old hands remained wrapped around his stick, his body still upright. Then the headless corpse crumpled to the ground.

Guaypar forced himself to look at the Guardian-Priest's head as it rolled to a stop: a disdainful smile was still fixed upon its frozen features.

Some of his blood had landed on the unique gold motif of the Inca's *unku* – the geometrical pattern of the *kapak*, the chief. Atahualpa ignored it and walked towards the idol's little temple.

'None may trifle with me,' he repeated before passing through the doorway and turning to Villa Oma and Guaypar.

He raised his ax once more, and it came down on the Cataquil statue's neck, just like it had on the Guardian-Priest's. He hit it so hard that the idol tottered over and crashed to the ground, where the head rolled away. A little gray dust rose up around it before settling down, dirtying the bottom of the Inca's tunic.

He stood on the threshold of the room, breathing heavily, with a savage and joyless look in his bloodshot eyes.

'Do you not rejoice, Villa Oma?'

'I do not, my Lord. Nor do I despair. I listen to you, and

I listen to our ancestors in the Other World. I listen to you, and I listen to our father Inti.'

A *chaski* was hurrying towards then from the foot of the mountain. He arrived completely out of breath, his forehead glistening with sweat, the muscles of his strong and sinewy legs still taut from his exertion. He murmured something into the ear of the young captain, Guaypar. Guaypar's face lit up.

'My Lord!' he exclaimed.

'What is it, my loyal brother?'

'The usurper Huascar has been taken prisoner by General Chalcuchima. He is defeated, my Lord! You may peel his skin off his bones whenever you feel like it!'

'Raise your eyes to mine, Villa Oma, look at your Emperor, and remove that look of fear – fear of the gods has no place here.'

Villa Oma kept his eyes turned down to the ground.

'An upheaval is in the making, Sage, an upheaval not seen in the Empire of the Four Cardinal Directions since the time of Pachacutec the Improver! I am the new Improver of the world! I am he who destroys the old gods and kills the bad gods, I am he who transforms men into stones and stones into men—'

'You cannot say these things, my Lord,' said Villa Oma in a low voice. 'That is the sole prerogative of the unique Viracocha, the creator of all things.'

'I *can* say these things – and anything else I want. Guaypar!'

'Yes, my Lord?'

'I want you to bring up all the sacrificial wood that you can find in that cursed village, whose people serve a damned *huaca* and its idol, and I want you to pile it up around this corpse—' he pointed at the headless Guardian-Priest '— this idol, and this entire mountain, and I want you to build a fire that will reach the sun itself!'

Guaypar had to restrain himself from grinning.

'I shall do so immediately, my Lord!'

'When it is finished, I want you to find what is left of the idol's head, reduce it to powder, and throw the powder to the wind!'

The *chaski* stayed respectfully behind Guaypar, holding his hands behind his back and keeping his head lowered. The captain turned towards him.

'What is it now?'

The young man whispered something else into Guaypar's ear. The captain lost his smile.

'There is more news,' he said.

'Later, loyal brother,' said Atahualpa. 'There has been enough news today, and I don't want to wait any longer.'

He climbed into his palanquin.

Anamaya watched the fire.

It had consumed the houses of the village, ran up the bush-land on the slope of the mountain, and now approached the three rocks on its summit.

It was as bright as day in the middle of the night, and the heat was almost unbearable. She turned to Guaypar.

'You did this?'

'I obeyed the orders of the Sapay Inca.'

There was nothing to say. She looked at the villagers who watched impassively as their homes, their mountain and their god burned.

'You look worried,' said Anamaya.

'I heard some strange news . . .'

'Huascar's arrest?'

'No. Some Tallane Indians from the coast said that some white men — their faces covered in hair and their torsos in metal — have arrived from the sea . . .'

Anamaya's heart began to beat violently.

'. . . They wear belts around their waists to which is

attached an object made of a sort of silver, which resembles the sticks that our women use to weave with. They travel on top of llamas much bigger than ours. The Tallanes called them *viracochakunas*.'

Despite the heat Anamaya trembled so violently that Guaypar noticed. He tried to put his arm around her shoulder, but she gently pushed him away.

'I remember,' she said, 'I remember when I was still a child and was keeping the great Emperor Huayna Capac warm when some messengers arrived. They told of strangers who came from the sea, and they used the name of Viracocha. Ever since then, nothing has been the same in the Empire of the Four Cardinal Directions.'

'But we are the most powerful!' exclaimed Guaypar. 'We have conquered all the other tribes!'

'I don't know why Huayna Capac doesn't speak to me from the Under World. I fear his silence. For a long time I thought that I was the one at fault. But now I wonder whether it is in fact he who hides so as not to see the end of the world. The oracle said it was—'

'There is no more oracle, Anamaya.'

'Look there!'

Anamaya stretched her arm towards the mountain. Everything was ablaze except the rock on which lay the broken idol in its building. The flames lapped up against it, and it glowed in the night like a russet-gold vision.

Anamaya thought of Huayna Capac's words, the ones that remained hidden in her heart.

'Not fire, nor water, nor wind can destroy the Word of Truth, Guaypar. Nor any fury.'

CHAPTER 37

Cajas, October 1532

'DO YOU THINK THAT THEY CAN SEE US?' ASKED
Gabriel.

Sebastian shook his head.

'I believe what I see. That's all.'

Ever since they had left the river bed to enter the mountain
range, Gabriel hadn't been able to stop himself from glancing
continually over his shoulder, looking at every tree and bush,
and at every shadow cast by the boulders heated by the sun:
they were there.

The group of fifty men and a dozen horses, under de Soto's
command and accompanied by guides, had been ordered two
days earlier to make its way to a town where, according to
what they had been told, a large garrison of the Indian king's
men were to be found.

The weeks spent in Tumbes, that strange town set between
sea and river, sand, mangroves and jungle, had changed the
nature of Gabriel's dream: the closer that they came to what
they sought, the more unattainable it seemed. The passing days had imperceptibly developed their own mundane
rhythm. The men became so used to hunger and thirst that
they ceased to notice their privations. Some of them got into
the habit of staring at the sea, and of watching those distant

black dots on the waves, local fishermen riding those strange sea horses that the Spanish had christened *caballitos*. They got used to the furtive smiles of Indian women, or the impenetrable and hostile stares of little boys. The routine of changing the lookouts and the endless waiting created a feeling of somnolence that was difficult to snap out of.

Pizarro finally ordered de Soto to lead a reconnaissance patrol to the town that the guides said was three days' trek across the mountains. He was to go as a peaceful ambassador. Only when the Governor took Gabriel aside to entrust him with a private mission did Gabriel shake off his torpor.

'I want you to stay close to de Soto,' said Pizarro. 'I want you to become his shadow, and make sure that you thwart any bad intention that he may have in mind . . .'

'Bad intention?'

'Don't try to understand. *I* understand him, and I understand men. I know exactly how much his loyalty is worth. You will go where he goes and watch what he does. And you will tell me everything. Understood?'

'And if it turns bad?'

The Governor smiled cryptically.

'We are less than two hundred in total, Gabriel. Despite the advice of my brother Hernando, who would do anything to get rid of de Soto, I would never send a quarter of my force to be massacred. It wouldn't be Christian, but above all it wouldn't be intelligent. It won't turn bad. I shall pray for you.'

Gabriel looked at the Governor's inscrutable face behind his impeccably trimmed beard, and at his small and compact form which seemed to give off a boundless energy. What did he really want? Officially, to make contact with the Indian king – 'Altabaliba' or something like that – and propose a peaceful treaty with him. Gabriel sighed: he resolved not to jeopardize his serenity by trying to second-guess Pizarro's real plans. It was a futile exercise that would send him mad.

They had set out two days before, and they had not yet
reached the top of their ascent. They had left the main path
at the bottom of the valley upon reaching two enormous white
rocks, placed on either side like sentinels. They had started to
climb the mountains through frustratingly thick bush along
paths that gradually became narrower but were always well
paved. Each time that they emerged from the bush near the
top of a hill and once again saw the blue dome of the sky,
Gabriel expected to discover the peaceful and reassuring
vista of a plain laid out before them. But they saw only
more mountains, receding endlessly behind one another and
seeming to close in on the small group.

He turned for the hundredth time to Sebastian, walking
beside him.

'How many of them do you think they are?'

Sebastian laughed.

'I've answered that question again and again, Don Gabriel!'

'I know: you believe what you see. But still, what's your
guess?'

'You're even more pig-headed than that *hidalgo* . . . well,
if they're capable of building cities like the one that we saw,
even though it was pillaged – and if their capital is even half
as beautiful as the old man described it to us . . .'

Gabriel looked at de Soto's broad, powerful back. De Soto
was riding his horse so effortlessly that they seemed to be
one being.

'And him? Do you think that he knows something that
we don't?'

'He's just like the Governor. He pretends . . . but, trust
me, his heart is as strong and his eye as quick as the
Governor's.'

Quick eyes, day and night . . . sometimes Gabriel would
wake with a start, convinced that there were eyes out there,
hidden in the darkness, determined to lure him out, looking
into his very soul. It was a curious sensation – he was

scared, yet at the same time he didn't fear for his life. If he had been able to look at the situation objectively and rationally, he would doubtless have realized the utter insanity of their enterprise. He would have envisaged the tens of thousands of soldiers armed with bows and arrows and spears and pikes who were waiting for them and who would encircle them before massacring them all, smiling as they did so. But he imagined that the eyes that watched him were dark and melancholic, and it felt good to surrender to their midnight blue.

On the morning of the third day, they captured two Indian scouts. Despite Felipillo's mediation, it was difficult to work out whether their mission was a hostile one, or who their masters were. Rumors ran through the Spanish expedition, and de Soto was forced to discipline some of the men. They changed their leather cuirasses for coats of mail, and Gabriel now kept his sword permanently in his hand.

They were sure to have to fight.

But against what, exactly?

The path suddenly deteriorated into an awful slope of loose stones, and the men and horses struggled up it. There was shouting and neighing, the men's breath was as short as their tempers, their hair was plastered to their heads with sweat, and their shirts stuck to their torsos. Stones fell in a rapid cascade, as if thrown by invisible hands.

Only de Soto climbed effortlessly. He led his horse on foot, and it was odd to see him off it, for he and the animal were often thought of as one, his gray armor the same color as its coat. He climbed at a constant speed, never slipping.

Gabriel followed close behind him and caught up with him at the peak, his chest burning and heaving for breath.

'Here we are, then,' said de Soto calmly.

Gabriel couldn't reply. De Soto looked at him with mocking affection.

'Is not speaking to me part of your orders?' he asked without rancor. 'I had imagined that your mission was only to spy on my actions . . .'

Gabriel avoided his gaze and shrugged his shoulders in an exaggerated manner.

'I don't know what you mean, Captain de Soto.'

'Come on,' smiled de Soto. 'Don't lie, it doesn't suit you. I like you, my boy. And not only because you saved my life.'

Gabriel went red, not knowing what to say.

'But I can promise you,' concluded de Soto rather cheerfully, 'that that does not put me under any obligation . . .'

The screen of mountains had finally given way to reveal a plain. The air was crisp now and cooler, and acacia blooms shivered in the slight breeze. A herd of those big sheep, which they had now learned were called *llamas*, were unperturbed by their arrival and continued grazing nonchalantly.

A little further on, the grass was strewn with yellow stains that betrayed the recent presence of hundreds of tents. A few campfires still smoldered here and there. Gabriel's heart missed a beat.

'There's no one here,' said de Soto. 'They've left.'

'Where to?'

De Soto made no reply. As the rest of the expedition caught up with them and discovered the sight for themselves, de Soto and Gabriel continued on across the plain. The llamas lifted their long necks to look at them like strange sentinels with wet, feminine eyes. Gabriel listened to the wind and watched the sky, his nerves on edge. He expected a screaming horde of Indians to come charging at them at any moment. But the prairie was so peaceful, the breeze hardly ruffling its sparse vegetation at all, that such a thing seemed impossible.

They crossed the abandoned campsite. Gabriel took a

blackened ball from the cinders of a still warm fire, and lifted it to his nostrils.

'*Papa*,' said a familiar guttural voice from behind him.

He turned around. It was Felipillo, one of the two interpreters, the one that he didn't like.

'What is it?'

'An apple that grows in the ground and that we cook in the fire . . .'

'And is it good?'

'Of course! Why?'

Gabriel didn't reply. He simply couldn't feel at ease with Felipillo. It seemed that the interpreter's face was divided into two parts: the bottom part was dominated by a sensual mouth with greedy lips, and the top by small restless eyes. Felipillo always seemed to be looking everywhere at once, as though he were being hunted. Or else as if he was spying on everything. It was impossible to hold his gaze for even an instant. And as a result one always felt a little unsure of the truthfulness of his translation.

Gabriel followed de Soto. They saw signs of a recent and hurried departure. There were a few utensils left behind, wooden vases and earthenware jars, even food supplies. De Soto turned to him.

'What do you think?'

'We captured some of their scouts, but not all of them . . .'

De Soto's face lit up. Gabriel couldn't help but feel sympathetic towards this man whom he was charged with spying on, who knew it and who didn't hold it against him.

'In your opinion, who is more frightened, them or us?'

'We don't get frightened, *Capitan*.'

'That's what I thought you'd say.'

As they passed the last of the tent patches, the two men noticed a bird soaring through the uniformly blue sky. It was bigger than an eagle, bigger even than an albatross,

and as black as a storm cloud. It circled high above their
heads, and little by little it came closer to them. They
admired it silently. De Soto's gaze left it for a moment
and looked at three trees standing in the middle of the
plain.

'My God,' he said.

Gabriel almost shouted out in shock.

On the far side of the plain a slope rose to meet a sort
of natural esplanade that overlooked the valley. The first
houses of the town, with mud walls and straw roofs, stood
there.

The men were silent, fearing a trap.

Each man held in his mind's eye the image of the three
Indians hanging from their feet, swaying in the breeze. Their
eye sockets had been empty, and it was impossible for the
men not to ask themselves stupid questions: Was it men or
birds who had torn out their eyes? And had they been still
alive when it had happened?

All the horsemen instinctively clung harder to their saddles. Swords could be heard rattling as they were loosened in
their scabbards and a mood of doubt and fear had come over
the expedition. But also, as Gabriel was surprised to discover,
a feeling of joyful anticipation.

Although not as devastated as Tumbes, the place had
obviously been touched by the grim hand of war. Here
and there, walls had collapsed, as well as entire houses, and
roofs had burned. But life had returned here – destruction
had only been a temporary visitor. At the town's entrance,
one building stood out from the rest, a remarkably high
construction. De Soto signaled for them to advance into
the town.

The patrol marched alongside a long outer wall with doors
set in it. Gabriel now recognized the recurring style – doors

that were wide at the base and narrow at the top, occasionally topped with a lintel on which an animal had been sculpted, a jaguar or a snake.

There was nothing menacing about the noises floating over the wall. They heard the crying of children castigated by their mothers. Occasionally they glimpsed a man springing up behind the wall before he disappeared, terrified, behind the parapet.

Felipillo was marching proudly alongside de Soto, as though he were the Spaniard's leader. His eyes darted about more than ever.

The perimeter path ended in front of a thick, evenly built wall, with a large opening set in its center. The patrol emerged into a vast square, at the far side of which a sort of pyramid had been erected, although without a triangular peak. Instead, steps led up to a flat area at its top. De Soto raised a hand and brought the small column to a halt. A small group of men stood on top of the pyramid, silhouetted against the setting sun. They didn't move.

'Gabriel!' called de Soto.

Gabriel made his way to the head of the column.

'Go on foot with Felipillo, and bring me the chief of this town. Remember: we are their friends.'

'Do you think that they are armed?'

'It shall be your honor to find out.'

Gabriel dismounted from his horse.

'Go easy there, boy, go easy . . . you don't want to lose me, and I don't want to lose you either. If you sense the slightest threat, shout "Santiago!"'

Gabriel handed his reins to Sebastian. He felt heavy and self-conscious, and there was little strength in his legs. Felipillo fell in behind him, following closely on his heels. Gabriel's arm came flying back and struck the Indian's chest. He retreated, surprised and suddenly scared.

'Stay back!' hissed Gabriel. 'Stay back!'

The square was covered in a dust not dissimilar to sand. Thousands of tiny shells crackled under the men's feet. In the square's middle stood a fountain, an exact replica in miniature of the pyramid. The water flowed down its delicately chiseled steps. *Savages and monkeys were what Hernando called them*, thought Gabriel nervously. *'Well, they know how to carve stone, by God!'*

When they reached the base of the pyramid, Felipillo prudently kept his distance from Gabriel. Without even turning back to look, Gabriel mentally assessed the distance between himself and the reassuring protection of de Soto, the horses and the armed expedition. He climbed each step slowly, so as to save his breath.

Once on top, he was blinded by the sun directly in front of him. It had been concealed behind the pyramid as he climbed it. Curiously, he felt a great sense of liberation in his heart. He had a sudden recollection of the young monk in his jail cell in Seville telling him something. *What was his name again? Ah yes, Bartholomew.*

'You do not know yourself, I mean really know yourself, until they approach you with the irons white from the burning coals . . .'

Yes, there were moments in life when the true nature of one's character was laid bare.

Gabriel wasn't scared.

The man who faced him was dressed in a magnificent, strange fashion. He sported a sort of multicolored band about his head, a few colorful feathers sticking up from it. His red-and-black tunic reached down to his knees. An image of two feline creatures looking at each other was woven into the upper part, their tails curled and their mouths menacingly agape. The man wore expertly braided leather sandals on his feet.

'We are the ambassadors of Charles the Fifth,' began Gabriel proudly. 'We come from across the sea bearing the friendship of our King, the word of Christ, and His message of peace and love . . .'

Felipillo's vaguely unpleasant and harsh voice resonated from behind him. *'What can he be telling them?'* wondered Gabriel.

A long silence ensued.

Eventually, the man uttered something very quickly, in a deep voice that Gabriel felt betrayed fear.

'What does he say?'

'He says that he has been waiting for you.'

The man with the cats on his chest — Felipillo explained that he was the *caraca*, the chief — gave many signs of his deference and friendly intentions. He ordered that the Spaniards should be magnificently accommodated in his palace, and that servants should bring them food: maize, dried meats, types of biscuit. His assumed indifference to their strangeness was belied by his fear of the horses — he gave them a wide berth.

Despite their protestations — for the repeatedly deferred promise of boundless gold had heated their blood — de Soto ordered his men to explore each house in groups of six. He promised to punish seriously anyone guilty of pillaging, murder, or any kind of theft.

The palace was made up of an inner courtyard around whose four sides were rooms. That night, torches lit the walls on which hung tapestries woven from the same type of wool as the *caraca*'s tunic. Some had geometrical patterns, others images of flowers or animals.

Night brought with it a biting cold. The Indian servants had lowered their eyes when they had given the Spaniards blankets woven from a fine wool that was thin but which kept them wonderfully warm.

De Soto, Gabriel and Felipillo sat with the *caraca*.

At first, his face was impassive. He opened his mouth as
if to speak, but then closed it again.

And then his eyes squeezed closed and his facial features
grew furrowed with tension.

He was crying.

CHAPTER 38

Cajas: night of 10 October 1532

I T WAS A BLACK NIGHT. SEBASTIAN CROUCHED DOWN next to Gabriel who was lying on a soft mat, resting after the long and draining march.

A torch on the wall still burned, along with some braziers in the corner of the room. Gabriel was half asleep.

'I found some girls,' said Sebastian.

Gabriel sat up.

'What are you talking about?'

'Do you remember that big building we passed at the entrance to the town? Well, it's some sort of convent, and I tell you that it's full of girls – dozens, nay, hundreds of girls: old women, young girls, ugly ones, but also—'

Gabriel was now wide awake.

'And what happened?'

'Nothing, of course. What do you imagine? We would never disobey the Governor's orders, nor *Capitan* Hernando de Soto's!'

'I have my doubts about that, *amigo*.'

'We were happy just to drink a few cups of a strange fermented liquor that they make in huge quantities. Its corn flavor isn't that great but, by the devil, does it ever warm the cockles of your heart!'

A mischievous gleam in Sebastian's eye made Gabriel smile.

'And apart from drinking a couple of friendly cups?'

'Nothing, I tell you, nothing at all! There's a way of talking to girls that you whites will never understand, being such brutal beasts! With us, it's different . . . we have a subtlety that escapes you, and that allows us to—'

'Enough, Negro!'

'Well then, why don't you tell me what serious things you've been up to while I was carrying out extremely important diplomatic missions?'

Gabriel sighed.

'Their chief told us his dismal story.'

'Very dismal, I'm sure!'

'Even de Soto, who wasn't born yesterday, was moved.'

'Tell me about it all.'

'We've landed in the middle of a war-torn country. A war is being fought between two brothers who both aspire to be the only Emperor. And our *curaca* joined the wrong side.'

'The men we saw hanging from the trees?'

'They, and many others. He said that his town has been pillaged, partly destroyed, and that many of its inhabitants have been massacred, while others have escaped into the mountains. He said that the conquering king's army took many of his boys and girls, and emptied his stores. The camp whose traces we saw was that of the conquerors. They left upon hearing of our approach, and are now two days' march from here. But the chief is terrified of seeing them return to exact more vengeance. His tears told of cruel tortures beyond anything we've known . . .'

Sebastian stayed silent for a moment, and then said:

'What does de Soto say of all this?'

'He says that it's good news for us.'

*   *   *

It was a pathetic pile of gold. A few ingots, a few objects, some vases . . . the *curaca* seemed genuinely sorry not to be able to do better. He was seated on a stool, near the center of the esplanade, under the shade of an acacia tree. De Soto sat beside him and tried to look as though he was completely satisfied with the haul. His men, however, milled about the square grumbling among themselves, thoroughly dissatisfied. Lookouts had been placed atop the platform that the Indians called the *ushnu*. Felipillo was very agitated, interpreting more than he was asked to, asking questions of his own, and finally saying to the Spanish captain:

'He says that he can offer you something else.'

'What?'

'Women to cook for you as you march. He wants to be as hospitable as possible, and learn the customs of the Christian people. He asks for your friendship and protection.'

'Tell him that if he goes on like this, then he has nothing to fear from us.'

Felipillo interpreted. The *curaca*'s face returned to its usual noble aspect. His tone was once more that of a man used to commanding others.

'He proposes that one of your men go with his servants to the *acclawasi* – the house of young girls. They will bring some women to the square for you to choose from.'

De Soto motioned to Gabriel. A few of the men drew near, curious to know what was going on.

'Go quickly,' murmured de Soto, 'before our boys find out and go choose for themselves . . .'

Gabriel didn't dare tell him that their 'boys' had already visited the house, causing God knew what damage. He caught Sebastian's knowing smile.

He arrived at the house of young girls to find it in a state of confusion. All its inhabitants were gathered in the courtyard, from the oldest, who seemed to be in charge, to the youngest, some of them mere children. They all wore long tunics, either white or red, that revealed the grace of their movements as they walked. The oldest ones wore a kind of mantle over their shoulders, held together with delicately worked pins of gold or silver. Through the door of one room he saw their looms. The noise reminded him of a farmyard, and he could hear women crying and laughing nervously. The *curaca*'s servants barked some orders, and the women fell relatively silent.

When they returned to the great square, the Spanish men began to whistle and make catcalls. Some even tried to grab the girls, while others pulled the pins from their cloaks. Chaos threatened to erupt in the square.

Suddenly, a cry cut through the cacophony – a cry of rage from the top of the pyramid. A tall Indian, flanked by the lookouts, stood there. He was almost a head taller than the two Spaniards, and he exuded a noble aura. His tunic was lined with threads of silver and gold, and its geometrical motif was astonishingly accomplished. He wore those gold plugs on his ears that the foreigners had seen before, although his were much bigger.

'Enough!' yelled de Soto.

Calm returned to the square.

'Let him go!' shouted de Soto to the lookouts.

The Indian came down the steps of the pyramid as nimbly as a cat. He paced quickly across the square. He went directly to the *curaca*, completely ignoring de Soto, and said a few words to the Indian chief. He was clearly extremely angry. The *curaca* stood up suddenly, and muttered a few apologetic-sounding words.

De Soto gestured to the Spaniards not to move and to the *curaca* to sit down again beside him. He turned to Felipillo.

But the interpreter seemed terrified of the newcomer.

Sebastian had crept next to Gabriel during the earlier disorder.

'That long-eared bat looks like a handful,' he whispered.

The 'long-eared bat' now addressed Felipillo in an incensed voice.

'He says,' began the interpreter, 'that we're all going to die because we touched women belonging to his master. He says that if one more of us dares to lay another hand on him, his troops are going to come and massacre every last one of us.'

'I make no question of his power,' replied de Soto calmly. 'But he shan't see us die twice. Who is his master?'

'The King. The Inca of all the Incas.'

'What is his name? Where is he?'

Felipillo nervously translated this for the Indian nobleman, not daring to look at him directly. The newcomer spoke, a little calmer now.

'His name is Sikinchara. He is the ambassador of their king, Atahualpa, who is twenty leagues from here.'

Twenty leagues ... Gabriel felt his heart flutter. He remembered flashes of their voyage so far: waves as tall as castles, storms, hunger – and now he was only twenty leagues from finding either fortune or death.

'Tell him that our master, Governor Don Francisco Pizarro, emissary of our King, Charles the Fifth, wishes to invite him as a friend. Tell him that we hope that he will honor us by accompanying us and accepting our gifts and our friendship. Tell him that we have the utmost respect for him, that we had no intention of offending him, and that we fear and honor his master, who we know is a powerful ruler, and who we hope to help in his just and honorable war.'

Felipillo took a long time to translate this. His fleshy lips moved fast, and sweat trickled down his forehead. Sikinchara listened to him closely, all the while glancing around elsewhere, looking at the strange things that the foreigners wore, their horses, their swords on their belts, and their armor. He smiled several times while Felipillo spoke, visibly happy with what he was hearing. Then he made his reply.

'He wishes to meet our master, and has an important message for him, as well as gifts.'

'Tell him that he is three days' march from here, at Serran, and that I shall accompany him there and guarantee his safety as I would that of my own brother.'

Gabriel took stock of Sikinchara. He had never seen a face like his. Certainly, he had grown accustomed to the honey-colored skin and high cheekbones that distinguished the Indians, but he had never before seen such a fire in anyone's eyes. He glanced over at his own companions: their faces, their dress, their postures . . . they paled compared to the newcomer.

'Is the Inca of all the Incas in his capital city now, twenty leagues from here?'

Sikinchara obviously thought that the question was hilarious. He looked at each of the Spaniards, one after another, as if wondering if they were all as astonishingly ignorant as the one who called himself their chief. Then he gave a long answer.

'Their capital,' said Felipillo carefully, 'is beyond those distant mountains, more than a moon's march away. It takes a day to walk around it. People from all parts of the world live there. There are palaces of dead Incas, as well as many temples, and a herd of priests. The most important of these buildings contain uncountable quantities of precious metals, offerings to the gods.'

At the mention of buildings whose floors were made of silver, their walls and roofs of gold and silver layered together, all the Spaniards fell absolutely silent.

Gabriel was no longer listening.

His gaze had wandered away, beyond the esplanade, above the pyramid, beyond even the mountains among which the town was cradled. His mind floated over those distant mountains and their peaks of eternal ice, the sun illuminating the ice so that it looked like sheets of gold, and now he was in those palaces and those temples where gold flowed in rivers, he was in the world of his dreams, he was the first to discover it, he opened his arms and that world came to him. He no longer felt like a man, rather he had become an animal – perhaps a bird that soared through the air, or a cat that pounced nimbly and powerfully on its prey – or else he was a cloud, or a torrential river that raged down a mountainside and tumbled off a cliff, a jet of water screaming into the void . . .

He was free.

He hardly heard de Soto give the order to make ready for departure.

CHAPTER 39

Ybocan, November 1532

S IKINCHARA LAID OUT THE FLEMISH CAMBRIC, the stout boots, and the necklaces in front of Atahualpa. Then he carefully placed the two glasses near the Inca.

'Their chief, whom they sometimes call *capito*, sometimes *governo*, said this before giving me these gifts: "Tell your master that I am so eager to meet him that I shall not stop in any village along the way."'

The Emperor Atahualpa sat on a low bench. Anamaya stood in the shade behind him, intensely curious. Guaypar and Villa Oma looked at the objects without daring to touch them. The transparent goblets were the most amazing pieces of pottery that they had ever seen. Atahualpa reached out and touched one with his fingertips before lifting it and peering through its incredible clear clay.

'And did you give them my presents?'

'Yes, my Lord. They looked silently at the piles of stones representing a fortress. And they questioned me about the ducks stuffed with wool. I told them that when powdered they could be burned to produce a pleasant odor . . . but they made no comment about the tunics sewn with silver and gold.'

'Where did they say that they came from?'

'From across the sea. They are ruled by two kings: one who is charged with this world, while the other is master of the Other World.'

'The Tallanes say that they are half men and half animal, their upper parts like men and their lower parts like llamas. They used the word *viracochas* . . .'

Sikinchara burst out laughing.

'Beings from the Other World! I also heard that legend . . . but believe me, they are men just like us, my Lord. They are different in that their skin is pale and they have hair growing on their faces. It's true that some of them ride big sheep, which allows them to cross a prairie at great speed. But can you imagine those creatures on the Inca road? My spies saw them traveling, and they only just made it to Cajas!'

'They also say that they have fire-spitting sticks.'

'Those are one of their toys. They set a type of powder alight, and the stick makes a deafening sound. One is only surprised the first time.'

'And those things that they wear on belts . . .'

'Weapons like ours, my Lord, although a little lighter. When I saw how scared they were of us, I didn't think that they would be very useful in battle.'

'How many of them are there?'

'Less than two hundred. Many of them are weak and diseased.'

'Tell me about their chief?'

'He is a tall man, but old and thin. His hair is like snow. His eyes are as hard as a sling stone, yet he smiles a lot. All his captains obey him except one, his brother, who is always trying to appear as important as him. But despite his eyes and his hair, he is just an old man. His head will break with only one strike of a club. What's more, I think that he's frightened of you. He showed a lot of respect for you and assured me that they have come only to help you.'

Suddenly, Guaypar burst out:

'I too have seen these strangers, and although I don't have his experience and wasn't able to see them up close, I don't agree with Ambassador Sikinchara's opinion.'

Atahualpa turned to Guaypar.

'It's true that your experience doesn't match your courage, Guaypar.'

'These men are dangerous, my Lord. In our presence, they smile a lot and pretend to be our friends. But in the villages that they have passed through, they massacre the people with those weapons that Sikinchara calls not very useful. They pretend to want to help you, but they have promised others to help Huascar the Damned!'

'Well, it's now that he needs their help,' sniggered Sikinchara.

'What do you suggest, Sikinchara?'

'I suggest that we let them come to us—'

'Madness!' interrupted Guaypar. 'We should have annihilated them straight away! Before I retreated with my army from Cajas, I had them trapped. They were at my mercy. I burned to receive the order to attack, my Lord, but that order never came.'

Sikinchara grinned disdainfully.

'We shall destroy them when our Emperor commands it.'

'Do you doubt it, Guaypar?'

Guaypar hadn't time to reply. Villa Oma, mute until now, suddenly interrupted:

'I doubt it.'

Atahualpa raised his hand to impose silence on the court, so that he could reflect upon the situation. Anamaya glanced up furtively at him, and caught a distressing look of doubt deep in his eyes.

A rain cloud drifted over the *tambo*. While Atahualpa stayed alone in his palace, Villa Oma and Anamaya left the *cancha*.

Anamaya couldn't help but admire the harmony that prevailed in even the furthest corners of the Empire of the Four Cardinal Directions. This thought came to her whenever she saw the *kallanka*, the succession of grain pots along the bottom of the lower terraces where wheat and quinoa grew, the pots standing out in relief against the *huaca* on the mountain that loomed over Ybocan. After a few days' march they would be at Cajamarca, one of the principal towns of Chinchaysuyu, to celebrate Atahualpa's victory and the definitive reunification of the Empire.

But Anamaya noticed the dark clouds passing overhead, blocking out the sun.

'What do you think, Villa Oma?'

'I leave for Cuzco with a heavy heart, my child.'

'What do you mean?'

'I don't like what I heard this morning. Sikinchara is a loyal soldier, but I've always had my doubts about his intelligence. And Guaypar is brave, but impulsive . . .'

Anamaya said nothing.

'Atahualpa believes that a *pachacuti* is in the making, an upheaval that will make him master of all the world. But he does not read the omens, nor does he listen to others . . .'

'It's not his fault that others lie to him, or else have shells across their eyes . . .'

Villa Oma shook his head gloomily.

'What's more, I fear for Cuzco . . .'

'But why? Isn't Chalkuchima ruling the city?'

Villa Oma smiled bitterly.

'I think only madness is ruling that city. Yet I was the first to encourage Atahualpa to put an end to Huascar's follies . . .'

'And that was absolutely necessary,' said Anamaya, her tone consolatory.

'No doubt. Nonetheless, the seed of hatred has blossomed into a flower of insanity. Atahualpa is seeking a revenge as disproportionate as his brother's madness. He has ordered me to take charge of the Cuzco priests, the ones whom Huascar tried to reform. But I'm not going alone. General Cuxi Yapunqui is to accompany me, and he has strict orders: none of the usurper's people are to be spared, including their women and even the youngest of their sons. Only their virgin daughters will be allowed to live, and they will be added to the ranks of the Emperor's concubines. He particularly specified that his own brothers and sisters were not to escape his revenge. Entire clans are to be annihilated, including Huayna Capac's. I don't like it, Anamaya. It's not in accordance with the traditions of the Empire, it's unbecoming for an Inca nobleman, and it's offensive to the Sun God – it's more like the work of a chief of a lowly tribe wreaking vengeance through bloodshed and murder . . .'

'But Atahualpa could never have ordered such a terrible thing!'

Villa Oma regarded Anamaya with a look of tenderness unusual for him.

'You yourself saw what was done to Cataquil's idol! His hatred of Huascar blinds him. And ancient fears gnaw at him . . .'

'People have been looking at me for many moons now, waiting for me to speak a truth that I don't have, Villa Oma.'

'I know it, child, I know it. Nonetheless, my confidence in you – and you remember how long it was in the making – is absolute. I took you to the secret city, and now I will tell you a secret from the bottom of my heart: Atahualpa will not be the man who saves the Empire of the Four Cardinal Directions—'

Anamaya cried out, 'Who, then?' startling a young shepherd who was returning up the esplanade with his herd of brown llamas, the animals strolling elegantly along the edges of the wide terraces. Anamaya calmed down a little before asking again:

'Sage, who will save the Empire?'

'I don't know, child. We'll have to wait to find out. In the meantime you can help Atahualpa.'

'How?'

'He confides in you as he does in no one else. You are the one who foresaw his triumph, and who rescued him from prison . . . if only you could read his future, and tell him that it calls for peace in the Empire and his forgiveness of the Cuzco clans . . .'

'Are you asking me to "see" what I don't?'

Villa Oma looked at her intently.

'I am asking you to help us avert a disaster . . .'

'I cannot lie, Sage. I feel that if I did, then Huayna Capac himself would return from the Other World to punish me . . .'

Villa Oma let out a sigh.

'You must help us, *Coya Camaquen*!'

Villa Oma's voice quivered with concern. Worry burned in his eyes to a degree that Anamaya hadn't seen since the death of the Elders on the road to Cuzco.

'Well, you can help me too, Sage,' she murmured.

'What do you mean?'

'Return my golden husband to me: bring back the Sacred Double!'

'But that's impossible! He is where he should be: in the Temple of the Beginnings, near the desiccated body of the Emperor Huayna Capac.'

'If you want my help, Sage, bring him to me.'

'But do you realize what you are asking? A Sacred Double has never been separated from his Lord! Can you imagine what will become of us if anything happens to him?'

'I *must* be at his side, Villa Oma! I cannot lie. But the Sacred Double's force might help me hear Huayna Capac, or visit him in the Other World! It's the only way that I can regain my powers! Don't ask me why, but I'm sure of it . . .'

The sun had come out, the air had freshened, and nothing seemed capable of disturbing the peace.

'I'll send him to you as soon as I arrive at Cuzco, along with a strong escort.'

'Shouldn't we tell Atahualpa?'

'No. This had better remain between us, child.'

Anamaya acquiesced. Despite her victory, she felt weak in her legs as she returned to the palace. 'Growing up,' she told herself, 'means carrying secrets too heavy for one person alone, and feeling things that cannot be shared with anyone.'

Shadows grew long over the *cancha*. Anamaya was resting by herself, trying to shut out the noise of rejoicing in the streets. The *chicha* was already flowing freely. All the soldiers knew that the victory celebrations, which would coincide this year with the Capac Raymi festival, would be unforgettable.

A silhouette appeared in her doorway. Anamaya sprung from her mat and took refuge in the corner, almost knocking over a jar.

'Don't be scared.'

It was Guaypar. He wore a simple white *unku* and a belt decorated with yellow, red and orange geometrical patterns. She sensed a savageness in his stance.

'Don't be frighened,' he said again. 'I'm not here to threaten you, or to talk about love . . .'

She was deeply moved by the melancholy in his voice. She had never found the words to tell him that she understood him, and that she felt flattered by his attentions. *Perhaps even more so now?* The thought flashed across her mind, but she immediately dismissed it. In her heart she knew that she was the *Coya Camaquen*, the wife of the dead Inca.

'They say that I'm impulsive and unthinking, but I've thought more about it than Sikinchara. When I said that the strangers were dangerous, I meant it. But they wouldn't listen to me . . .'

'They're all celebrating the victory . . .'

'They shouldn't be. Believe me, the arrival of the foreigners has woken the sleeping anger of many of the tribes and villages. They may be only two hundred, but who serves them, who carries their loads and feeds them? Who have even fought alongside them? Indians – I know, we've subjugated some tribes with terror or diplomacy. But a spirit of revenge lives in them. That's why we must cut out their lying tongues, and be done with them before they go any further.'

'You told all that to the Emperor, but he didn't listen to you.'

'He'll listen to *you*.'

'Let me be, Guaypar.'

He moved closer to her and raised his hand. She held her breath.

'Don't touch me,' she whispered hoarsely.

'I'm not touching you.'

He ran his hand just above her skin, standing so close that she could hear his breath rising and falling, and could see his hand trembling. His hand followed the line of her body, always just above it. He got down on his knees and ran his hand down her legs, as if caressing her with superhuman tenderness. She felt her breathing grow shallow and speed up, and her heart beat faster than she would have liked, but she couldn't help herself.

When his hand arrived at her bare foot, he brushed her so lightly with his fingertips that she thought that she was going to fall to the ground. She felt his breath against her body, she wanted to scream out, but she couldn't—

'Guaypar!'

He jumped to his feet.

'Even if I wanted to forget you, I couldn't.'

He said this quickly from between clenched teeth, and

his violent tone belied the tenderness of his words. Then he left, shouldering his way past Inti Palla, who was staring at Anamaya.

'What was he doing?'

'He—'

Anamaya gathered her breath.

'He wanted me to talk to Atahualpa.'

'He was asking your feet?'

'He was begging me.'

Inti Palla pouted disapprovingly. Anamaya couldn't help but admire her. The *anaco* that fitted other girls like an oversized sack hugged her admirable body, leaving little to the imagination. Her long hair had been coiled into two big bunches held together by long, gold pins, one shaped like a snake, the other like a hummingbird.

'Perhaps he'll listen to you.'

'Me? Why?'

Anamaya was relieved. Inti Palla wasn't going to persist with the subject of Guaypar. She had obviously come to talk about something else.

'He hardly looks at me any more, he doesn't touch me . . .'

'There are many difficult problems facing the Empire . . .'

'Then why does he spend his nights with Cori Chimpu? Or with Cusi Micay?'

'He'll come back to you, Inti Palla. You're the most beautiful of all . . .'

Anamaya said this sincerely. Inti Palla sat cross-legged on the matting, and motioned Anamaya to sit next to her.

'You've become my only friend,' she said, 'and I was so horrible to you . . .'

'You, horrible? I don't remember that . . .'

Inti Palla laughed and put her arm around Anamaya's neck.

'Yes, horrible, because I was jealous of you and I thought that you wanted to take him from me . . .'

'Me!'

Anamaya was stupefied. How could a thin little girl from the forest possibly represent a threat to a young woman as accomplished and sensual as Inti Palla?

'Come closer to me,' whispered the concubine.

Anamaya felt a little confused, but allowed herself to follow Inti Palla's lead. The two young women lay down side by side. A gentle breeze ruffled the feather tapestry hanging over the door.

Now she had one arm around Inti Palla's curved shoulder and, for the first time in a long while, she felt free of the tension that had gripped her since the start of the war.

She ran a finger along her friend's cheek – and caught a tear.

She licked it off, and whispered tender, soothing words of consolation.

CHAPTER 40

Huagayoc, 11 November 1532

ONE AFTER THE OTHER, TWO BOLTS OF LIGHT-ning shredded the steel-gray sky. Thunder rolled down the slopes to the valley, as though hammering them.

As the noise died down, Pedro Martin de Moguer's dog could be heard barking madly at the sky, as though he saw an Indian in it and wanted to bite him. The lightning and thunder had excited the Neapolitan mastiff, which was about the size of a calf, white as milk but with demented black eyes – as demented as those of his master, a fat, square-jawed sailor who had joined the expedition with Benalcazar. For some reason unknown to Gabriel, de Moguer was always the first to volunteer for scouting missions. Did he hope to be the first to plunge his hands into the promised treasure chests?

Gabriel looked de Moguer and his great big mutt over with a barely disguised distaste.

They were marching ahead of the main group heading for Cajamarca by about a quarter of a league. But a few more turns up the switchback ridge and they came out above the fog gathered over the river, losing sight of the long and motley column still behind them.

'A hundred and eighty men and fifty-seven horses,' repeated

Pizarro over and over, not to draw attention to the ridiculously tiny number of men who had set out to conquer this vast and powerful nation, but rather to distinguish them from the latecomers who swelled their ranks every day. As they made their way towards the heart of the Inca Empire they were joined by hundreds of black or mulatto slaves arriving from the isthmus, and above all by thousands of Indians – the Tallanes, the Chimus, those whose villages had been burned because they had failed to pay the necessary tribute, all those who had reason to hate the Incas and hoped to wreak revenge upon them.

The path was narrow. It went up and up, sometimes running between a rock wall and the edge of a cliff, with just enough room for a horse and a man to pass side by side.

The advance guard had been traveling on foot for several leagues now. They marched with their necks bent down, their morions tilted forward on their heads to keep the rain from blinding them and their nervous horses' bridles passed back over their shoulders.

What was more, the horses were exhausted. They had been underfed during the last weeks and their ribs showed through their hides. The saddle straps had worn through their coats so that their bare skin shone in strips on their underbellies. On some days they had climbed peaks high enough to discover early-morning frost, and had caught cold with the effort of the ascent. On other days they had trudged through suffocatingly humid valleys where flesh-eating bats, as big as falcons, had attacked them, tearing into their flanks and necks . . .

The storm had turned the sparsely vegetated clifftop path into a morass of yellow mud. Flat rocks had been worked into steps, but now doubled as miniature cascades with water streaming furiously down them, making them dangerously slippery. The earth alongside the rocks had caved in from the rain and the heavy, dull impact of the horses' hooves.

The rumbling thunder had only just extinguished itself

when a fresh bolt of lightning ploughed through the clouds. This one ran horizontally along the mountain tops, like a gigantic snake attempting to link them together.

The horses shied and flared their nostrils. Their upright ears flicked back and forth nervously. With one gloved hand, Gabriel tightened his grip on his bridle, while with the other he stroked his horse's muzzle reassuringly.

But de Moguer's hound, maddened by the thunderclaps, began to howl furiously. It bounded out in front of Pedro, at the head of the expedition, and blocked their way, standing there with its chest heaving and its back arched. It howled at the distant valley lost in the rain, its demented eyes popping out of its head.

'Fucking dog!' shouted Pedro the Greek, turning towards Sebastian, Gabriel and de Moguer. 'Hold your horses, else that mastiff's going to panic them!'

The mastiff bared its fangs ferociously and seemed to hesitate for a moment before trotting forward through the streaming rain, its light coat now covered in mud. Then it growled and bolted between the men and their horses. It brushed past Pedro's horse's hocks, and the Andalusian jumped sideways and kicked up a rock.

The rock bounced three times and plunged into the ravine, falling as lightly as the rain.

'God's blazes, de Moguer!' exploded the Greek, his beard a sodden sponge. 'Control your fucking mutt! He's going to send us all over the edge!'

Fat de Moguer was bringing up the rear, sweating profusely under his rain-soaked cotton shirt, sodden despite the oiled-leather coat that covered him from shoulder to thigh. He was pathetically trying to lead his horse on. De Moguer had extorted the sorry creature from a delirious man afflicted with verrucas during the height of his agony. Now, the half-stolen horse was in almost as bad a state as its previous master. It had been wickedly bitten by vampire bats and its wounds had reopened, oozing a thick yellow pus that even the heavy rain did not dilute. Its breath was labored, and it moved only reluctantly. The horse bared its teeth and its eyes were wide with fever.

De Moguer called his mastiff to him. It ran towards him with its fangs bared and startled the horse. With a high-pitched neigh, the horse threw its head around and reared up on its hind legs. The bridle snapped out of de Moguer's chubby fingers, and the panicked horse almost knocked him over with a flailing hoof. And then the soft ledge under it, held together by only a few tufts of grass, crumbled under the animal's weight.

De Moguer let out a cry as his horse went down. The doomed animal pawed at the air desperately with its forelegs, and its emaciated belly hit a rock. Then the horse landed a kick on the cliff face, pushing itself away from it, and plunged into the abyss.

The horrified conquistadors looked on as the animal seemed to float in the air for a moment before hitting a tree with its flank and turning over in its fall so that it now plummeted head first. It hit a pile of rocks so hard that the stones loosened under the impact, causing an avalanche.

The horse had snapped its neck and died on impact, and its body rolled down the pile and came to a halt in a muddy ditch nearly two hundred feet below.

'By the Sacred Virgin,' muttered the Greek.

The men looked at the horse's body as though they expected it to rise up and walk away, despite the horrendous fall.

'I warned you!' growled the Greek.

De Moguer looked terrified, and shrugged his shoulders heavily.

'Bah,' he said, pretending to be calm. 'He was a sick horse. He wouldn't have lasted much longer in any case . . .'

But each man saw through the false indifference of his words. Sebastian chuckled:

'A horse easily acquired becomes a nag easily lost.'

De Moguer lifted his head, full of rage:

'You, nigger, you'd better watch—'

But he hadn't time to complete his slur. Gabriel pointed into the ravine and shouted:

'Look! Look at them!'

Around twenty Indians appeared from their hiding places under rain-laden branches, from the tall grass, and from behind boulders. They had succumbed to their curiosity, abandoning their invisibility to take a closer look at the dead horse.

When de Moguer's hound saw them, he instantly started barking again. The Indians froze in their tracks and raised their copper-coloured faces up towards the Spaniards. But there was too great a distance between them for either party to threaten the other. As one of the Indians stretched his hand towards the carcass, the Greek clicked his tongue and set out up the path again, saying:

'Of course they're watching us! What did you all imagine? Night and day, they're out there. While you're snoring, they're counting the hairs in your nostrils. They're like flies, and we've landed in the honey pot!'

They reached the summit at midday, all their nerves now thoroughly frayed by the presence of the invisible, silent Indians.

The rain finally stopped as they descended through a narrow valley. They passed by terraces of plantations, like soft green shelves held up by carefully hewn rock walls: from a distance the view looked like a giant fan with a river as its backbone. The storm clouds gave way to a sky bluer than the ocean that they had sailed across.

Two hours later they arrived at a village similar to all the others that they had seen thus far. This one had around sixty houses fanning out from a very large elevated square with a sort of truncated stepped pyramid in its center, like a throne for a giant. Its walls were perfectly aligned, and its stones so well set that no blade, no matter how fine, could be slipped between them.

On the top step was one of those temples where the Indians performed their bizarre pagan rituals. Here, they burned leaves and even their best-woven fabrics, while clucking away in their incomprehensible language and raising their arms to the sky. Here they worshipped the sun and the moon and God knew what other impious nonsense.

But if there was gold to be had in this village, or silver, or delicate pottery, or even emeralds, then the temple was where it would be.

As usual, the bearded strangers were met by a horde of children. They hid behind bushes and tree trunks to better spy on the horses and the metal swords — these never failed to amaze them. The adult villagers were usually more circumspect. They only came out of their homes or courtyards with the greatest precaution, and always after the *caraca*.

This time, however, when Gabriel and the Greek, who were riding side by side with their swords ostentatiously displayed across their saddles, reached the edge of the raised square they found the village's entire population gathered there. They also saw two palanquins decorated with gold leaf and a check pattern of blue and yellow feathers.

Gabriel heard de Moguer exclaim from behind him:

'Hola! Isn't that the big monkey of an ambassador we met before?'

In fact, it was Sikinchara, the Indian king's emissary, the noble and disdainful 'big-eared bat' who had come to meet the governor at Cajas, who was waiting for them in front of the villagers, surrounded by a small group of solders, llamas and servants.

His dress was even more splendid than the first time that they had met. A long, bright red cape, woven with subtle geometric designs, covered him down to his calves. Underneath, he wore a long tunic of some kind of shiny silk, checked with green, yellow, and crimson. A breastplate of hammered gold and silver covered his chest. His forehead and thick hair were hidden by a leather helmet topped with a line of short yellow and cobalt-blue feathers. He held a shield in his left hand, a shield covered with the same fabric as his tunic. His right hand was wrapped around a spear with a heavy bronze point.

He smiled at them. They approached cautiously, holding back their horses.

'A good or a bad surprise, I wonder?' murmured the Greek to Gabriel.

'We should stay on our horses until the Governor gets here,' he replied.

'He's grinning,' snarled Sebastian, making sure that they could all see the barrel of his harquebus. 'I hate it when they grin at me . . .'

'Well then, smile back at them,' sniggered de Moguer. 'With your nigger's white teeth, maybe they'll think that you're a cannibal!'

The faces of the Indians gathered around the Inca lord carried expressions of fearful respect. Only one man came forward with him, a man whom they had not yet noticed. He was younger and thinner than Sikinchara, and there was a feverish quality in his eyes. Like Sikinchara, he wore those bizarre plugs that pierced through his stretched ear lobes, marking him out as an aristocrat. His gold plugs were smaller than the ambassador's, however, and his dress less splendid. His helmet had fewer feathers, and his breastplate was modest. But he carried himself as haughtily as the other, and there was a restrained violence about him that drew one's eye.

The ambassador began to say something in his incomprehensible language when a gaggle of noisy children suddenly came running from the edge of the village.

And then everything happened in a blur.

The dog growled and bolted. De Moguer whistled ineffectually at it. But the mastiff didn't heed him and was onto the children in a few bounds. They were now paralyzed with fear.

The Indians began to shout out. Gabriel was already spurring his horse on urgently.

Sword in hand, he screamed at the hound to stop, but it didn't obey. Gabriel could hear Pedro coming up behind him. The hound took one of the children in its jaws, and the others scattered, wailing.

Blood gushed from the child's leg as Gabriel, lying flat along his horse's neck, made a scything cut with his sword. But he lifted his arm at the last moment. The dog was shaking the child in its jaws and had put the little boy between itself and Gabriel's blade.

Gabriel turned his horse around, and the beast released its victim long enough to take the boy by the throat. The child's unbearable screaming stopped instantly, choked off in a gush of blood.

Now they could only hear the hound growling as Gabriel lunged at it. This time his sword passed clean through the animal's chest and its point stuck in the ground. Gabriel furiously jerked it free and raised it in the air once more. He brought it whistling down on the monster's neck, severing its head, which rolled aside in a flow of dark blood.

Only then did the Neapolitan mastiff unlock its jaws and release the mutilated child.

* * *

'Lord Guaypar says that Don Gabriel is a brave warrior and a fine man.'

It was night, and fires burned all around Huagayoc, encircling the bustling village with light.

Don Francisco's troops had set camp less than an hour before, raising basic cotton tents or simply gathering around the fires in small groups. The Governor, his brothers, and his lieutenants had been invited by Sikinchara to a feast in the *curaca*'s palace.

And now that their stomachs were filled with roast llama, maize cakes cooked on hot stones, a variety of strange, round, light-skinned roots, and more beer than was healthy, they took to conversation.

The young lord who had come with Sikinchara spoke first. Then Martinillo, the second of the interpreters, stood up and spoke in a sing-song Castilian, as fluidly as the flames dancing above the braziers.

'Lord Guaypar thanks Don Gabriel for killing the wild creature that eats children . . .'

Earlier that afternoon, when Sebastian had gently lifted Gabriel, who was prostrated before the child's savaged corpse, and Pedro the Greek had held back de Moguer, who was enraged at having lost both his horse and his dog in one day, Gabriel's gaze had crossed the young Inca's, and a sort of complicity had sparked between them.

The villagers had run to the dead child, crying and moaning. The Indian lords, however, didn't move an inch, and watched the argument between Gabriel and de Moguer with cold curiosity.

But this young man, Guaypar, had suddenly taken a step forward. He had spread his hands and, keeping his eyes fixed on Gabriel, had said something, which of course the Spaniards hadn't understood. And now the young man stood up again and once more spread his hands, speaking in a very serious tone.

'Lord Guaypar says that perhaps Don Gabriel and he will be brothers in the Other World . . .'

Gabriel was embarrassed. But, prompted by a telling glance from the Governor, he stood up. He gave a flourished bow, as was done in Toledo, for he truly respected the Indian. He heard a cynical laugh from behind him:

'By the faith, brother,' sniggered Hernando Pizarro, pointing his glove at Gabriel, 'perhaps he's not a bastard after all? Dear Gabriel has found his family . . .'

A wave of laughter ran through the Spanish camp, and the two Indian lords furrowed their brows seriously.

'Quiet, Hernando,' said Don Francisco dryly. 'We are being watched. Martinillo, ask these princes for news of their King Atahualpa . . .'

Gabriel sat back down as the Indian spoke. He was furiously red with anger at the affront, and had to strain to stop himself from slapping Hernando. Captain de Soto tugged on his sleeve and whispered:

'Don't worry about that idiot Hernando, my friend. Ignore him, he's just a loudmouth and your silence will embarrass him – but watch your back over these coming days. De Moguer does not forgive, and he has as much sense as his dog that you killed. You can be sure that he'll seek revenge . . .'

A glance from Don Francisco silenced him. Now Martinillo bowed repeatedly to the Indian lord whose proud composure deeply impressed the gathering.

'He says that the Son of the Sun has won the war against his brother Huascar who wanted to split the Empire of the Four Cardinal Directions. His hundreds of thousands of soldiers were victorious. Huascar, the bad son and brother, is captured. Soon, he will be a pile of ashes.'

'I am happy to hear it,' said Don Francisco, his face impassive, 'and I'm happy to learn that your King is a great warrior.'

'Lord Sikinchara says that there is no greater warrior than

the Emperor Atahualpa because he is the Son of the Sun.
He defeated Huascar the Mad by encircling all his army in
a wall of fire that burned through the mountains for three
days. Huascar's men could no longer fight, or even breathe.
They begged for mercy, but the Emperor let them burn with
the grass beneath their feet. Our Emperor Atahualpa is good
to those who pay him tribute, and merciless to his enemies.
He is happy to meet the strangers in the Cajamarca plain. It
is only two days' march from here. He has food and lodging
for them.'

A heavy silence followed these words. Sikinchara smiled
at the Spaniards disdainfully, confirming the threat that they
suspected.

'I sincerely rejoice for your King's victory,' said the Governor,
his voice oddly quiet. 'I have no doubt that he is a great and
courageous prince. But it would be good for him to know that
my King is even greater, and rules a world much, much larger
than this one. He has more soldiers and servants than can
be counted. I have myself already defeated many princes as
powerful as King Atahualpa, even with as few men as I have
around me now. What's more, we have an even greater Lord,
whose kingdom is in the sky as well as on the Earth, and who
rules over the sun, the moon, and the stars as he does over
men, plants, and animals. It is He who gives us our strength.
That is why there are so few of us. Thanks to our Sacred
Lord, each of us fight like twenty or thirty ordinary men . . .
But please tell your King that we shall go to Cajamarca in
the next few days. If he wishes for peace, then I will be his
friend. But if he wants war, then I shall give it to him, as
I have to all those who have opposed me, my Emperor and
my God.'

Sikinchara's expression was no longer disdainful. Instead,
it was tense with hatred. The young Guaypar stood and
quickly whispered something that Martinillo didn't translate.
Then he looked at Gabriel once more.

He was no longer friendly. He looked like a man ready to fight to the death, one who would never bow before an adversary.

Gabriel stared right back at him. He forced a smile, but wondered whether in fact it looked like a strained grimace. He mouthed something that the other couldn't understand:

'I'm not scared of you.'

But he wasn't so sure of the truth of his words.

PART 4

CHAPTER 41

The Inca's baths at Cajamarca: 14 November 1532

THE INCA'S BATHS WERE JUST OUTSIDE THE CITY on a plain that was composed as much of water as of earth. If a newcomer were to stray from the royal road, he would certainly get lost in the swamps, or – worse – stumble into one of the burning hot sulfurous springs that flowed into cool rivers.

The Emperor and his army had pitched camp here, a forest of white tents covered the plain and the gentle slopes rising from it. It was nightfall, and the Inca was resting; he was into his third day of fasting.

All evening, Anamaya had glanced furtively at the high road above Cajamarca, a road paved with large and even flagstones. The strangers were due to arrive at any moment.

What would they look like?

Over the last few days she had listened to the returning spies make their reports. She was aware of Sikinchara's contempt, and of Guaypar's hatred for the strangers. She had heard descriptions of their remarkable ugliness, their heinous cruelty, their avidity and their lying tongues . . . Yet she looked forward to seeing them, to sizing them up for herself, perhaps even to understanding them.

'Anamaya?'

Inti Palla was approaching from across the yard and waved at her from beyond the fountain of mixed waters in its center. The concubine was sullen, and had been so ever since she had lost her position as the Emperor's favorite.

'He wants to see you,' she said, her expression deliberately blank.

Atahualpa was resting in the dark, shrouded in the perfumed smoke of burning spices, their heavy odors wafting through the humid air. Anamaya approached him with her head bowed and her back bent.

'Straighten up,' he said languidly, 'and look at me . . .'

She hesitated. It had been so long since she had heard that friendly order that the intimacy that had once bound them together now seemed only a faded memory . . .

'Straighten up,' repeated Atahualpa testily. 'We are alone!'

'As you wish, my Lord.'

'I do wish it! Come closer to me,' he added, less angrily, 'as you used to.'

She approached him carefully, avoiding his bloodshot gaze.

'You weren't Emperor back then, so—'

'Without you, I wouldn't be now . . .'

'My Lord, you've thanked me many times already, but it is Inti, Quilla and the Lords of the Other World who have made it so, not a child from the jungle . . .'

He smiled.

'Look at this feather, young woman. Here, take it . . .'

He held out the *curiginque* feather that he had lazily plucked from his royal headband. Anamaya shuddered involuntarily.

'Don't be frightened. Do as I tell you . . .'

Making sure not to touch the Emperor's hand, she took the feather and held it carefully between two fingers.

'It doesn't weigh much, does it?'

Anamaya shook her head. The beautifully colored plume felt weightless in her hand.

'So light, young woman, yet it weighs so heavily on my head that I can't sleep at night . . .'

She said nothing, moved by the trembling sincerity of his voice.

'Wasn't I justified in taking it from my brother? Didn't I do what was right? But I can never forget what they whisper behind my back: that I wasn't formally named as successor, that I broke with the orthodoxy—'

'But you won your place with your courage . . .'

'And because I trusted your visions, and because you transformed me into a snake . . .'

He laughed, a little bitterly.

'Have I ever told you why I refused my father when he named me as his successor?'

'Your mother was—'

'—Not from a powerful clan – that's what everyone says. But I know the real truth. I know it . . .'

He sighed, and reflected for a moment. Then:

'Four seasons after I successfully completed the *huarachiku*, my father, the great Inca Huayna Capac, gave me command of an army and sent me to put down a rebellious tribe. But I was defeated, and if my father hadn't come to help, my defeat might have turned into a complete rout . . .'

'Was it against the *Canari* Indians, near lake Yaguarcocha?'

He looked at her, stunned.

'You knew about that?'

She didn't reply. She remembered the first night the dwarf had come into her room and told her the secret . . . She thought of him now, her only friend during the darkest depths of her loneliness. She wondered if he was still alive . . .

Atahualpa stared at her, as if trying to read her thoughts. Then he waved his hand dismissively:

'Well, it doesn't really matter. I remember how foolhardy I was then, young woman, I remember the insane pride that swelled in my chest . . . I remember the numbness that gripped me after the defeat, after the death of those thousands of valiant warriors, killed because of my ineptitude. Above all, I remember the shame I sensed in my father's eyes . . .'

She could hear scuffling on the other side of the curtain that hung between them and the Emperor's servants, guards and women.

'Those eyes haunt me every night,' said Atahualpa dolefully.

'My Lord Emperor!' called a *yanacona*.

'Who is it now?'

'The *curaca* of Cajamarca.'

'I don't want to see him.'

'We told him that, my Lord, but he insisted.'

Atahualpa looked at Anamaya listlessly.

'The feather of power is so light and yet so heavy . . .'

The *curaca* approached, bearing a rock on his back, and began by begging the Emperor's pardon for disturbing his rest. But Atahualpa interrupted him in mid-sentence by raising his hand.

'Speak,' he said.

'My Lord Emperor, the strangers are only a day's march from here.'

'I want them to be amazed by the splendor of my Empire,' said Atahualpa imperiously.

'What are your orders, my Lord?'

'I want them to arrive in a deserted city, so that their hearts are crushed with fear, and their souls flooded with doubt . . .'

'When should we prepare this?'

The Inca screamed with rage:

'When did you say that they were arriving, you brainless fool? Tomorrow? Then it must be done tonight, of course!'

'Tonight,' repeated the *curaca*.

Later that night Atahualpa asked Anamaya to lie down next to him. At first she was worried that he might take her for one of his concubines. But in the end he only wanted to talk to her, and did so freely, endlessly, his voice murmuring like a brook. She had trouble reconciling this man with the one who had shouted so angrily earlier that evening, and with the one who had ordered the massacres in Cuzco.

Only three times did Atahualpa pause in his flow, and each time Anamaya thought that he had fallen asleep, hearing only his breath from the shadows. But whenever she made to leave, she heard his voice say softly, 'Stay, don't leave me now.' He sounded so deeply sad that her heart constricted.

Anamaya started telling him how much she regretted not being able to help him now as she had before, and how she lamented the silence of the Gods and Ancestors. He interrupted her gently.

'I want nothing of you but your companionship, girl with the sacred lake in her eyes. I have come to love you for yourself.'

As dawn neared, Atahualpa rose from his place on the matting next to Anamaya and kneeled in front of her. Without touching her, he moved his face just above the surface of her body with a sort of animal devotion, from her head to her toes, as if he hoped to find answers in her white *anaco*, in the snakes on her wrist, in her long legs or in her delicate hips . . .

She forced herself not to move as she felt his breath move up and down her body. When he had finished his voyage over her, the Inca put his face above hers.

'Your eyes,' he murmured. 'Your eyes . . .'

She closed her eyelids and felt his lips caress them as lightly as the brush of a butterfly's wing.

When she opened them again, he was gone.

CHAPTER 42

Cajamarca: Friday, 15 November, 1532

I T WAS MIDDAY, YET THE SKY WAS AS BLACK AS coal.

The forward party had reached a plateau overlooking the valley. Their horses sensed their riders' excitement. On their own initiative, and despite their fatigue and the altitude, they stepped onto the grass beside the paved road and broke into a trot. Not one of their riders – Gabriel, Pedro the Greek, Diego de Molina, and Juan, the Governor's young brother – even considered holding back his horse.

Gabriel filled his lungs with the crisp Andes air, and felt a little intoxicated. Suddenly he spurred on his horse, although not in a spirit of competitiveness or out of pride. The animal shuddered from its neck and withers to its rump. With an imperceptible shift in her pace, she accelerated into a gallop, lowering her ears a little and loosening the bit between her teeth. Gabriel heard laughter and people calling out from behind him, but he didn't turn to find out who it was. He lifted himself a little off his saddle to take the horse's stride more comfortably.

The horse's hooves thudded on the compacted earth, and the rolling sound of the gallop matched Gabriel's beating heart. He raced past a hedge of agave plants. The path bottlenecked between two walls, forming something like a gate. Beyond was a steep field strewn with boulders. Here, the panting horse scattered a herd of terrified llamas.

A few paces on, Gabriel was suddenly seized by an almost superstitious fear, so he reined in his horse and jumped down from his saddle. He walked up to a boulder bigger than a house and, leaning against it, he saw an incredible sight.

The valley below snaked between steep mountains that soared into the clouds. It was no wider than a couple of leagues, and was totally covered with tents.

Thousands of white tents were standing packed against one another like the feathers of an enormous wing, with specks of gold here and there. Standards fluttered from the tops of the tents, bursts of color in the white sea. Thick yellow plumes of smoke rose from the camp and gathered under the clouds. He could hear noises rising from the camp below, wailing horns, shouting.

'By the blood of Christ!'

Gabriel was so absorbed that he hadn't heard his companions join him, and Pedro's oath made him jump.

At the foot of a mountain across the valley, glimmers of light pierced through the dark day. Young Juan Pizarro was the first to react:

'Is that gold? Are those shining things gold?'

None of his three breathless companions said anything. Despite the sweat that trickled under their padded suits of mail, they all felt a cold shudder.

Looking closely, they discovered that the tents were not haphazardly placed, as they usually were in a Spanish military camp, but were arranged in careful squares and rectangles. From afar, they could see the logic of the bustling tent-city's layout, complete with avenues, lanes and squares. This movable city blocked their way south; it was more unassailable than any wall.

How many thousands of soldiers were waiting there?

Twenty, thirty, forty thousand?

Double that?

'My God,' thought Gabriel, clenching his teeth. 'And we are only a handful!'

'That damned Inca chose his spot well,' murmured Pedro, as though he was reading Gabriel's thoughts.

'Look at the city! The real city!' yelled Diego de Molina from behind another boulder.

It hugged a slope below them to the right, and stretched to the western shores of the marsh.

Its buildings of beaten earth and stone were in very good condition, with new and carefully maintained roofs. Nonetheless, the immovable city seemed tiny in comparison with the forest of tents stretching across the valley. They could make out less than a dozen *canchas* in it. A long adobe wall on the eastern border between the city and the plain marked out the main square.

A vast and empty square.

'That's where we're meant to go,' muttered Gabriel. 'But it doesn't look like anyone's expecting us.'

His chest hurt, and his breathing was ragged. He sat down on a flat rock. He tried to absorb the enormity of the scene that lay before him.

Finally, he had arrived.

Here he was on the edge of this ocean-like valley, a menacing, magnificent monster of a place.

Pedro and Alonso had frantically remounted and rushed off to tell the Governor what they had seen. The clouds behind Gabriel parted, and the sun struck the back of his neck at the same time as it flooded the white sea of tents below him with dazzling light.

With the sunlight came a strange dance of shadows in the valley below. The shadows undulated and snaked their way between the tents. They disappeared and reappeared, as though alive.

The ray of sunlight focused into a long, straight beam, like a giant spear. Gabriel noticed a new shadow forming at the bottom of the slope that led to the city, a slope that a moment before had been only a patch of grass scattered with rocks and a few shoots of those apples that grew in the ground. The form floated above the furrows and soft greens. He recognized it. It was the same shape that Sebastian had drawn in the sand at Tumbes. It was the same shape as the birthmark on his shoulder.

The shadow moved slowly. He saw it uncover its fangs, and its ears spread in the breeze. It had two yellow stones for eyes.

Gabriel felt the weight of the world on him, and he felt weary. Like a child lost in his own imagination, he closed his eyes – and the animal leaped into his dreams.

Pizarro's hand shook Gabriel from his reverie.

He jumped to his feet.

'Isn't it splendid?' exclaimed the Governor.

His eyes glowed with pride. Gabriel couldn't see a hint of doubt or fear in them. Pizarro's fingers squeezed his shoulder so strongly that Gabriel thought his bones would crack.

'Didn't I promise to bring you here? Didn't I promise you that?' he said, his beard shaking with excitement. 'Here we are, my boy! Here we are at last! They're all here waiting for us, and they're going to see what we're made of!'

The men arrived noisily, one after another. The horsemen arrived first, including the two younger Pizarro brothers, de Soto, and Benalcazar. Then came the foot soldiers, followed by the wounded and the sick, the bearers, the slaves and the Indians from the coast. How many were they in all? Perhaps two thousand, at the most. Opposite them, ten, twenty or a hundred times that.

The men caught their breath and silently absorbed the

scene for themselves. Some sat down on rocks and put their heads in their hands. Others simply stood in the breeze, filling their lungs as they looked down into the valley. No one spoke. Trumpets blared from a distant hill, as though sounding a sinister welcome.

The first to speak would be the first to admit the fear that was knotting his guts. No one wanted to confess to that.

Ambassador Sikinchara approached the Governor and stared at him with his black eyes. He wanted to enjoy the Spanish *capito*'s fear. He wanted to see him sway before the assembled might of his master. But instead Don Francisco Pizarro turned to Sikinchara and said with a friendly smile:

'Let's go to our meeting.'

A light and even rain fell on Pizarro's forces as they made their descent. The royal road descended so steeply that its wet flagstones were too slippery for the horses. However, no spoken order was needed for the horsemen to dismount and lead their animals on foot.

All of the troops avoided looking down into the valley. Occasionally trumpets sounded from the immense Inca tent-city. But the Spaniards were making too much noise of their own to hear.

Most of the Indians had stayed at the top of the mountain, and only the servants and bearers had followed the Spaniards. Don Hernando had claimed the right to go on ahead, along with the Inca ambassador Sikinchara, a dozen foot soldiers and five capable horsemen. Pedro the Greek and Sebastian were among this forward party, as was de Moguer, now on foot and without a horse or a dog. Gabriel had been asked if he wanted to join them. But it didn't matter to him. He was happy to be alongside the Governor, two or three hundred paces behind.

The herders had all deserted their reed and mud-walled

huts along the royal road. The fields were empty. No woman or child cried out. The purple quinoa stalks wilted and broke under the weight of the rain.

Further down, the royal road narrowed and now became so steep that stairs had been built there. The huts gave way to adobe houses, and even stone ones. But these too were empty.

The river's thundering din was overwhelming. A thick fog, like fire smoke, rose from the marsh that stretched from the bottom of the northern mountain to the Inca's bathing houses.

Gabriel noticed that the Governor hadn't taken his eyes off the Indian city.

It was much bigger than it had appeared from the mountain top. They came across a fortress hidden in a fold of a valley, beyond the houses and streets that fanned out from the huge square.

The Spaniards instinctively slowed their pace. Don Francisco turned to Gabriel and said in a voice loud enough for all to hear:

'It's only a rock.'

And it was true. It was only a cone-shaped rock, perfectly round. It appeared dark yellow and black in the falling rain. A spiral path had been carved to its summit. It looked like a snail's shell. A narrow building sat on top it. Don Francisco pointed at it with his gloved hand and said:

'That's where we'll put the Lord's crucifix and plant a bed of roses for the Sacred Virgin!'

There was some laughter from the ranks, but it didn't last. Friar Vicente Valverde crossed himself and murmured:

'May the Lord hear your words!'

'He hears me,' smiled Don Francisco.

As the Spaniards and their bearers came into the first street, their horse's hooves clip-clopping against the expertly hewn flagstones, the rain suddenly gave way to hail. Thousands of small white hailstones drummed against their iron morions and covered the ground in white. Their noses and cheeks froze in the cold.

Finally they entered the great square. It was immaculately white, without a single trace of footsteps anywhere.

It was immense, much bigger than any of the sacred Inca squares that they had previously seen. It was even bigger than any *Plaza Real* in Spain, thought Gabriel with a shiver that wasn't caused by the cold.

Its shape was irregular: a truncated rectangle developing into a trapezoid and then a triangle.

An adobe wall higher than a man and at least five hundred paces long divided it from the marsh to the south. Magnificent buildings with many doors stood around its other sides. Each was very wide, at least two hundred paces across. And on the left was another of those giant stepped pyramids where the Indians went to worship their gods and perform their pagan rites.

The hail ended as suddenly as it had started. No one moved. Don Hernando and his men had not advanced any further. The only sounds were the prayers that Friar Vicente Valverde murmured to himself.

A dog barked from beside a huge trapezoid door across the square that opened onto the vast valley. It was an Indian dog, slight like a hare hound, but with hair so short that it seemed to have none at all. The Neapolitan mastiffs barked back at it, but were immediately silenced by their masters.

It was the hour of vespers. Yet the sky was so heavy with clouds that it was as dark as though the sun had already set.

The Spaniards' expressions were severe and fixed. Gabriel knew the look of fear, and what he saw around him was more than fear.

Of course, none of them had forgotten about the tens of thousands of Indians in the valley on the other side of the wall. But every man knew from the bottom of his soul and in the blood that ran through his body that this day would be like no other.

Yes, this November day – a strange summer's day in this latitude – would be a day of truth. A day after which nothing would ever be the same for mankind.

Only the Governor's face remained completely impassive.

After having considered the square, he turned to Ambassador Sikinchara as though he was expecting something from him. But nothing came. The noble Indian's proud lips didn't move. His eyes gave nothing away.

Amid the one hundred and seventy Spaniards, he and his servants were the only ones dressed in bright colors. His gold ear-plugs shone like bright stars in the odd and unseasonably wintry light reflecting off the carpet of hailstones.

Sikinchara walked with an even and powerful gait, his face closed but serene. How could the Governor's brother – noble *hidalgo* that he was – think him arrogant or ridiculous, wondered Gabriel.

Don Francisco spurred his horse and trotted to the base of the pyramid. His horse's hooves crackled on the hailstones, leaving a trail.

He pulled on the reins, and did a wide turn to face his still immobile men. He shouted:

'Ambassador, let Prince Atahualpa know that His Majesty Charles the Fifth's envoy awaits him here. And may he inform us where we are to stay!'

Emperor Atahualpa's skin was still red from the very hot bath he had taken during the hailstorm. Now he rested in a fine-webbed hammock between two pillars of carved wood in a room opening onto the courtyard. Through his half-closed eyes he watched the hailstones melt and the mist rise from the scalding hot water of the fountain.

Inti Palla fanned him to keep him cool in the sticky heat that had returned immediately after the hailstorm. The air was suffused with sulfurous vapors.

Anamaya was sitting with some of Atahualpa's wives a little further back. She wondered if he was dozing after his bath, or if he was thinking, as she was, about the newcomers that they had just seen arrive across the valley.

There had been too little light and, as the strangers had been too far away, they had not seen them clearly. But they had been able to watch their cortège descend the royal road between the potato and quinoa fields.

It was not a big cortège, nor as big a group as Sikinchara and Guaypar had said it was. It was a black and gray strip amid the soft green fields. It was a procession without any of the colors preferred by the Son of the Sun. It was like a lusterless earthworm slithering down to the floor of the valley.

Perhaps the Emperor was asleep after all, because he didn't move at all when noises in the courtyard announced Guaypar's arrival.

Guaypar prostrated himself under the hammock for a moment, waiting for the Emperor to speak. But as he said nothing, Guaypar respectfully announced:

'My Lord, Sikinchara's messenger has arrived. The strangers are in the square.'

Atahualpa let some time pass before asking:

'What are they doing?'

'They are at the foot of the *ushnu*, congregated around their *capito*. A few seem to be searching the streets for hidden soldiers. Sikinchara says that they are frightened.'

Now Atahualpa opened his eyes and smiled at Guaypar.

'Fear does not always have the appearance of fear, brother Guaypar. Has Ruminahui done the necessary?'

'At dawn, my Lord. Twenty thousand soldiers surround the city. They are invisible, hidden behind hills, trees, and in the long grass. The strangers are trapped. You have only to give the order, and we shall burn them alive tonight, like guinea pigs!'

'You are hungry for blood, Guaypar. But you know my decision. Our Moon Goddess does not like to see us fight at night, and Inti wills that I finish my fast. We shall do it tomorrow. It shall be a great celebration for Inti's children.'

'It shall be as you command, my Lord,' said Guaypar, a little regretfully.

'Let Sikinchara tell the strangers to stay in the square tonight. Let him tell them that perhaps they shall have the honor of prostrating themselves before me tomorrow.'

As Guaypar left, Inti Palla accidentally brushed Atahualpa's face while fanning him with feathers. He propped himself up on an elbow and growled furiously. Inti Palla let out a little cry, dropped to her knees, and quickly retreated.

As another concubine took her place, Atahualpa's bloodshot gaze crossed Anamaya's, who looked directly at him.

'They're just men, aren't they, *Coya Camaquen?* Viracocha has sent no one to help me, and soon I must go to Cuzco and pay my respects to my ancestors.'

His voice was bitter, and Anamaya found no reply. She reflected on the night that she had spent beside him. Perhaps it had been a dream after all . . .

Gabriel pushed aside a tapestry with his sword. A little light slipped into the large, warm room that was filled with the smell of earth and grass. It looked empty.

He was about to let the tapestry fall back down over the door when he heard a little squeak. A tawny guinea pig trotted out from behind some pots. Then another, then ten more, all scurrying out suddenly and squeaking.

Only then did Gabriel notice two eyes shining in the darkness of the opposite corner of the room. They belonged to someone half hidden behind fagots of wood.

He saw a tiny foot, then a tiny hand: a child!

Gabriel smiled with relief. He switched his sword to his left hand, bent low and said softly:

'Hello there, boy.'

The child was petrified. His eyes were wide open. He was a beautiful boy with silky cheeks and lips as well defined as a woman's. His thick black hair framed his even and delicate face. As Gabriel crouched down, his leather boots made a cracking sound and the tip of his sword clanged against his spurs. He ungloved his right hand and gave a broad smile.

'Don't be scared,' he said as gently as he could. 'Don't be scared, little one . . .'

Gabriel's voice sounded strange to his own ears. He hadn't considered what he looked like to the child, with his dirty and still-wet padded coat of mail, his helmet, the beard that covered his face, and his sword.

The guinea pigs were squeaking madly and running all over the place.

'Don't be scared, child,' repeated Gabriel. 'I'm your friend . . .'

As the child still hadn't moved at all, Gabriel straightened up and stepped towards him with his hand outstretched.

The boy bounded across the room like a cat.

'Boy!'

Gabriel was too surprised to make a move, and watched as the child screwed up his eyes and clenched his little fists in a final attempt to summon up courage, then charged directly at him, just missing him before fleeing out the door. Gabriel turned around and watched the child who was already running across the courtyard. He jumped onto a woodpile and vaulted over the outer wall.

Framed in the courtyard's doorway, Sebastian let out a little laugh.

'But I didn't mean him any harm,' protested Gabriel as he put his glove back on.

Sebastian stopped laughing. He looked straight into Gabriel's eyes.

'When I was a kid, *I* always ran from Spaniards,' said the African. 'And most of the time, my friend Gabriel, I had good reason to.'

'So?' asked the Governor when they had returned to the square.

'There aren't any soldiers,' announced Gabriel. 'Just a few kids, women and old folk.'

'No men and no warriors except a couple of guards in front of those depots full of all kinds of stuff,' added Sebastian.

'They seem unconcerned,' continued Gabriel. 'The women go on weaving as if we weren't here.'

'How many?' asked the Governor.

'Four or five hundred, no more.'

Sebastian pointed at a high wall to their left:

'That's the palace,' he explained. 'There are servants in it, and its yard is unlike any of the others. Its walls are painted and there are snakes engraved in its stones.'

'We don't care about snakes,' said Don Hernando in a grating voice, his horse twitchy under him. 'Has "his Lordship" Gabriel found anywhere for defensive emplacements?'

'Up there, Don Hernando,' replied Gabriel, not taking the bait. 'The outlook is perfect from the top of that rock, you can see the town and the plain and even the road that leads to the tent-city and the Inca's dwellings. It is large and paved, and lined with trees up to the marsh. They can't take a step towards us without our seeing it . . .'

'Of course you can see well from up there,' grumbled de Moguer. 'You don't need to climb it to realize that.'

'Don Francisco,' interjected Captain de Soto, 'all of this bothers me.'

'Ah?'

De Soto pointed at Ambassador Sikinchara, who was talking with some newly arrived runners.

'This is too much like a trap for my liking,' said de Soto in a low voice. 'Not one warrior in the whole place! The entire city, just for us. We're given a perfect lookout point from which to see nothing, we're enclosed by walls with tens of thousands of soldiers on the other side. No, Governor, I don't like it at all. The Indians are what they are, but these ones know how to fight, and are used to winning battles. Don't underestimate them.'

'De Soto is right,' admitted Don Hernando, 'we know what those birds' songs are worth. They speak only lies.'

'We could place the falconet up there, my Lord,' said Pedro the Greek, pointing at the flat-topped pyramid. 'That would give us a good range.'

They all looked together at the summit of the *ushnu* and the steep steps leading up to it.

'Yes, said Don Francisco at last. 'Take as many men as you need to get it up there before nightfall . . .'

'But it won't be enough,' growled Don Hernando, again looking darkly at Gabriel. 'That fool doesn't know what to look for. Look how the city is laid out on the slope. They could surprise us from over there, and come at us through the streets without our even realizing it.'

'Well then, brother,' said Don Francisco calmly, as Gabriel once again made no reply to the insult. 'If it makes you feel safer, why don't you guard that approach yourself?'

Don Hernando stammered something inaudible and yanked too hard on his reins, causing his horse to sidestep and bare its teeth. Gabriel stared at him, smiling wryly beneath his beard. Don Hernando chose three other horsemen to go with him, and their horses' hooves clattered as they trotted away.

The men were tense. The captains' anxieties were like sand grinding between their teeth. Only Friar Vicente Valverde seemed calm, wandering away towards the group of bearers to check on the trunks carrying the big crucifix, the holy water, and his robes for Mass.

Hardly a moment after Don Hernando and his men had disappeared through one of the doors off the square, Martinillo approached Don Francisco's horse and bowed respectfully.

'Lord Sikinchara has received a message from Emperor Atahualpa,' he announced.

'Ah? And what does he say?'

'The Emperor Atahualpa wishes his Lordship the Governor to know that he and his men may stay in the square tonight, and that the Emperor will visit him tomorrow morning . . .'

Gabriel caught Martinillo's hesitation. But the young interpreter lowered his eyes and continued:

'The Emperor Atahualpa says that he is fasting to thank his father the sun for his victories, and that he cannot leave the sacred baths. He says that he will come tomorrow to . . . to meet with his Lordship the Governor.'

Don Francisco's anger might have been feigned as he turned towards Ambassador Sikinchara. Gabriel thought he saw amusement as much as fury in the Governor's eyes.

'Stay in the square! Here, under those rain clouds? This is not how things are done, Ambassador! His Majesty's envoy does not sleep under the stars when there are magnificent buildings all around him. Nor does he like to be kept waiting!'

As Martinillo translated this, Captain de Soto declared:

'Don Francisco, let me go to the Inca's camp, and find out what he wants from us.'

'It's dangerous, de Soto. You'll be at his mercy.'

'No more dangerous than waiting here like cattle in a slaughterhouse. And we'll be able to see the Emperor and his camp up close. I'll take twenty horsemen, to frighten them . . .'

'Above all, don't dismount to talk to him. But be respectful. We mustn't offend him, de Soto, but be firm. Take the ambassador with you. I don't like having him here watching us. And take Felipillo to interpret. He's less honest, but he's smarter than Martinillo. We must win over the Inca as much as make an impression on him. We must make him understand that everything can happen peacefully!'

De Soto nodded, smiling again, feeling happier at the prospect of action.

As he chose those who would accompany him, Gabriel pushed his horse next to the Governor's:

'My Lord, the fool that I am asks your permission to go. Perhaps there are things there that I will know to look for.'

Don Francisco sized him up and furrowed his brow.

'Don't make me lose a horse,' was all he said in reply.

He turned to de Soto and added grumpily:

'Don't forget to tell the Inca that I don't sleep under the stars. It's important . . .'

'It's not the first time, Governor!' replied a smiling de Soto. 'I know how to handle myself.'

Don Francisco kept his eyes fixed on de Soto as he grabbed the captain's bridle and said:

'It will be the first time, Captain de Soto, that you will be alone among thirty thousand Indians. Your neck will never have been so exposed. May God bless you, my friend!'

'I know what it is,' said de Soto, still grinning. 'You're still worried that I won't come back to you, Don Francisco!'

Gabriel kept his smile to himself.

CHAPTER 43

Cajamarca, 15 November 1532

B Y MID-AFTERNOON, THE WESTERN HORIZON HAD cleared. The valley, glistening from the rain, shone under Inti's caress. A soft fluid light flooded the valley from its mountain crests to its deepest depths. Larks and windhovers circled over the marsh rushes and gorged themselves on insects.

Throughout the tent-city, women stoked the fires to heat soup and cook corn biscuits.

Atahualpa had drunk a lot of *chicha* during the final ceremony of the day. Now, he had only women around him, the *curaca* of Cajamarca and all the oligarchy having left the court, leaving only servant girls behind. Everything was calm.

But then another *chasqui* arrived. He ran up to Guaypar and announced that one of the newcomer's officers and a band of mounted warriors were coming to greet the Emperor. Sikinchara was with them.

This time, Atahualpa came out of the bathing enclosure. He climbed to the top of a hillock and looked towards the city.

It took him a while to spot them. Then suddenly he clicked his tongue and pointed at the black dots following the road along the edge of the marsh.

He turned to Anamaya.

'Look,' he said with unexpected gentleness. 'You'd think that they were huts walking across the plain.'

His peaceful smile was full of tenderness. For an instant, he looked like a father happy to be sharing some time with his daughter.

Then he turned to Guaypar:

'Brother Guaypar, have my guardsmen come to the court, as well as all the priests and noblemen. Tell each of them that the Son of the Sun does not wish to see the slightest hint of fear in anyone.'

The causeway was wide enough for five of the Spaniards to ride abreast. It led across the plain, through the swamps, towards the countless tents. Indians had come out to see them, and massed into gangs along the low walls. This time, they made no effort to hide.

All of them gazed out from behind stony faces, expressing no emotion or curiosity.

De Soto grimaced as he turned to Gabriel and said exactly what was going through Gabriel's mind:

'They always look like they know something we don't, don't they?'

Despite their anxiety the Spaniards moved along at a slow walk, keeping pace with the ambassador on foot. They rested the staves of their lances on the points of their boots. After half a league at this rate, the road suddenly disappeared into a swamp. There was only a narrow path through the rushes. Gabriel started out on it, but pulled his horse back after only a few strides.

'It's much too marshy,' he said to de Soto. 'We might bog the horses down and arrive covered in mud.'

'Or break our horses' legs . . .' added de Soto.

'The Powerful Ambassador suggests that we follow that path over there,' intervened Felipillo.

Ambassador Sikinchara smiled at them and pointed at a rocky ford between the reeds.

'The bugger let us get ourselves caught in a bog!' grunted de Soto, and ordered them to follow the ambassador.

'And now,' mused Gabriel, 'he knows where our weak spot is. If we have to retreat or if they suddenly startle the horses, we'll be taking a bath that we'll never get out of.'

De Soto came up beside him. Their gazes met.

Both were thinking exactly the same thing.

The women finished dressing the Emperor.

The sound of the soldiers taking their places around the basin of hot water could be heard from the courtyard.

The whole camp was hustling to the Emperor's orders.

Officers harried their troops to form tight ranks, as during wartime, with their clubs and slingshots in their hands. Those closest to the royal road, between the burning river and the marsh, looked furtively to the north. Beyond the swaying reeds, they could see men with giant silver cups on their heads and with faces hidden behind hair. They seemed taller than the reeds . . .

The women had abandoned their cooking. They held back their children from running through the tent-city with shouts, cuffs on the ear and caresses. The children were crying. They wanted to see the strangers too.

Atahualpa ordered that the shirt given to him by the strangers be attached atop a long pole and flown above the *cancha*'s walls, like a standard taken from a vanquished enemy.

Then he noticed Anamaya, who had been silent for a long while. He said to her:

'Stay close to me, *Coya Camaquen*, and be my eyes. Look carefully at the strangers' faces. Maybe it will be enough for them to see the color of your eyes to realize that they are nothing.'

Anamaya knew that he hadn't said this ironically. She sensed only loneliness and fatigue in his voice.

After having forded yet another river, the Spaniards were close enough to make out the buildings where the Inca was staying. They could now see the strange coned rock rising from Cajamarca, a sea of white tents standing between them and their companions.

'Captain!' cried one of the men of the escort. 'Look there! Look at the standard flying over the Inca's lodgings!'

Gabriel, like everyone, looked in the direction that he was pointing. High up on a pole, though hardly moving in the light breeze, he saw the silk shirt that the Governor had given to the Indian king.

De Soto swore. He raised his lance and signaled them to stop. He called Felipillo and told him to ask the ambassador to go on ahead alone and warn his master of the foreign lords' arrival.

Felipillo hesitated.

'Tell him, you animal!' de Soto said, angrily raising his voice.

As usual, Sikinchara stared at the captain while listening to the interpreter.

When Felipillo had finished, Sikinchara smiled broadly, revealing his white teeth. Without further ado, he raised his hand as if to wave goodbye, and barked orders at the bearers.

When he had moved away a little, Soto asked Felipillo:

'Why was he smiling like that?'

The same kind of smile stretched across the interpreter's lips:

'Oh . . . because he is very proud to be the one to announce your arrival to the Emperor.'

Once again, de Soto's gaze crossed with Gabriel's.

'We shall soon find out who's the better liar, him or us,' sighed Gabriel.

Sikinchara prostrated himself as soon as he entered the court. With his head lowered, he made his way across the garden, around the basin, passing before the soldiers and Powerful Noblemen, before once again prostrating himself behind Emperor Atahualpa who was sitting on a stool under an awning.

Despite having his forehead in the dust, he could feel everyone looking at him, and he fairly bristled with pride.

'Come before me, Sikinchara,' ordered Atahualpa, and tell me who the strangers are who have come here.'

'They are thirty men led by one of the *capito*'s captains,' replied Sikinchara in an even voice. 'There are some riding their beasts, carrying spears and with shields attached to their seats. It shows that they are weary, my Lord, and scared of you.'

'What do they want?'

'To invite you on behalf of their *capito*, who has stayed behind in the square at Cajamarca. They'll tell you this through the Indian who speaks their language.'

Atahualpa asked no more questions.

Anamaya could tell that the Emperor and the noblemen were nervous. The sky above the courtyard had turned as crimson as his eyes. It was the hour when Inti turned from gold to red.

But in truth, it wasn't the Emperor Atahualpa who was the most scared. She felt the cold hand of fear grip her, and she trembled as though the afternoon's hail had smothered her soul and still lay there, without melting.

Why?

If only the Sacred Double was around . . .

Why did she feel her stomach knot when the strangers

arrived? They were only a handful of men, while there were more than a hundred soldiers in the courtyard alone, and thousands upon thousands in the camp outside.

Sikinchara asked in his indolent voice:

'What are your orders, my Lord?'

'We shall hear them out. And we shall kill them tomorrow. Like this!'

Atahualpa thrust his hand into the air and closed his fist, as though catching a fly.

This move pleased him, and he did it again, smiling.

'Like this!' he repeated.

Someone laughed in the courtyard. Then someone else joined in. Then another. Then more. The Emperor began to laugh as well. And all the Powerful Noblemen broke out in a great guffaw. The soldiers, concubines and servants laughed with their mouths wide open, and threw their heads back so that their laughter could rise to the reddening sky along with the vapors from the baths.

With tears of mirth trickling from his bloodshot eyes, Atahualpa once more crushed his imaginary fly.

'Just like that!' he said.

The causeway came to an abrupt end.

They had reached a narrow bamboo bridge that spanned the river. The water was so hot that it was actually boiling in places.

The white tent-city began about ten paces back from the opposite shore. The Indian soldiers were formed up in perfectly aligned groups of fifty. With the points of their spears planted in the ground, they watched the Spaniards.

As always, their faces betrayed no emotion. They looked completely unfazed and fearless.

Gabriel shifted in his saddle and sliced the heads off a couple of reeds with his sword. He threw them into the steaming water. The plants curled up and sank, little black shreds carried away by the current in the blink of an eye.

De Soto, who had watched him do it, whistled between his teeth.

One of the escort pointed at the earth-covered bamboo bridge and muttered:

'There's no way we'll make it across that. It'll collapse under the weight of the horses and we'll be cooked for sure!'

An old Indian lord, his ears and neck covered by enormous gold ornaments, approached the opposite bank of the river. Gabriel, like the others, contained his surprise. Apart from the extraordinary feathers upon his head, the man seemed to be entirely covered in gold: they saw gold bracelets on his wrists and large gold rings on his fingers when he pointed downstream.

Felipillo translated the golden lord's few words:

'The Powerful Lord says that you may ford the river a bit further down. It is shallow enough there for men to wade across it.'

De Soto motioned to Gabriel and three other horsemen:

'Follow me! And you others,' he added for those left behind, 'don't let yourselves be seduced by all that gold. Watch those troops. If they move an inch, shout out as loud as you can, then join us.'

The crossing was at a point where the hot stream converged with a cold river. While the water was no longer scalding hot, it was still warm enough for steam to rise from it.

On the opposite side, a few large stone steps led to the Inca's lodgings. Two squads of soldiers, formed up in squares and perfectly disciplined, guarded the entrance.

The swirling water and rising sulfur bothered the horses. They stepped back from the edge and thumped the ground with their hooves. A few Indian lords appeared, as resplendently covered in gold as the first, and watched the foreigners.

De Soto was trying to head his horse into the river, but the beast snorted and resisted, and finally reared up on its hind legs, neighing furiously.

Gabriel placed the butt of his spear on his boot and calmed his own horse. He thought about Don Francisco: if he were here, the Governor would certainly launch into the river without a second thought. With three kicks of his heels, he would be on the other side!

But just as he was about to do exactly that, a loud guffaw burst from inside the Indian king's lodging.

Laughter spiraled through the air, as though intended as a deliberate affront to the Spaniards.

So, shouting out to Felipillo who was riding double behind him, Gabriel spurred his horse till it bled. De Soto, moved by the same indignation, launched his horse into the river. The others followed. Upon touching the hot water, the animals leaped as if going over a wall. They kicked and reared, but they made it across. When they came out on the other side, their iron shoes sparked against the stone steps, and steam rose from their coats.

For the first time, Gabriel saw amazement on the open-mouthed warriors in front of him.

He looked at de Soto. The captain shook his head, and laughed.

The Spaniards entered the Inca's court at a brisk trot.

They had to lean down along their horses' necks to duck under the lintel, but they sat up tall as soon as they were in, gripping their lances firmly in their right hands and their reins in their left. Their swords were tossed about against their saddles as they rode.

As they passed between ranks of perfectly still soldiers, the horses seemed to realize the pomp of the occasion. So they stiffened their ears and chewed their bits and rolled their eyes. As though releasing a lingering resentment for their enforced hot baths in the river, they snorted as they passed a basin full of steaming water, while stamping the ground like dragons come down from the sky.

But in here, the Indians seemed unimpressed.

The Spaniards easily identified the Inca king: he was the only one sitting down. He had over ten women standing around him, all with their gazes lowered. He wore a sleeveless tunic made with plaques of gold. His forearms were completely covered in gold. But his face could not be seen.

Two women held a large woven cloth in front of him, a veil lined with threads of silver. The Spaniards could not make out his facial features or his eyes. But he could see them.

Gabriel saw a band around his head above the veil. On his forehead was a crimson tuft of silky wool with a fringe of fine gold threads hanging from it and with an amazing diamond-shaped feather stuck in it, as colorful as a rainbow.

He was so still that he could have been made of wax.

Not a shiver. Nothing. For all the Spaniards knew he could have been a corpse. But then they noticed the veil in front of his face moving back and forth to the rhythm of his breathing.

Still he didn't flinch, although now the horses were passing to and fro in front of him, baring their gums that had been bruised by their bits.

His stillness conveyed a sense of exceptional dignity, a strength that made observers shudder. Gabriel felt a fear rise up in him that until now he had managed to hold off.

Gabriel sat up tall in his saddle, and deliberately stared at the faces that surrounded the Inca King. He saw the assuming and scornful ambassador Sikinchara. He recognized the young warrior with the proud manner who had thanked him for killing de Moguer's hound.

Gabriel nodded, offering a gesture of recognition. But

the other didn't respond, simply staring at him unblinkingly.

De Soto drew his horse a step closer to the Emperor, causing Felipillo to protest:

'Not so close!'

He was kneeling between the horses with his palms flat on the ground and his neck bent forward.

De Soto glanced at Gabriel. The captain was more pallid than usual, but his voice was as strong as ever:

'I am a captain under the command of Governor Don Francisco Pizarro, who is the envoy of God and of His Majesty the Emperor, Charles the Fifth of Spain, and who was sent by them to discover this land and to bring the Word and Spirit of Jesus Christ to it . . .'

The silence that followed his introduction was so complete that they could hear the water bubbling in the basin.

Gabriel's lungs hurt from unwittingly holding his breath, and he slammed Felipillo in the back so hard with the butt of his lance that he almost knocked the interpreter to the ground.

'Translate that! Translate it now, you bugger!'

Felipillo kept his head bowed as he translated in a muted voice. Gabriel couldn't help but doubt the fidelity of his translation.

But de Soto had already regained his self-assurance. He maneuvered his horse side on to the Emperor and saluted him in the Spanish manner:

'Our Lord the Governor invites you to share a meal with him tomorrow, to seal your friendship and to offer you his help. He knows that you like to conquer . . .'

Only the Inca's veil moved.

And then, just as the silence was becoming unbearable, the old man covered in gold who had met them at the riverside said something.

'It's well,' said Felipillo.

'What do you mean, "It's well"?' growled de Soto.

'The Powerful Lord who speaks for the Emperor said: "It's well."'

Captain de Soto gave Gabriel a lingering, quizzical look. Then he ungloved his left hand with all the dignity that he could muster. Next he took off a gold ring from his fingers and, leaning forward on his horse, offered it to the Inca.

The veil trembled as the Inca said something. The old man stepped around from behind the Emperor and approached de Soto. But the captain immediately closed his fist.

'No!' he exclaimed irritably. 'Not you! I will only hand it to your master!'

Felipillo, curled up, terrified, in a ball, didn't translate this. But the Spanish captain's meaning was as clear as his irritation.

De Soto moved his horse so close to the Inca that the breath from its large nostrils lifted the veil and fluttered the feather on the royal band. De Soto stretched his arm out once again, offering the ring.

For what seemed an eternity, nothing happened.

Then, as though his movements were meant by divine right to be slower than those of ordinary men, the Inca finally moved.

He stretched out his arm and opened his palm. The ring fell into it. The Inca brought his arm back, but then, with the same slow indolence, turned it over and let the ring fall.

It bounced off the flagstones and rolled along them with a metallic sound.

But Gabriel was no longer listening.

Why had the Emperor wanted Anamaya to be his eyes?

What she saw turned her blood to ice.

What she saw burned her eyes.

They charged into the courtyard like furious demons. The

beasts, their monstrous bodies stretched out, had huge eyes, and they struck the ground with their feet made of metal as though they were trying to break the flagstones.

As for the men astride them, they wore clothes so tight that it looked like they were naked. They wore second skins wrapped around their feet and calves. They had strong thighs and narrow waists, and larger frames than an Indian.

And their faces . . .

Their faces were covered in hair, mainly black hair, although occasionally mixed with white, and one had a beard as golden as the sunrise. Their lips were long and expressive. Their lively eyes shone from under their silver helmets. They looked rudely at each Indian face, even looking directly at the Emperor and his women. Their eyes looked at people as though they penetrated into their souls.

And they weren't ugly.

No, they weren't ugly like Sikinchara and Guaypar had described them.

The one whose face was covered in golden hair had a tender, fragile quality about him, evident in his nostrils flared with apprehension. His nose was delicate, his lips very red, long and thin, his skin was as pale as alpaca's milk . . .

Yet these faces terrified Anamaya.

What she saw was worse than facing a puma's fangs.

What she saw in the faces of these men belonged to her past, to her memory.

She remembered the child Anamaya. The precociously tall ten-year-old. The child who was laughed at by the other *Chiriguano* girls in that humid jungle village for being too tall and for having skin too light.

The child who was mocked for having a flat forehead and lips too thin and long.

The one whose eyes repelled the matrons and girls of the *acclahuasi* in Quito . . .

So, after the Emperor had let the ring fall, and as its

tinkling sound on the flagstones filled the heavy atmosphere in the courtyard, Anamaya lifted her face and stared at the golden-bearded stranger as she had never stared at anyone before.

She knew.

When the gold ring proffered by de Soto fell from the Inca's scornful hand, Gabriel didn't hear it tinkling on the flagstones.

What he saw made him dizzy.

Blue eyes.

Incredible blue eyes.

A girl stood out amid the sumptuously dressed Indians wearing golden cloaks and richly colored tunics. She was slightly taller than the rest and clad entirely in white except for a simple red belt around her waist. She didn't have the heavy, carefully parted onyx-black hair of her compatriots. Hers was softer, and coiled onto her shoulders in tresses held together by gold threads. On her forehead she wore a diadem with an emerald set in it and with three short feathers atop it, red, blue, and yellow.

And she had those blue eyes . . .

She was beautiful.

But it wasn't her strange, unique beauty that took Gabriel's heart by surprise. It was her presence.

Gabriel felt as if he had made the long journey from Seville to this lost valley just to see her!

It was as if God, destiny, or fortune had had no other goal when setting the obstacles along his way here. As if the shame of his bastard birth, the humiliation heaped on him by the Holy Office, and the unshakeable madness of Don Francisco Pizarro had all conspired to make this moment happen. It was as if he was meant to be here now, facing the unknown, facing this woman from another world with the sky in her wide-open eyes – or maybe it was a lake floating in them.

He felt so dizzy that he had to grip onto his horse's mane to keep from falling. He had to clench his teeth to keep from wailing like a frightened child.

All that was around him was only a barrier separating her from him.

Walling off his hope, and already his desire, for her.

He saw nothing except her eyes, he heard nothing except the beating of her heart.

Was it possible to yearn for someone as soon as he'd seen her for the first time?

Was it possible, in the space of a glance, to know that he could never breathe again without feeling her breath or her burning kiss on his lips?

Gabriel was cold, freezing cold, and he felt that only her touch would warm him.

The ring rolled in ever decreasing circles to a stop. Then, a cacophony exploded from just outside the courtyard, a cacophony of stamping hooves and shouting. Don Hernando Pizarro's grating, high-pitched voice called:

'What's happening, de Soto?'

'Their damned Inca refuses to speak to me. He'll only talk to the Governor – but what are you doing here?'

Gabriel hadn't turned to look. He couldn't have done it even if he had wanted to. The young girl had lowered her eyes when Don Hernando had entered the courtyard. Gabriel kept staring at her lush hair and the feathers in her diadem, as if trying to will her to raise her face to his: *She knows, I'm sure she knows! It couldn't be possible otherwise* . . .

'I've come to rescue you,' shouted Don Hernando. 'I was worried that you had met with trouble. If he won't talk to you, perhaps he will to me . . .'

Gabriel barely heard these words or Felipillo translating them as God knew what. Silence fell on the courtyard after the Indian interpreter had finished. Silence, and emptiness, because the girl hadn't lifted her face.

She remained still, prostrated, shivering, her fingers trembling, her fist opening and closing, as though she was terrified. *No! She mustn't be scared! She mustn't be scared of me! She can't be frightened of me, like a little child!* thought Gabriel frantically.

He was about to wave at her, perhaps even cry out, when he heard Don Hernando snarl:

'Tell that monkey to lift his monkey's head and answer when he's spoken to!'

Felipillo didn't interpret this. But his tone didn't need translating. The Inca didn't move, but all the noblemen around him bristled under the insult, staring at the Spaniards as they would at an anthill before crushing it.

Without thinking, Gabriel yanked on his reins, turning his horse about on the spot, and found himself beside Don Hernando. His hand was already wrapped around his sword grip and his expression conveyed so much anger that the Governor's brother smiled derisively and murmured:

'It was only a joke to wake you up. You looked a little too frozen by fear, schoolboy! We must show them who is stronger! Felipillo, tell King Atahualpa that I am not a lowly captain but Governor Don Francisco Pizarro's brother. The Governor is his friend. He invites him to dinner. He waits for him at Cajamarca, and will not eat or sleep until he receives his reply.'

When Gabriel turned back towards the Inca, the young girl had lifted her face and was looking at him again.

There was surprise in her blue eyes.

She looked at him like no woman had ever looked at him. Not even Doña Francisca in Seville, all that time ago.

She looked at him, and he felt an urge to stroke her hair, to touch her lips.

He could have leaned down from his horse and carried her away, leaping over the boiling river with her in his arms . . .

In his delirium, his muscles tightened and he felt a stab of pain in his back.

But he felt a welling of tenderness in his chest.

For a moment, to suppress the desire that was flooding through him, Gabriel closed his eyes.

When he opened them again, he saw that the two women who held the Inca's veil were lifting it extremely cautiously. The Inca king's face appeared, strangely handsome, broad and powerful.

He had a nose like a bird of prey's beak. His mouth, slightly arched with disdain, was as perfectly defined as a statue's. But his eyes were truly amazing. Two black pupils surrounded by blood looked out from under his pleated eyelids. The Inca's face was like a splendid mask symbolizing both cruelty and hurt.

Gabriel sensed Don Hernando's and de Soto's surprise beside him.

But when the Inca began speaking in a slow, clear voice, he saw that the blue-eyed woman had disappeared.

The Inca didn't speak to the strangers. He only addressed one of the Elders who stood beside him who then relayed his words to the interpreter Felipillo. He said:

'All along your road here, you have mistreated my Powerful Lords. In my villages, you mistreated my *curacas*, you put them in chains, you fought them and in so doing you disrespected me, the Son of the Sun, the Emperor of this land that isn't yours. You disrespectfully entered into the Houses of the Virgins and carried away women. You entered a palace where my father Huayna Capac slept during his lifetime here and you stole precious mats from it. All along your trip you ate what wasn't offered to you and your dogs fed on our children . . .'

The Inca spoke about the strangers' cruelty for a long time. He told of his fury that they had disturbed the peace of the Empire of the Four Cardinal Directions.

But when he stopped talking, Don Hernando Pizarro replied that it was all lies. His voice carried the confidence of arrogance:

'The Governor is a good Christian. He wishes harm on no one and fights only those who oppose him. When we were approached in peace by people bearing smiles and gifts, we too smiled and gave gifts. When we were attacked, then, yes, we fought back and conquered all those who wouldn't submit. We did this, and will do it again if necessary. We do it fearlessly, because each one of us on his horse is strong enough to fight an army of people like those gathered here!'

The Inca laughed as though he was spitting out all his scorn.

He said:

'Come down from your animals to rest and eat something with me.'

'We too are fasting,' replied Don Hernando coolly, 'and we've vowed not to set foot on the ground until we return to our camp. Soon it will be nightfall and we must have a reply for my brother the Governor. Will you come and share his bread?'

The Inca's eyes still seemed to be laughing from inside their rings of blood:

'Today I am giving thanks to my father the Sun, my mother Quilla, and the Thunder God Illapa for having given me the strength to defeat my brother Huascar who broke the Law. Today, I fast because my warriors, of whom there are thousands and thousands, and who obey my every command, were victorious in great battles. My fast ends tomorrow. Tomorrow I shall come to Cajamarca with a few of my Powerful Lords. Tonight, you may stay in the great buildings on the square. But you shall not enter the one decorated with snakes, for that is mine.'

The Inca fell silent for a moment and looked curiously at the horses. Then he added:

'Before you leave, you must drink the sacred beer, for it is my custom to thus entertain those who aren't my enemies.'

He had just finished saying this when two young women approached, each carrying a beautifully worked golden goblet. The Inca drank from one goblet before one of the women offered the other to Don Hernando.

The Inca drank again from silver goblets, one of which was offered to de Soto this time.

Then the blue-eyed girl approached the Inca.

She offered him two golden goblets. The King of Peru furrowed his eyebrows and looked at her. All the Elders showed their surprise. Nevertheless the Inca took one of the goblets wordlessly. The young girl prostrated herself as he wiped the white, bitter foam from his lips. Then she rose and approached Gabriel. And, as her gaze plunged into his, she offered him the other golden goblet.

Anamaya had seen the look of disgust that Inti Palla had given the strangers when the blue-eyed girl had offered them the golden cup.

She had also caught Guaypar's bloodthirsty look of hatred and Sikinchara's scornful gaze. She had noticed the Emperor's fascination with the big hoofed animals and thought how happy he would be to possess one.

She detected hatred as well as diplomacy in the course of Atahualpa's speech, and finally contempt. She felt how determined the Emperor was to frighten the foreigners, and how certain he was of his overwhelming power, of the power of his thousands and thousands of warriors and the protection of his father the sun.

Yet he was wrong. Anamaya divined that they were all wrong.

It wasn't the violent words of the strangers' chief that made her realize this. His boasting and lies disguised the reality of their threat.

No, she sensed it in Gold-Beard's silence, and the look in his eyes. She had realized it when he had confidently put his hand on his weapon as the strangers' chief was throwing out insults that the interpreter hadn't dared translate.

Gold-Beard had a boldness that the others pretended to ignore. He had a strength of character that Atahualpa couldn't see. He bore all the power of his unknown world.

She sensed him as though she was touching him. As though he was hugging her to him so tightly that she couldn't breathe, or as if he was about to carry her off on his strange beast.

But everyone else seemed to be ignoring him.

The Emperor himself was blind to him.

So when she had realized that none of the cups of *chicha* were destined for him, she had filled one for him herself, fearless of the ire of the Emperor who hadn't ordered her to do so.

And when she offered it, she saw his surprise.

He took the second skin off his long, white fingers, and his hands were trembling. He leaned down to her, and for a moment she thought he might fall into her arms.

Both of them were careful not to let their fingers touch.

He was so pale!

Yes, Gabriel too thought at that moment that he could fall into her arms.

And although he hated the taste of the bitter fermented drink, he didn't show it. He drank it down as though he was drinking her soul. And he ended up liking the bite of the beer. She stood fearlessly unmoving next to his horse. Her chest was level with his knee: only a slight movement by the horse and he would be touching her.

His heart pounded in his chest.

The beer warmed his knotted stomach. The butterflies in it settled. Everyone was looking at them. Gabriel felt the weight of the Inca's bloodshot gaze.

He handed the empty goblet back to her. She lifted her arm and threw her head back, as though offering him all her innocence on the spot, as though she wanted him to see how pure she was.

But then Don Hernando broke the spell and said:

'We shall now take our leave, and await your visit tomorrow.'

The Inca inclined his head slightly, and almost smiled:

'May one of you stay with us tonight, as my guest,' he said, and pointed at Gabriel with his gold ax.

'No!' protested Don Hernando quickly. 'The Governor won't allow it. He awaits all of us at Cajamarca. His anger would be immeasurable if you kept one of us . . .'

At that the Emperor really smiled, and all the Powerful Lords smiled with him. Even the ranks of soldiers in the courtyard grinned.

All of them had seen right through the stranger.

They looked bemused, as though saying: 'Well, well, look at these brave warriors, they're as scared as guinea pigs of us!'

Don Hernando had already begun to turn his horse around when de Soto exclaimed:

'Wait a minute! Shouldn't we thank the Indian for his hospitality? I have noticed that he is interested by our horses. And we wouldn't want them to think of us as cowards . . .'

And with a shout, he began trotting around the courtyard. He had an intelligent, well-trained horse, and mount and rider understood one another well. With a combination of spurs and reins, de Soto had it walk forward and backward a little before launching into a short gallop. The horse's hooves clattered against the flagstones. Then he turned around and around, increasing the pace as he did so. The Indian servants and guards stepped back a little to make room for him. The animal was breathing hard and neighing, and foam flew off its bit. As a finale, de Soto let out a holler and made the horse gear up. Now the Indians rushed out of the way, terrified. They clambered over one another, some falling to the ground, others fleeing the courtyard.

Don Hernando laughed and galloped out the gate. Gabriel turned to the dais one last time. But instead of the blue eyes that he was looking for, he found only the Inca's wry smile.

But in fact the Emperor was furious. He immediately ordered his wives, servants and guards away.

Sikinchara tried to appease him by saying:

'We'll kill them all, but we'll keep their animals, and the one foreigner who puts those metal things on their feet that spark against rock.'

'We should have killed them all long ago,' said Guaypar, 'even their animals.'

The Emperor shut them both up with a glance. He turned to Anamaya and asked:

'Why did you offer *chicha* to the quiet stranger, *Coya Camaquen*? I hadn't ordered it.'

Anamaya prostrated herself.

'Forgive me, Emperor.'

Atahualpa raised his eyebrows.

Guaypar said, almost regretfully:

'My Lord, he was the one who killed the enormous dog that devoured the child at Huagayoc.'

This didn't diminish Sikinchara's contempt for the stranger, but Atahualpa nodded his head slightly.

'I like their animals,' he said slowly. 'But as for their masters – they are humans that cannot be understood.'

He rose, and then, as an afterthought, said to Sikinchara: 'Round up all those who ran away from the animals. Take them out to the camp and behead them. No one among us must show fear before the strangers.'

CHAPTER 44

Cajamarca: night of 15 November 1532

NIGHT HAD ALMOST FALLEN WHEN THE MISSION that had gone to meet the Inca Atahualpa galloped into the huge square of Cajamarca. Governor Don Francisco Pizarro hadn't budged from it since they had set out earlier that afternoon. He sat stiffly on his horse, as though he'd been frozen there by the hailstorm and had yet to thaw.

The sound of hooves brought men running out of the buildings, burning torches in their hands. The flickering light threw shadows across the men's faces.

'The Inca refused to come with us, Francisco,' Don Hernando immediately announced, 'but he agreed to come tomorrow.'

The Governor nodded his approval, and asked:

'What is he like?'

'Like a worthy prince,' interjected de Soto.

'A bit like a Moor,' said Don Hernando. 'He sat on his stool the whole time, while all his entourage stood. His eyes were flushed with blood, as though he had eaten his enemies raw. And, of course, he's arrogant, like all Indians—'

'He's also very dignified,' added de Soto. 'He knows his own worth.'

Don Hernando grumbled:

'De Soto calls it dignity. The truth is that the Inca didn't say a word before I arrived. He only started chatting when he learned that I was the Governor's brother . . .'

De Soto said nothing to this, and so Don Francisco abruptly asked:

'How many of them are there?'

'Oh, a lot,' sighed Don Hernando with a dismissive wave. 'And they're well armed too, with spears, slingshots and clubs. But nothing too dangerous!'

The Governor's eyes lingered on de Soto, who said:

'I guess that there are around forty thousand of them. And they're battle-hardened. Their star-pointed clubs look like they could do some real harm.'

A murmur ran through the Spanish ranks, the men repeating the number to one another. Forty thousand! None among them had ever seen such an army.

Friar Vicente approached Gabriel's horse and, taking hold of its bridle, asked:

'Did you tell the Inca king that God was on our side?'

Don Hernando grinned cynically:

'I told him, Friar Vicente, and repeated it to make it clear. But I might as well have read the Gospels to pigs in their sties. The Inca let us know that the sun was his father and the moon his mother.'

Friar Vicente crossed himself and shook his head.

'They're a low breed of pagans,' continued Don Hernando, 'so don't imagine that you're going to convert them by simply preaching the Word.'

'They're men and women like any other,' declared Gabriel confidently. He tried to catch Don Francisco's gaze in the dark. 'They're human beings just like us, my Lord. And they're in their own land.'

'The schoolboy drank their brew – like the man that he is!' roared Don Hernando. 'His perception is clearly blurred!'

But his joke fell flat, and was buried by the silence that followed it. They felt cold on their necks: the night had brought an icy breeze with it that made the torches flare and hiss.

At last the Governor moved, and as he rode off towards the buildings, he said in a voice too low for the rest to hear:

'Don't delude yourself, brother. Gabriel is right: they *are* just like us. They have courage and brains – and we would do well to remember it.'

The evening wind carried the sound of horns and trumpets.

Children, pretending to be frightened but in fact thrilled beyond measure, sat together in tents. They wouldn't sleep. Instead they talked in hushed, excited voices about the strangers: how they came and went, half men, half beasts, bigger than llamas, jumping clear over high walls and producing sparks from their silver feet.

In the *cancha*, the Emperor had retired to his chamber, and had ordered that he should not be disturbed. An uncomfortable calm hung over his camp.

Like all the women who weren't to stay close to him for the night, Anamaya prostrated herself before walking backwards out into the courtyard. Atahualpa didn't even glance at her. The many goblets of *chicha*, the fast, and the tension of the meeting with the strangers had taken their toll, and he looked utterly exhausted.

Anamaya had decided to visit the small temple by the boiling spring. But Inti Palla intercepted her as she came into the courtyard.

Her eyes shone out of the shadows, and her teeth were bared like fangs. She grabbed Anamaya's wrist roughly.

'Where are you running to? To join them?'

'Join them? What are you talking about?'

'Don't lie to me! I saw right through you!' hissed Inti Palla.

Anamaya tried to free her arm, but Inti Palla tightened her fingers and squeezed the gold bracelet into her skin so hard that it left a mark.

'I saw how you looked at them—'

'Let me go!' cried Anamaya, her blood boiling.

But Inti Palla, her face suffused with hatred, grabbed Anamaya's other arm and shoved her back against a wall.

'I always knew that you were a black-hearted demon,' she sneered, 'even though the Emperor wouldn't listen to me. He will now, though!'

'But I don't know what you're talking about!' said Anamaya.

Inti Palla pushed her back towards the center of the courtyard. Anamaya bristled, but didn't try to fight back. Her chest was on fire, her insides were burning as though she had drunk from the boiling spring. She had guessed what would come next.

'Oh, don't try to play the noble *Coya Camaquen* with me!' said Inti Palla, almost triumphantly. 'I saw your eyes on the stranger. A woman cannot miss these things: you looked at him like you wanted him between your legs!'

'Shut up!' shouted Anamaya.

'For years I pretended to be your friend because you were close to the Emperor. But you spurned me the moment I laid eyes on you, and have done ever since! And I knew that one day you would betray us—'

'It's not true!' burst Anamaya, pushing her away.

Inti Palla clenched her fist and struck Anamaya across the face. Anamaya teetered and fell to the ground, her head landing less than a foot from the stone basin. Gasping with shock, she filled her lungs with its vapor.

'And I know the reason why!' yelled the princess, beside herself.

As Anamaya stood up, memories and emotions unrolled in

front of her mind's eye: her mother's smiling lips whispering words of love, the cracked skin of the old Inca, the face of the golden stranger, his gaze lost in hers . . .

'I too know the reason why,' she shouted.

Inti Palla was so startled by Anamaya's declaration that she abruptly fell silent. Anamaya smiled meaningfully, and something in her blue-eyed look disconcerted Inti Palla, who stumbled back a step.

For the first time, Anamaya looked at her with neither fear nor admiration. She saw Inti Palla for what she really was: a girl corrupted by jealousy and hatred.

'I know,' she repeated, 'and I'm not frightened by what I know. I know where I came from, and I know the path that I've taken. I know that a stranger – a man like one of them – was my father.'

She listened to her own words floating through the night.

'I know it from scattered images that I see in my mind, from a feeling I get under my skin, from the things I remember the children in my village saying about a hairy stranger who came from the jungle and returned to it—'

'You're one of them! You're as repulsive as them!'

'But I also know,' continued Anamaya, ignoring the interruption, 'that all my life I've obeyed the Inca of all the Incas, Huayna Capac, I've followed the orders that he gave me on his night of dying, the night when he promised to watch over me . . .'

She stopped talking, and looked scornfully at Inti Palla's defeated expression.

'Do you remember when you asked me in Quito why I was so ugly? I shan't ask you the same question. I *know* why you are so ugly. I know why the Emperor won't touch you anymore, why he hates the smell of your skin and why your belly disgusts him . . .'

'You're mad!' Inti Palla's eyes welled with tears.

'I can see the darkness within you, Inti Palla. Under the

smooth skin of your cheeks, there is vile hatred and ill will. I can see the rot of your soul in your eyes.'

'You're a witch, come from the Under World to destroy us!' blubbered Inti Palla. She held her arms together up in front of her, as though protecting herself from a fire. 'You're a stranger and you want to give us up to them like you've given yourself to them. You want them to come here and trample us with their animals!'

As Inti Palla sobbed, Anamaya approached her and tried to part her arms. The princess stepped back towards the boiling spring.

'You're consumed by hatred,' murmured Anamaya, 'by floods of hatred and lies—'

'You're not one of us! You want us to die!'

Anamaya didn't hesitate: in a flash she grabbed Inti Palla's wrists so forcefully that she almost broke them. Inti Palla stared out of terrified eyes and wailed. Sweat mixed with tears and the burning hot vapors on her face.

From a distance, they looked like they were performing a strange, antagonistic dance. Anamaya led Inti Palla toward the basin of boiling water, as if she intended to throw her into it. The princess resisted with all her strength, crying out. She fell to her knees, and grazed the skin of her soft, sensual thighs on the sharp edges of stones. Her blood and sweat dripped into the dust. The boiling water was so close that they felt it burning against their faces and the stench of its sulfur irritated their throats.

Anamaya twisted Inti Palla's arm, and the princess grimaced with pain. The blue-eyed girl squatted down to the princess's level and thrust her head back against the edge of the basin.

'Is this what you had planned?' whispered Anamaya into her ear. 'Did you mean to get rid of me by throwing me into the boiling water?'

Inti Palla couldn't stop crying.

'Answer me!'

Inti Palla nodded between sobs.

'Then look carefully,' said Anamaya.

She scratched Inti Palla's skin as she roughly released her. She took the gold bracelet off her own wrist, the twin snakes that the princess had given her so many seasons ago. She waved it in front of her.

'Do you remember giving me this? I was a terrified little child, a creature out of the forest so ugly and deformed that I deserved nothing but insults. I thought that you were like the others. And then one day you came smiling into my room, and spoke tender words to me, and as you gave me this bracelet, you told me that you were my friend. You were so beautiful, I so much wanted to believe you – yes, I wanted to be your friend . . .'

Anamaya flung the bracelet from her and it fell into the basin with a tiny splash, making no more noise than a pebble or a hailstone falling into a lake. It sank like a falling leaf, moving from side to side, and was briefly brought up again by a column of boiling water before disappearing into the sulfurous reds and browns at the bottom of the basin.

Anamaya stood up briskly. Her friendship with Inti Palla died in her heart with as little noise as the piece of jewelry had made when it sank.

Without looking at Inti Palla, curled up and still sobbing on the ground, Anamaya straightened her tunic and walked away into the night.

'Master Francisco!'

Like the rest of the Spaniards, the barber and surgeon Francisco Lopez, known as Pancho, was settling into one of the buildings off the square. He had already set his tools neatly atop his leather-banded chest: pewter bowls, lancets, forceps – both serrated and flat – razors, jars of oils and medicinal herbs.

He turned around in answer to Gabriel's call and grinned.

'What can I do for you, Gabriel?'

'I'd like you to shave me.'

The barber searched Gabriel's deadpan expression for any sign of comic intent, wary of being made fun of. Finding none, he looked at Sebastian, whose own expression was one of undisguised hilarity.

'The visit to the Inca has turned him mad,' he concluded.

'He also wants a haircut,' chortled Sebastian. He winked at the barber, who shook his head.

'Now listen, Gabriel: it's late, and the Governor wants to see us in less than an hour—'

'Therefore you have enough time.'

'But I haven't! And in any case, you'll have plenty of opportunities to be shaved, cut and sliced tomorrow!'

'Now there's the wisdom of a brave man,' teased Sebastian.

'And anyway, why do you want to lose your beard?' continued the surgeon. 'It becomes you handsomely.'

'To feel the wind against my cheeks.'

'Have you really gone mad, or are you just pretending?'

'Pancho, I want to be as clean as a newly minted coin tomorrow. Please shave off my beard and cut my hair. Then I shall go wash off the rest of the filth in the river.'

'*Madre de Dios!* In the middle of the night? With forty thousand savages bawling all around us?'

Pancho picked up one of his phials and ceremoniously presented it to Gabriel as though it was the sacrament of Mass:

'Gabriel, I want you to take three drops of this elixir. It'll calm you down, and then you'll do us all a favor and fall asleep!'

Sebastian burst out laughing.

'You don't get it, sawbones! *El Señor* Gabriel plans to meet a lady tomorrow!'

Gabriel glanced suspiciously at the big black man.

'I know which lady it is,' said the barber, mimicking the action of reaping. 'We're all going to meet *her* tomorrow. But I can promise you, Don Gabriel, that she won't care at all if we're unshaven and smell rancid!'

'Both of you stop your fooling,' said Gabriel, taking a razor from the trunk.

He opened it, ran its blade lightly across his palm, then pointed it at Francisco's stomach. He commanded him in such a low, serious tone that the other two immediately stopped smirking:

'Please shave me, Pancho — or you'll never see the color of the gold of Peru.'

Anamaya ran barefoot to the spring. She had to wash herself free of all those impurities, free of all those words that had sullied her, free of all the violence that she had witnessed.

She had to be reborn.

Now, by the silver light of the moon, she came out of the scalding hot water into the cool night air. Steam rose from her naked body. Her bath hadn't washed away the tears that still streamed down her cheeks. She slipped into her white *anaco*, but didn't put on any of her jewelry. She had thrown away Inti Palla's bracelet, but the bloody impression of the intertwined snakes remained on her wrist.

On the other side of the valley, on the mountainside where the black-and-gray column of strangers had wormed its way down that morning, there was now a long, long chain of fire. It was formed by the torches of thousands of rebel Indians who had joined the bearded men. All those whom Atahualpa had conquered but whose allegiance he had lost. All those who had sworn loyalty to Huascar and who now sought to avenge themselves against the Emperor by joining forces with the strangers.

The chain of fire looked like a long stream of molten gold in the black night, running from the top of the mountain to the walls of the town.

Cajamarca was so far, yet so close.

'They're all going to die,' said a voice from the shadows.

'Guaypar!'

The young warrior stepped out of the night. His torso and legs were bare. He wore only a *huara*. Anamaya couldn't help but admire his strong body. His muscles seemed as unbreakable as mountain boulders.

'I heard everything,' he said. 'I know the evil that lives in the heart of that woman. And I know that you have never betrayed us.'

'Thank you, Guaypar.'

'But I also know that you weren't looking at the stranger as a girl looks at her father . . .'

She heard the bitterness in his voice.

'. . . And I've come to tell you that he's going to die.'

Anamaya closed her eyes. A bolt of pain shot through her body, and her muscles seized.

She remembered the stranger's face. The blind excitement that she had felt when he had almost fallen into her arms was still with her, like a flame burning in the pit of her stomach.

The stranger existed as a sliver of tender hope within her.

And now she feared for his life.

'Leave me alone, Guaypar,' she murmured.

'He's going to die,' Guaypar repeated quietly. 'He and all his companions.'

Guaypar vanished into the night.

Anamaya turned her back on Cajamarca. She stared at the night shadows of the western peaks, the direction from which the Sacred Double would arrive, as long as Villa Oma hadn't left him behind.

'Come to me,' she begged, 'come, Sacred Double, and help me!'

Friar Vicente had ordered that all the pottery and statues, all the pagan idols should be removed from the alcoves in the walls. Now tallow candles burned in their place, giving the great hall, with its magnificent gold-leafed beams, the feeling of a crypt where ghosts gathered.

A dozen doors opened onto the square through the hall's front wall. Those who couldn't fit into the hall were bunched around these. The town was deserted except for a handful of sentries armed with horns to sound the alarm. They watched from their posts along the road to the fortress, and from the top of the pyramid.

Everyone fell silent when the Governor climbed onto a platform of chests hastily thrown together. Don Hernando and his captains stood around him.

Friar Vicente raised the gold crucifix that he'd fixed onto a pole. He lowered it three times towards the assembly, each of whom took off their hat, morion or cap. Then he faced Don Francisco, and lowered the cross once more, moving close enough to the Governor for him to kiss it.

Everyone crossed themselves.

'God's Will be done on Earth as in Heaven,' began Don Francisco in a strong, clear voice. 'May He protect and guide us, and may the Blessed Mother of Christ do the same . . .'

Now everyone's gaze was on him. Don Francisco seemed to look at each face individually. His pupils were as gray as his beard, but seemed to give off more light than the torches. He thrust his gloved hand into the air and thundered:

'Do you really believe that there are forty thousand Indians around us? Absolutely not!'

He paused, then continued:

'There are many more of them than that! Probably at least double! Eighty thousand warriors!'

He paused again, as if waiting to hear someone complain against the absurd odds.

'Eighty thousand! One against four hundred! One Spaniard against four hundred Indians! How many of them were there at Puna? A few hundred? And at Tumbes? Not many more than that! Their King, Atahualpa, has assured us of his friendship, and has given us many handsome presents. He has welcomed us into this magnificent square. But it's a simple trap on a massive scale. He wants us in here to massacre us more easily. And you are scared. You are frightened like little children who stare at the dark and let their imaginations run wild! Do you know why you are scared? Because you don't have enough faith in God! One against four hundred! That is how God wants it – and God wants it like that, lads, because He wants us to demonstrate His power to those who don't know Him yet. God wants the Indians of this gold-rich land to come into His bosom like the rest of mankind! God says: "One against four hundred, that is what each of you shall overcome, you, Pedro the Greek, you, Alonso, you, Juan, and Benalcazar and Mena and every single one of you . . ."'

Don Francisco pointed at each man as though he was grabbing them by the throat. Then he continued, thundering even louder:

'All of us! God wills it, because He wants to test our faith, *compañeros*! God allowed us to get this far, despite everything that we've endured, because He wants us to be the instrument of His power and His majesty! My brothers, God chose each one of us and blessed each one of us because we are fearless, and each one of us is determined to expand His Kingdom courageously! *Compañeros*, open your eyes, open your minds! The Indians have gathered here in such huge numbers – eighty thousand! – because they are scared of us! Scared! That's why they've been making that dreadful clamor all night, preventing us from sleeping . . .'

He stopped, and now grins could be seen behind beards. Two or three men even laughed. So Governor Don Francisco Pizarro nodded his head and laughed with them. Then, in a calmer tone, he added:

'Tomorrow morning, their king will come here. He will enter the square surrounded by his servants and his women, and covered in his baubles. That is when I shall take his hand, and not let go of it again! And you shall see, eighty thousand warriors won't dare lift a finger! That's what will happen tomorrow . . .'

The mountains, the clouds, the whole world shook with the incessant sounds of trumpets and drums. Fires dotted the plain, braziers endlessly fuelled by the Indians. By the light of all those fires, the tent-city gave the impression of being even larger than it was. The wind had dropped and a drizzle had started to fall, but not heavily enough to prevent sparks dancing a slow saraband as they rose from the flames.

But Anamaya heard nothing. She saw nothing.

Since midnight, she had been squatting in a cloud of smoke. She had prepared the herbs herself, with no help from any priest. She had hidden the *coca* and the *chicha* behind an unfrequented temple wall, away from prying eyes.

She had drunk the beer, and inhaled the smoke.

Now she was simply waiting. She was unaware that she was rocking back and forth on her heels.

She was alone. She hadn't felt as alone and lost in the wide world since the early days after Sikinchara had captured her. She hadn't felt so vulnerable and abandoned since the day that the Emperor Huayna Capac had held out his hand to her.

Yet she still held a tiny jewel of hope in her soul. She was waiting for him to come to her and help her through this terrible, dark night. If only he would help her, she who had looked after him so conscientiously for so many years.

But only the rain fell, a thousand tiny pearls landing in her hair, wetting the burning coca leaves so that the smoke that rose from them was heavier and more bitter. And from the Other World came only freezing gusts of silence.

Armed shadows darted whispering through the deserted streets.

The infernal cacophony produced by the Indians on the plain filled Cajamarca. They didn't stop drumming or blowing their horns once throughout the whole night. Not even the horses could sleep.

They had lit thousands of fires, and it looked like all the stars in the sky had landed on the plain.

But the Spaniards avoided looking toward the tent-city. Don Francisco had ordered:

'Don't look at them! Shut them out of your ears! They're only trying to taunt you. Block your ears with the fabric of your shirts if you have to.'

The Governor himself wandered from group to group. He placed his hand on shoulders made wet by the drizzle.

'Keep your blades dry,' he advised, 'and grease your boots and morions. It'll keep your minds and hands busy.'

He bantered with the foot soldiers as easily as with the horsemen and captains. He asked how they liked the corn tortillas served by the Indian women who had come with the bulk of the Tallane troops. He laughed with them, and asked if their hearts were as warm as the bean soup! When he laughed, his lips barely moved under his beard, and as his good humor met with astonished looks, he said:

'Tonight, boys, there are no more foot soldiers or horsemen, no more lords or common men. We are all together in God's hands, *compañeros*, and tonight we are all lords!'

The tip of his long sword tapped the edges of the steps as he climbed the great pyramid to inspect the falconet manned by the Greek, Gabriel and Sebastian. He checked the angle of fire: straight down onto the road. He reflected for a moment, then ordered:

'After sunrise, there's no point aiming at the road. It'll happen here in the square. Move the falconet so that it points at that big door over there that opens onto the plain. And, Gabriel, I'm going to need you down there.'

He noticed Gabriel's clean-shaven face in the torchlight, laughed, and added:

'What a good idea! To be clean for the big day.'

He gave Gabriel an affectionate look and slapped him on the shoulder, causing Sebastian and the Greek to laugh. He said:

'We'll show you off to the Indians tomorrow morning. They'll think they're seeing an angel!'

Suddenly she couldn't see anything but white. She heard a child cry out:

'Anamaya!'

There was nothing in front of her but a void. Everything was soft and white, with no angles and no sharp edges. It was as if the whole world had been carpeted with snow.

The child called again:

'Anamaya!'

She tried to answer, but couldn't hear her own voice.

'Don't be frightened,' said the child's voice. 'Don't be sad.'

Although she couldn't hear herself, she silently asked who the voice belonged to.

'I am the one who is always with you. I am the one that you care for in the world of humans.'

Anamaya thought that this was impossible because the one that she cared for in this world was a very old man who had already crossed the threshold of death. The child laughed and said:

'I am that person. I have come as my child self because the world is becoming young again. A great *pachacuti* is in the making. What has been will no longer be. What will come is still a child in its mother's womb.'

Anamaya trembled as she thought of the war that would begin tomorrow. The child said:

'What is old cracks easily, what is too big fractures easily, what is too strong loses its strength – that is what the *pachacuti* is about. All the knots on the *quipu* strands lead to the one knot. Beyond this, the strands vanish over the horizon, flowing free, flowing unencumbered by knots. The world is closing in on itself, preparing to be reborn. Nothing will ever be the same again.'

Anamaya thought: *Then we are all going to die. The strangers are going to kill us*. The child said in a soft voice:

'Some will die, and some will grow. Have no fear for yourself. But look after my son, the one whom you transformed into a snake, because he is the last knot of the present era. And look after my son whom you saved from the snake, because he is the first knot of the future strand.'

Anamaya thought: *How can I? I'm not even a real Inca*. She felt the child's gentle caress as he murmured:

'You are what you are meant to be. Have no fear for the future: the puma is with you.'

'Nice speech the Governor made last night,' said the Greek. 'I like it when Don Francisco talks like that. But still, it was only a speech. And very soon now the real troubles will begin.'

He pointed at the eastern mountains, where the sky grew pale through the clouds.

All three were still sitting at the foot of the falconet atop
the pyramid. All three were soaked through and through from
the rain, and frozen by the cold. The pandemonium from the
tent-city that hadn't stopped all night had suddenly ended
about an hour earlier, all the drums and horns falling silent
at exactly the same eerie moment. How had they known that
dawn was approaching? The thousands of fires had produced
a brown bank of pestilent smoke that stagnated above the
valley, as thick as the clouds above it. It irritated their eyes
and throats.

'One against four hundred,' continued the Greek with a
little smile. 'We'll soon find out what that feels like.'

'You will if you stay alive long enough!' laughed Sebastian.
'It's a pity those buggers don't attack at night, then at least
I would have had an advantage!'

They stopped their idle talk for a moment, and tried to
make out if there was any movement at all at the baths.

'Why so quiet, *compañero*?' the Greek asked Gabriel.
'Normally, fear makes people talkative.'

Gabriel looked at him and smiled.

'I am scared, it's true, but not of what you imagine,' he
said in a husky voice.

'Of what, then?'

But Gabriel gave them nothing but an enigmatic smile.
When the Greek and Sebastian had lost interest in him, he
lifted his head and gazed at the stars. *There was another dream
behind my dream,*' he thought to himself. *But I didn't know it
until now.*

CHAPTER 45

Cajamarca: 16 November 1532

THE LONG WAIT BEGAN AT DAWN.

No one admitted to the fear that gripped their hearts. The bronze axes were still covered in blood. Those who had fled from the strangers' animals had paid the ultimate price.

What kind of people were they really, behind their hairy faces and the second skins they wore, behind their repulsive smell? They certainly weren't gods, they were less than men, even, worse than animals . . . Why did they speak as gently as llama kids, then as aggressively as snakes? What did they want?

These questions were never spoken out loud: they would have earned the speaker the death penalty. Instead, they remained bottled inside each Indian; they poisoned the blood of servants and noblemen alike, they paralyzed cowards and worried the brave. The Indians began to prepare. They donned their checkered tunics and their gold and silver breastplates. Some of the more foolish laughed, expecting a celebration, a day to remember.

Guaypar looked at them with disgust, rage pulsing through his veins. But he couldn't do anything about it.

*   *   *

The long wait began at dawn.

Anamaya opened her eyes, her heart beating quickly.

She hadn't slept at all, and her entire body ached. The child who had spoken to her that night had come from an ancient source, an ancient dream whose meaning had been lost in time. Before, she had thought she knew. Now, she knew nothing . . .

. . . Except that she was frightened.

She wasn't frightened of Inti Palla and her threats anymore. It was a deeper, more painful fear that gripped her.

Fear that the sun would disappear, never to return. Fear of the new world being born, fear of the pain of its birth.

Fear of the child's words, the mysteries they contained: '*Look after my son, the one whom you transformed into a snake, because he is the last knot of the present era.*' Atahualpa, of course. How could she forget that day that she had helped him escape from Huascar's men by making him pretend to be a snake? '*And look after my son whom you saved from the snake . . .*'

But above all, she was frightened of the stranger with the dark eyes and the golden hair and whose mouth spoke a language that her ears didn't understand but whose eyes and body spoke another that she understood perfectly, a language in which she had always been fluent. She felt as if up till now she had only been waiting for him.

Emperor Atahualpa ended his fast.

He woke and called for food and drink. As he ate he listened to the camp preparing to accompany him to the strangers waiting at Cajamarca.

Sikinchara, Guaypar and the generals came in and prostrated themselves beneath his hammock. They told him that everything was set for the 'hunt', as they called it.

'The strangers cannot escape, my Lord. They are as hope-
lessly trapped within the walls of the square as your brother
Huascar was in the ring of fire. Neither they nor the traitors
who have joined them can take any road out of there.'

'What are they doing at the moment?'

'Nothing at all. They're hiding in a building off the square,
and the smell of fear rises from them.'

The Emperor called for more drink for the Powerful Lords
and himself. Then, he announced:

'We shall go without weapons.'

He saw Guaypar's astonishment, and repeated:

'We shall go with no more weapons than are needed for
hunting.'

The Powerful Lords nodded their heads in agreement.
They looked out over the rushes that surrounded the Inca's
baths and lodgings towards the walls of Cajamarca. And as
they drank their *chicha*, they all laughed at the arrogant
strangers who didn't know that they were going to be captured
as easily as frightened deer during a *chaco*!

The long wait began at dawn.

Friar Vicente led the Spaniards through Mass in the
palace's biggest room. They had hardly slept at all that night,
and now they squeezed close to one another to ward off the
cold and to keep their fears at bay. They recited prayers that
had long been forgotten.

When they heard Friar Vicente recite the words 'Sacred
Mary, Mother of God,' they all turned to look at Pizarro.
He was looking confidently towards the sky, his eyes bright
with exultation. For once, not one of them dared even think
of mocking his faith.

But their fervor didn't prevent some of them from pissing
themselves.

*   *   *

The long wait began at dawn.

Pedro the Greek had set up all the artillery that they had atop the pyramid: three culverins as well as the falconet that they had installed the previous evening. At the break of day, half a dozen harquebusiers had come up to dry their powder that had become wet during the damp night.

Below, in the square, Don Francisco had personally placed each man in strategic spots in the buildings, whether horseman or foot soldier. Now there was nothing to do but wait for the Inca.

Gabriel sat on the parapet that bordered the platform on top of the pyramid.

Since daybreak, he had been daydreaming of the blue-eyed woman. He thought wistfully how pleasant it would be if they were to meet one another in a sun-dappled country bower. If they were to come together, smiling, during a warm, peaceful afternoon . . . he would put out his arm and she would take it, and they would stroll together with no other goal than the fulfillment of love.

But instead he felt cold, damp air against his clean-shaven cheeks. His tired eyes saw only the bustling activity of the Inca camp. The smoke from the night's fires still hung in the sky, although the clouds above it were breaking up. When Sebastian and Pedro came and sat beside him on the parapet, he murmured:

'. . . I saw a star fall from heaven unto the earth: and to him was given the key to the bottomless pit. And he opened the bottomless pit; and there arose a smoke out of the pit, as the smoke of a great furnace; and the sun and the air were darkened by reason of the smoke of the pit.'

'What's that song you're giving us?' grumbled the Greek with a grimace.

'Nothing, just an old memory. A quote from the Bible . . .'

'Well, keep it for yourself,' muttered the Greek. 'We

already have Friar Vicente to do the Bible-quoting. And as for the furnace of hell, we have one of our own right here in front of us.'

'Hey, look!' cried Sebastian, pointing at the Inca's lodgings. 'They're moving! Look, they're coming!'

Women, children and men bustled about. They gathered together bundles of clothes, or the last fagots of wood. Inside the tents, servants unhooked sides of dried llama meat and flayed ducks from the beams. Little boys darted between the legs of the soldiers and lords, helping them put the finishing touches to their dress, hooking their gold breast-plates on, or else planting bright feathers in their headdresses.

Then the army formed into ranks. Dozens became hundreds and hundreds became thousands and yet more thousands. At last the sun pierced through the clouds and warmed their faces. Dust rose from the trampled plain, a plain that seemed too small to hold such a huge army.

Trumpets sounded their deep notes and the troops stationed around the bath lodgings lined up in formation. The Emperor's grand palanquin came out into the courtyard.

Eighty men, dressed entirely in blue, had the honor of bearing the enormous weight of the Emperor's golden throne on their shoulders. Two more palanquins followed behind them, one carrying the provincial Governor and the other Cajamarca's *curaca*. Then two hammocks followed for Atahualpa's uncles who advised him.

Despite all the commotion, Anamaya saw and felt almost nothing.

Her eyes were nearly as red as the Emperor's, she was ghostly pale, her cheeks were hollow and her lips chapped. The smoke of the burning leaves had irritated her eyes and the *chicha* had left a stale, bitter taste in her mouth.

The child's words were spinning round and around in her

head, and she felt a little dizzy. Despite his reassuring voice, her fear was intense.

Since dawn she had been agonizing over whether to tell the Emperor that his father had at last spoken to her. But how could she tell him that he was the last knot of the present era? How could she tell him that the present might end today, and the Empire of the Four Cardinal Directions be reborn? How could she tell him this as he set out thinking that he was going to capture the strangers as easily as he would wild llamas?

Also, how could she tell him that she was haunted by the face of the stranger to whom she had offered the goblet as much as by the words of the child who had come from the Other World?

How could she explain that she felt irresistibly drawn to the stranger, although she was terribly ashamed of the attraction? Despite her fear, she foresaw the fulfillment today of a promise that burned in her heart.

But how could she hope? Hadn't the child from the Other World said that the present would end today?

But as the Emperor climbed into his palanquin, she stayed in the background. And as the column set off at a slow march, she kept her secret to herself.

She looked up and saw Guaypar beside the palanquin, and Inti Palla amid the concubines. Both of them carefully avoided her blue-eyed gaze.

Sebastian turned to Gabriel.

'Can you hear it?' he asked.

The sound coming from the cortège was funereal, as though an entire city was mourning its dead. It was a moaning that seemed to rise from the depths of the Earth, voices and trumpets sustaining one long, sad note.

'And yet they're dancing,' murmured Gabriel.

'I wish they wouldn't,' replied Sebastian.

Gabriel looked at his black face whose expression was usually tinged with irony. This time there wasn't a hint of it.

'You're not going to piss yourself like the others, are you?'

Sebastian showed the perfect alignment of his white teeth.

'Keep dreaming, Your Grace.'

But he wasn't laughing now.

Pizarro and his captains had climbed the pyramid to survey the situation.

They shaded their eyes with their hands: the sun had come out suddenly and cleared the sky of clouds. What they saw took their breath away.

It looked as though the entire plain was moving towards the city. They saw the Indian sweepers dressed in red and white checkered tunics sweeping the causeway for the third time that morning. Dust rose above them and hung there for a moment before being whisked away by the capricious breeze.

Beyond them, the Spaniards saw an advancing army of gold: gold shining from the soldiers' breastplates and gold-tipped spears, axes and clubs, gold ornamenting the heads and wrists of the noblemen, gold laced through the women's hair, and above all, the mass of gold that was the Inca's palanquin.

The cortège, approaching at a maddeningly slow pace, looked something like a giant butterfly taking off languidly in the midday heat, its two massive, colorful wings slowly flapping at either side of its gold body. Tens of thousands of Atahualpa's men covered the plain to both sides of the Emperor's palanquin. They were impressively well disciplined, advancing at exactly the same slow pace as the eighty palanquin bearers, slowly but surely closing in on the walls of the city.

Gabriel realized that he was holding his breath. He was mesmerized by the terrifying beauty of the Inca army.

And then Candia called out:

'They're armed! They're coming armed!'

A fearful panic spread through the Spanish troops. But Don Hernando and de Soto assured the men that the Indians' gold and silver breastplates weren't armor at all, just ornaments.

Don Francisco had barely finished giving his orders when Pedro the Greek, standing on top of the falconet's battel, started yelling:

'They've stopped! Mother of God, my Lord: they've stopped! The palanquin's halted, and it looks like they're even setting up camp!'

'Shit,' said Pizarro.

It was the first time anyone had ever heard him swear.

A tent was erected so that the Emperor could sit in its shade. He called for the sacred *chicha*, as one did during a hunt, to thank Inti the Sun for the pleasure of the chase.

He drank in long, slow gulps, and the priests poured some *chicha* on the ground with each goblet that he emptied, the ground soaking it up as quickly as the Emperor drank it.

To Anamaya, it looked like everyone was at a loss about what to do next.

Men sent to spy on the strangers returned laughing, and told how the bearded men, with their animals, had hidden in the buildings around the square like frightened guinea pigs.

For the sport of it, Atahualpa ordered that one of the strangers come before him. Anamaya hoped that it would be the one with the golden beard.

*   *   *

'Who will go alone?'

The interpreters had absolutely refused to return to the Inca camp. Their fear was greater than anyone's. Pizarro's dark gaze, his eyes as black as coal, shifted from one man to the next. His men avoided his stare.

'I don't want him to stop outside the town. He must come in. If we don't grab him tonight, we're all dead. So, who will it be?'

Murmuring filled the air. Fear now ruled, banishing the men's hopes. By God, how dark the sky was, how high the mountains, – by God, how frightened they were . . .

'I'll go,' said Gabriel.

'Do you speak their language?'

'I'll go with him.'

It was Aldana, a man from Extremadura, who had spoken. His upper lip was cloven, and although he was a man of few words in Spanish, he had spent a lot of time learning the Indian's harsh language from the interpreters, the *curacas*, and Sikinchara.

Pizarro turned back to Gabriel.

'Why do you want to go?'

'I just do, Don Francisco.'

Pizarro's onyx eyes pierced through to the darkest reaches of his soul.

'Watch out for yourself, little brother.'

Their companions watched them as Gabriel and Aldana got on their horses and crossed the square. Gabriel repeated Don Francisco's word, *hermanito*, over and over in his mind.

He heard Don Hernando's disdainful voice say:

'There go two walking corpses . . .'

But Gabriel smiled a peaceful smile that no one else could understand. He went towards his strange destiny with a light heart.

*   *   *

Anamaya saw the first stranger – a small, thin man with a bushy black beard that didn't hide his cloven upper lip. And then she saw *him*. In an instant she made out his delicate, symmetrical features, the gentle dignity of his eyes, the elegant line of his neck no longer covered with hair.

She closed her eyes to collect herself. When she opened them again, she forced herself to look down at the ground.

'My Lord the Governor wishes to dine with you,' said the stranger hesitantly as he gave an awkward bow. 'He will not eat unless it be with you, and he wants you to know that he likes you, and that he is at peace with you . . .'

She heard Atahualpa answer in a heavy voice:

'Return to your people. Tell them that I shall come before nightfall, and that I shall come unarmed. Why would I bother with weapons? I am master of this land . . .'

Laughter filled the air.

'What is the man with golden hair – whose beard fell from his face with fear during the night – doing with you?' asked Atahualpa scornfully. 'Does he always sit there in silence while others talk?'

Anamaya felt the blood drain from her face. She felt that the Emperor was talking to her, and that a dreadful hand was about to tear into her chest and rip out her heart.

'You don't understand me,' grumbled Atahualpa. 'But I see the fear in your eyes. Don't worry, no harm will be done to you – yet.'

Now Anamaya lifted her gaze. The Emperor had stood up. He walked heavily towards the man with the light hair and tried to take hold of his silver stick. But the stranger didn't allow him to touch it, and moved away from him. The crowd murmured in shock, but Atahualpa silenced them with a wave of his hand. He returned to his throne, feigning a smile of indifference, as though it was but a game that bored him.

The thin little stranger had already turned around and

started off towards the town, but the light-haired man had stayed put, looking directly at the Inca. He spoke a few words in a firm voice.

And then he looked at Anamaya.

And he smiled.

And as he turned around, calmly, like a cousin leaving after visiting a cousin, she realized that she wouldn't be able to live without that smile.

Gabriel's legs were trembling.

'I thought we weren't going to get out of there alive,' said Aldana blankly.

Gabriel wanted to reply, 'Me too,' but he said nothing.

He realized that he was, in his heart, still back there with her, the two of them together amid all those strange people who wanted to see him dead.

He mouthed the words, but didn't speak them, keeping the secret in his heart.

'I love her.'

He repeated it to the clouds, to the wind, to the spirit asleep in the mountains: 'I love her.' And they all heard him say it. Fortunately, his compatriots didn't.

'We'll finish with them tonight,' said Atahualpa in a thick voice. The Emperor had drunk too much *chicha*, and his throat was clotted. His movements were as slow and heavy as his voice, and his eyes were diminished in strength. He looked bloated, dazed as much from all the scalding baths that he had taken during his fast as from the many jars of sacred beer that he had downed since morning. But behind his drunkenness, and despite the laughter all around him, there was a look of infinite sadness on his face, in the crease of his mouth.

Anamaya felt herself choke. A wave of pity for the Emperor came over her, and she was about to throw herself at his feet when she felt a hand grab her arm.

She turned with a start. It was Guaypar, and his serious and severe face was right next to hers.

'I saw you,' he said, straining to be gentle.

'What do you mean?'

'I saw you,' he repeated. 'Need I say more? Do you remember what I told you last night?'

Anamaya blushed. She lowered her gaze.

'I'm going now to join Ruminahui on the royal road,' continued Guaypar. 'The Emperor may seem to be treating this lightly, like a game, but he's pretending. Soon you will all continue down the road to the square in Cajamarca. The strangers will be so frightened that they'll flee and we'll be waiting for them. We're going to annihilate their race so that they'll never return to wreak their destruction here again . . . Be careful, *Coya Camaquen*, be very careful, and don't let your blue eyes reveal our plan to the strangers.'

'Some are carrying bows, others pikes about five feet long with fire-hardened points.'

'We knew that already,' said Pizarro.

'They're hiding weapons and armor under their tunics,' added Aldana.

'Ah? Which ones?'

'Slingshots for sure, perhaps clubs . . .'

Pizarro grinned scornfully. He waved away their fear with his hand.

'Is their King coming? That's all I care about.'

'He told me he would,' said Aldana, his voice a little hesitant.

The Governor ordered further precautionary measures. The horsemen and their steeds were to wait inside the buildings around the square, and bells were to be attached to their saddles. The foot soldiers were to wait in other buildings with their armor and weapons within reach, so that when the time came they would surge out from everywhere.

'But above all,' Pizarro shouted so that all could hear, 'above all, we must capture him alive. The square must be empty when they arrive, with no guard even. They must suspect nothing. And you, up there on the pyramid, I want you all to duck down under the parapet. After they've arrived, no one is to fire a single shot whether from harquebus or crossbow, before I give the order. And my order shall be the cry of *Santiago* . . .'

There was only one gate just large enough for the palanquin to pass through into the square. The procession that streamed through it seemed endless: first the many servants, then the lords bearing the Inca, then the two other palanquins, then the hammocks and the women.

The warriors had stayed outside the wall with their pikes, their clubs, their axes.

When the Emperor's group were all in the square, the trumpets and drums that had been sounding throughout their approach suddenly fell silent.

The Emperor raised his arm, and this simple gesture was enough to silence every voice.

There wasn't one foreigner in the square.

'Where are they?' asked Atahualpa.

We're not scared of you. She was sure that's what the golden-haired stranger had mouthed. Anamaya wanted to go up to the Emperor's palanquin and tell him that Sikinchara had been wrong from the beginning. But the crowd was so thick that she couldn't get there.

She shouted but her cry was drowned out by the crowd, who had started singing again.

*   *   *

Pizarro spoke in a hushed voice, but still loud enough for all to hear:

'You must build a fortress around your heart, because it is the only one you have . . .'

He told them exactly the same thing as he had told the men gathered in the other building a little earlier. In each of the strange and magnificent Inca palaces, foot soldiers and horsemen were bunched together shoulder to shoulder, some laughing nervously, some completely silent. All had a distant look in their eyes, and many had sudden pangs of nostalgia for the corner of Spain where they had been born.

'You will have no one to help you but God. God helps the faithful even in the most dire circumstances. You will find the courage that you'll need, because God is fighting on our side!'

Many had tears in their eyes, and were clenching their fists.

'Be careful, all of you,' continued the Governor quietly, 'and when the moment comes, run straight at the enemy with confidence and rage. You, the horsemen, cut off the palanquin to the right, and make sure that your horses don't trip each other up. I'm going on foot with our soldiers. No one is to touch the Inca before me.'

Gabriel had torn his gaze away from the Governor's hypnotic eyes. Through an opening he could see the gold shimmering on the halted palanquin. It seemed to be floating on a sea of men. They had started singing again, and their song sounded like a drone from the depths of the Earth.

Where is she, he asked himself, *so that I can take her in my arms and carry her away . . .*

'Hermanito?'

It was the Governor's dry voice.

'Don Francisco?'

'Now is not the time for daydreaming.'

Gabriel gripped the hilt of his sword.

'I wasn't daydreaming, Don Francisco.'

'Hmm. Well, stay close to me.'

The Governor had whispered this so discreetly and quickly that Gabriel wasn't sure if he had heard him right. But he had said it. And Gabriel's heart swelled with pride.

'Where are they?' repeated Atahualpa as his procession continued to stream into the square.

Sikinchara came up to him with his head lowered.

'They're hiding in the *kallankas*, my Lord. They'll die of fright in there, before dying again at your command.'

'I want them to show themselves,' said Atahualpa.

'Go now,' said Pizarro to Friar Vicente.

Felipillo was utterly terrified when he glanced at Gabriel. But he had no choice: he had to follow the Dominican with his crucifix and his Gospel. The friar had draped his star-decorated stole over his mauve habit. His eyes looked determinedly ahead, and he was murmuring a prayer to himself.

Gabriel, like everyone else, was impressed by his broad back as he walked out into the square. And they all held their breath.

Anamaya saw the stranger come out of the palace. He was wearing an astonishing garment, and he had the little interpreter with him, the one that they had brought with them yesterday.

The stranger wore a sort of *unku* a lot like theirs, except longer, and with a *quipu* as a belt. Unlike his companions, he had no hair, not even on his head. He was carrying a box and a stick in his hands, and as he approached he occasionally put his lips to them.

Her heart beat faster: she sensed that the Emperor was in danger. But although his palanquin was only a short distance away, the mass of warriors between her and it was far too dense for her to reach it.

The singing stopped.

The crowd parted for the stranger, and he went straight to the palanquin.

He spoke in a disagreeable high-pitched voice, and Anamaya wanted to block her ears not to hear.

He spoke strange words.

It was as if Friar Vicente were trailing fire behind him. The crowd parted to let him near the Emperor but didn't close up again behind him, as if no Indian dared step where he had stepped.

Gabriel saw the Dominican stop in front of the palanquin, and could hear him clearly enough:

'I am a man of God, and I preach the Word of God to Christians. God commands that there be no war or discord within his flock, only peace. In His Name I ask you to be a friend to all Christians, as they are friends to you. This is the will of God, and you would do well to heed it. We had agreed to meet in peace. Why, then, have you brought so many warriors?'

The Inca didn't reply, or even move. A terrible image flashed through Gabriel's mind: Friar Vicente had parted the sea to reach the master's ship. The master had only to wave his hand for the sea to close up and the priest would drown, and all of them with him.

'The Lord Governor,' continued Friar Vicente, 'likes you a lot. He is waiting for you in his lodgings, and wishes to see you. Go and speak with him, I beg of you, because he won't dine without you.'

Felipillo barely had time to translate this in his blank, terrified voice, when the Inca spoke.

His words were words of rage.

An angry murmur spread through the crowd of Indians in the square. They shared their ruler's rage. He spoke for all of them: he cursed the strangers for the murders that they had committed, their thieving and pillaging, their raping of women during their journey. It was no longer a game, a mere hunt.

It was time for revenge.

'I will not budge from here until you have returned all that you have taken from me. Only then will I decide how each of you shall die. Who dares give me orders?'

The stranger replied, through the interpreter, with some incomprehensible babble about his god and another man who was his son and yet another who was his spirit. What confusion reigned in the foreigners' diseased souls!

'Who is this god of yours?' thundered Atahualpa. 'Who is your Lord? What is his will?'

'Here is the Son of God,' said the stranger, and he lifted his crossed stick. 'And His will is painted in here.'

With that, he handed the box to the Emperor.

The Inca couldn't get it open. He turned it over and over, and shook it as though it was a casket containing something.

Gabriel saw Friar Vicente reach out to help, but the Inca struck him and pushed him away.

Eventually he managed to open the Gospel-book, and he rifled impatiently through its pages. Then he shouted something angrily.

A murmur grew into a rumbling from the crowd in the square.

'Gentlemen, get ready,' said Pizarro calmly. 'The time has come.'

'I too am a son of God,' shouted Atahualpa. 'I am the son of the sun!'

The crowd responded fervently:

'It is so, Great Emperor!'

The clouds had parted, for the second time that day, and Inti revealed his splendor. How could they doubt one who was master of the entire universe?

Anamaya perceived the fire in Atahualpa's eyes. She knew now that she had to get to him, and her own eyes hurt as tears welled up in them. All the truths that she had learned the night before and that she hadn't dared speak because she had been frightened, or because the golden-haired stranger had been looking at her, were choking her as effectively as a gag of cloth across her mouth.

When the Inca flung the box to the ground, hundreds of white wings scattered from it on the breeze. Atahualpa sat up majestically on his palanquin, his cheeks swollen with all his rage against the newcomers' crimes:

'I too am the son of God! I am the son of the sun!'

'It is so, Great Emperor,' roared the crowd once again, as the sun heated them. Anamaya had shaken off her paralysis and had slipped her way through the crowd to within five or six paces of Atahualpa's palanquin. Only a few guards and Powerful Lords stood between her and the Emperor.

Just then, two great cracks of thunder exploded.

But they hadn't come from the sky.

*   *   *

When the Inca had flung the Bible to the ground, they had all seen Felipillo rush to pick it up. Friar Vicente's cries filled their ears:

'Come out, come out, Christians! Crush these mongrels who deny the Lord! This one threw the Holy Bible to the ground!'

Now Friar Vicente was running towards the palace, all the while yelling as he cut through the crowd of Indians. Oddly, they didn't make a move to stop him, letting him pass as if he was untouchable to them.

'Don't wait any longer!' howled Friar Vicente when he was within ten paces of the Governor. 'Can't you see that more of those godless savages are rushing in? Ride them down, Governor! I absolve you ahead of it!'

Don Francisco regarded him impassively as he bawled these words.

Only a moment earlier, he had calmly laced up his steel corselet greased with tallow. His helmet hid his entire face except for his black gaze. He pointed his hand wrapped in a thick leather glove towards Friar Vicente, who seemed about to burst:

'Calm down, Don Valverde. You shall have your bishopric.'

Gabriel was the last in the saddle. Don Francisco turned to him and said in a low voice:

'I'm going by foot. When I'm with the Inca, I want you near me.'

They burst out of the palace and the buildings around the square at exactly the same moment, all shouting 'Santiago!' as one. The Governor's standard fluttered in the wind. Foot soldiers rushed from the neighboring buildings with their blades pointed skywards, hollering like madmen.

Two deafening detonations followed, and the summit of the pyramid was hidden in a cloud of white smoke. Four shots had actually been planned, but Gabriel didn't have time to think about the wet powder that had let them down once again. The crowd of Indians cried out in stupefied panic. They saw the round shot fly over them, moving almost with deliberation, it seemed, before the deadly accurate balls hit the gate where warriors were crammed together. Heads exploded, chests were pulverized, and the crowd was gripped by terror. The men that the projectiles had hit and who hadn't died instantly were drenched in blood and screamed in agony.

The sky suddenly darkened.

The cacophony of the bells attached to the horses deafened Gabriel. He was amazed that he didn't have to strike anyone. The crowd of Indians parted before the animals of their own accord. The Governor walked in great strides with his right hand on the grip of his unsheathed sword, as if on parade.

Ahead of them, meanwhile, Juan Pizarro was having trouble controlling his flighty horse. He held the reins in one hand, the other gripping the stave of his lance as though it was the banister rail of a steep staircase.

As they neared the Inca's palanquin, Gabriel saw from the corner of his eye the other horsemen at the foot of the pyramid. Behind them, the foot soldiers' blades were already dripping blood, and they yelled 'Santiago! Santiago!' over and over as the horsemen charged, their spears stuck straight out ahead of them.

A wave of movement passed through the crowd of Indians massed around their King's palanquin, like a gust of wind across the sea. They clambered over one another trying to escape the assault. Yet, incomprehensibly, they didn't fight back.

Gabriel, from his high vantage point atop his horse, saw their closely huddled heads as a sea of black mud. His mind was confused for a few seconds by the memory of the blue-eyed girl. He prayed, despite himself, that she wasn't among the women he could make out beyond the Inca's palanquin, their faces twisted with fear. They were thrusting their hands into the air as though hoping to be snatched up by the sky.

When the riders got close enough to the Inca to see his bloodshot eyes and disdainful mouth clearly, a dozen Indians, shoved from behind by the crowd, collapsed in front of Juan and Cristobal's horses. The Spaniards had no option but to trample over them. As the horses' hooves broke their bones and shattered their ribs, the warriors looked up from the ground utterly flabbergasted, their open mouths silently crying out.

They didn't believe us! thought Gabriel in a bitter rage, almost cruelly. *Those fools didn't believe us! Soon they'll all be dead, and they're not even fighting back! Why? Why such madness?*

As if in answer to his unspoken questions, a salvo from the harquebuses under Pedro's command bored holes through brains at random. The dead now piled up on the living, and utter confusion reigned. Their path to the palanquin closed up behind them like quicksand. Diego de Molina and Juan Pizarro were standing in their stirrups, hollering out and windmilling their swords in great sweeps to either side, carving a passage through the mass of human flesh that yielded to their blades like butter.

Gabriel, his head buzzing, restricted himself to striking the Indians with the butt of his lance. Now another salvo from the harquebuses heightened the panic to breaking point. The Indians began to flee the square. Heads popped up from the piles of bodies only to be crushed by the horses or speared or even beheaded by sabers sweeping like scythes.

The crush was such that Gabriel felt his horse tremble with fear. The beast reared on its hind legs and neighed desperately. Its hooves landed on heads, transforming them into bloody pulp. An Indian wearing enormous gold ear-plugs grabbed the stave of Gabriel's lance and tried to pull him off his horse.

Gabriel immediately let go of the lance and yanked his horse to the left. The animal instinctively understood: it kicked out and spun around and around on itself like a top, clearing a space around him. Then the horse stopped for a moment, foaming at the mouth, and Gabriel drew his sword and urged the creature on with his knees. He struck Indians aside and joined the Governor by the Inca's enormous palanquin.

Now Don Francisco was actually on it. He had managed to grab the Inca's left arm and was trying to tug him down. But after a moment of surprise, the Inca gripped on to the armrest of his throne as tightly as a clam to a rock. Underneath them, a hundred Indians still carried the palanquin, unyielding in the chaos.

'To me, *compañeros*!' roared Don Francisco. 'Fucking hell! Help me get him off this thing!'

Diego, Juan, and Cristobal howled like savage beasts, leaned down from their saddles – and began slicing off the bearers' hands.

Gabriel was chilled by the scene, despite the sweat trickling down his face. His companions' swords cut off the Indians' hands, their arms, or their fingers. The bearers didn't cry out in pain: instead they bowed their necks and continued carrying the palanquin on their armless shoulders as blood jetted from the stumps of their amputated limbs.

Juan, enraged to the point of madness by their obstinacy, howled like a wolf and began slicing their throats. But as they fell others immediately stepped into this circle of hell and took their place, offering themselves to the swords.

The Inca himself was still holding on to the palanquin, although it was about to tip over. His fine clothes had been shredded. Ambassador Sikinchara rushed to fight off the Governor, but the clover-shaped point of Molina's lance pierced clean through Sikinchara's gold breastplate and came out between his shoulder blades. It pinned the ambassador to a pillar of the palanquin – he looked surprised as the lance's tip thudded dully into the wood.

Now other Indian noblemen came at the Spaniards with bronze axes. At last, they were fighting back. Gabriel's sword whistled through the air that was already stinking of blood and sliced off an arm. The jolt of steel hitting bone vibrated up his arm and his whole body shuddered. He felt as though he was living in a nightmare beyond description.

An Indian wrapped his arms around his leg and hung there with all his weight. And as Gabriel lifted his arm to strike again, a knot of rage rose in his throat and choked him.

He stood in his stirrups and struck out blindly with his sword. He hollered out like the others.

But in the hellish cacophony, his cry might as well have been a breath of silence.

The sun had gone into hiding.

Over the heads of screaming women, Anamaya saw the strangers cutting off arms as if they were reaping maize.

She saw brave Lords rush to Atahualpa's aid and offer their hands, their heads, their blood to protect him. But they fell, and they died for nothing. The strangers' furious charge was unstoppable, and their silver sticks were lethal. Against them, the Indian's slingshots and clubs seemed like child's toys!

'I am the son of the sun!' cried Atahualpa to the darkening sky.

But he still hadn't ordered his thousands of warriors to fight!

And they were so obedient that they wouldn't move without his order, allowing themselves instead to be massacred in vain!

Was he drunk from all the *chicha*? Was he too flabbergasted by the strangers' fury to give the order?

Now Anamaya saw her Emperor fighting like a mere mortal, fighting the cruel strangers who were trying to carry him off.

Moaning and wailing filled the air. She was carried in the push of the crowd, now one way, now the other. She felt desperate hands grab at her, tearing her tunic. She floated on a torrent of bodies that lifted her and dropped her back down again. The Other World seemed to have sent the most terrible storm down upon them.

She remembered the child's words: *'What is will no longer be.'*

Why hadn't she had the courage to warn Atahualpa? She couldn't bear to look at his palanquin. She knew already that he was defeated.

Wasn't she as responsible as the strangers for his downfall?

Was it because of the golden-haired stranger that she had said nothing?

Although the Emperor Huayna Capac had ordained this horror, she couldn't bear it any longer.

She was about to abandon herself to the maelstrom that was all around her, about to let herself slip to the ground under the thousands of panicked feet, when she saw a glimmer of gold across the plain in the sinister shadows of the western mountains.

Yes: a ray of sun had broken through the clouds and was reflecting off something there in the west. The west, on the road to Cuzco.

A drop of gold like a peaceful star fallen among the chaos of death.

She knew.

She could feel him.

The Sacred Double.

The one she had been waiting for.

*   *   *

Molina, Juan, and Cristobal had surrounded the Governor and shoved their horses against the palanquin in an attempt to tip it over. If anything, it was even higher now that its bearers had climbed atop the bodies piled under their feet.

'Make sure you don't hurt the Inca!' shouted Don Francisco, still tugging on the Emperor's arm.

Horsemen arrived from across the square. The scene was like the climax of a hunt. With their lances or with their bare hands they tore the finery off the Inca: they knocked off his feathered crown, ripped away his gold cape, and tore his necklace from him.

De Moguer had barreled through the crowd from the other side and jumped onto the palanquin. He swung his blade around him in great swipes, all the while bawling out like a berserk animal. He grabbed the Inca's gold breastplate with his other hand and tore it off him. He let out a deranged laugh as he waved it triumphantly in the air. An Indian nobleman armed with a club tried to grab it from him, but de Moguer gutted him with his sword, and the Indian's intestines fell from the gaping wound in his stomach.

'No one hurt the Inca!' repeated the Governor.

Gabriel saw the frenzied mania on de Moguer's face. He wrenched away from the Emperor's servants who had closed in around him and urged his horse through the piles of dead and wounded. De Moguer's sword was poised above the Inca. His first strike missed the Emperor and glanced off the upright of his throne. However, it sliced through Pizarro's glove on the hand that held the Inca's arm. The Governor yelled an insult at de Moguer, but didn't remove his hand.

Gabriel rammed his horse into the palanquin and struck de Moguer hard in the back with the flat of his sword. De Moguer stumbled forward and dropped his blade.

'Don't touch the Inca!' screamed Gabriel, beside himself. He held the tip of his sword under the stunned de Moguer's chin.

'Didn't you hear the Governor, you sack of shit! You are not to touch him!'

Gabriel's rage was so great and he yelled so loud that everyone in the immediate vicinity paused for a moment.

Hatred twisted de Moguer's already repulsive face. Gabriel saw all the evil in the world concentrated in it.

Meanwhile, Pizarro, making the most of the moment, had managed to tear the Inca away from his throne. He yanked the Emperor to him with a powerful tug just as the palanquin tipped over, and as they fell he wrapped his left arm protectively around the Inca's neck and covered him with his shield.

'You just saved the day, son!' he shouted to Gabriel. 'Stay with me, we've got to get this bugger into the building!'

But then, as Gabriel was trying to extricate his horse from a mass of Indian servants paralyzed with fear, he saw her.

She stood immobile amid the bedlam, with her blue eyes bright as diamonds.

She wasn't looking at the Inca. She was looking at Gabriel.

Anamaya saw the golden-haired stranger through the chaos.

The Sacred Double had disappeared behind a hill like a flash of vain hope.

The women all around her were desperately trying to flee, running into one another amid the spilled blood and severed limbs. Some had completely lost their minds, and they grabbed on to her. She shoved them away. She couldn't take another step.

Whether they were riding their animals or on foot, the strangers were a whirlwind of death. Killing possessed them, and death danced in their eyes like black flames.

She saw the strangers roaring insults and tearing off the Inca's clothes one by one. He was already half naked.

She saw the blade raised above Atahualpa.

And she saw the golden-haired stranger bound onto the palanquin and shove the murderer away.

Although blood dripped from his sword, she saw that he didn't revel in slaughter like the others.

She heard his cry of rage against all the killing.

And now she saw him look at her.

A door opened in her soul, and carried her away from all the horror around her.

What she felt made no sense, yet she almost spoke it aloud:

'Take me with you! Don't leave me in this sea of blood!'

Gabriel felt feverish. He couldn't get the girl's blue eyes out of his mind as he cleared a path through the fighting with his horse for the Governor and the Inca. The Governor kept hollering:

'I'll have your head if you hurt him! Don't touch him!'

Eventually they got Atahualpa into a building, and Pizarro said to the men guarding it:

'Your life depends on him staying alive!'

He removed his glove and examined his wounded hand. Then he looked at Gabriel, his eyes aglow with ferocious joy.

'We've won the battle, my son!'

The battle?

Gabriel's gaze wandered blankly over the horror in the square, and then out at the plain beyond it.

It had never been a battle. A battle needed two sides. What this was was a massacre, a slaughter. The Indians were desperately trying to flee, but it was hopeless.

He opened his mouth to reply to the Governor. But a

thought occurred to him – the one and only certainty in all the confusion – and he closed his mouth without saying anything. He had to save her. The only real battle was that he ensure that she lived. That was his own true struggle, and was more important than the will of God or the King of Spain, or even Don Francisco, who out of infinite kindness had called him 'son'. He had to save her no matter what the cost.

Without a word he turned his exhausted horse around and charged back into the fray.

The outer wall of the square collapsed in a cloud of dust under the press of thousands. Bodies immediately piled onto the rubble, pushed there by the pressure of the pan-icked crowd.

But Anamaya didn't move.

She was waiting for him.

Barely slowing from a gallop, Gabriel leaned down from his saddle and scooped her up, hooking her under her armpits. She wrapped her arms around his neck and let herself be lifted off the ground. She wasn't heavy at all: he hauled her up and sat her on his horse between its neck and the pommel of his saddle. She immediately adjusted to the rhythm of the galloping horse.

There were only fifty or so paces between them and the breach in the wall through which the crowd was fleeing.

All around them, the Spaniards continued their killing. Some had obscene grimaces on their faces, and, intoxicated by all the violence, they dug up from within themselves reserves of cruelty that had been born of their own fears.

Gabriel saw Sebastian shouting something to him from the summit of the pyramid, but he couldn't hear what his friend was yelling. The young girl's hands were wrapped around his waist, and their bodies were joined like intertwined leaves flying on the wind.

He could smell the perfume of her skin and feel the warmth of her neck next to his mouth. He could feel the life-force of her young body warming his loins.

Sebastian was still shouting something at him from above but still Gabriel couldn't hear his words. He was doing his best to find a passage through the throng of fleeing Indians.

The girl murmured something in her strange language and he felt her body quiver. The horse broke its rhythm to leap across a pile of rubble strewn with bodies, and his mouth struck against her temple. Her taste on his lips intoxicated him.

But then he felt a sharp pain in his lower back. He spurred his horse around to find the grotesque de Moguer brandishing a lance.

'I'm going to kill you! I'm going to tear your guts out and eat them, you little fuck!'

He threw his lance but missed, and it clanged against some bricks.

Gabriel felt hot, viscous blood flooding over his hip from de Moguer's first thrust. The blue-eyed girl looked into his eyes, worried. He forced himself to smile, and without realizing it he hugged her so tightly that it hurt.

A gang of naked children were running towards the marsh, carrying a dirty crown of colorful feathers. All around them men were running away, noblemen as well as servants, their gold breastplates and white tunics stained with dust, mud, and blood. And all wore the same look of bewilderment.

At last Gabriel felt the horses' hooves thudding instead of clattering: they had reached grass. They were on the plain.

Gabriel looked down to absorb the glow in the girl's distressed blue eyes. But he saw that they were full of tears.

He started trembling.

She did too.

She laid her delicate brown hands in his as his horse slowed to a walk of its own accord.

The air was thick with death and destruction. But the two of them trembled with a love as pure as the first day of life.

CHAPTER 46

Cajamarca: 16 November 1532

I T WAS A SIMPLE REED HUT SET IN THE MIDDLE
of the marsh at the confluence of a river and a
stream of scalding water from which steam rose above
the rushes.

On the earth floor there was only a mat. In the corner
lay a couple of simple wooden bowls and a dusty clay jar,
its lip broken. The fireplace clearly hadn't been used for a
long time.

Gabriel was relieved: no one had slept there the previous
night. No dead man's soul would haunt him.

The shadows grew longer.

He brushed a fly off his head, then looked at his hand:
blood.

He had been so strong, and was now so weak. He had a
passing thought: would he die now? No, of course not. But
still, he was incredibly tired. His limbs felt so heavy.

She darted out of the hut and returned with a few leaves
that she tore into pieces and slowly chewed. Her fingers
touched his head, near the wound on his skull.

He closed his eyes and abandoned himself to her tenderness.

When he opened his eyes again, she smiled at him. Her

hand brushed against his cheek, but flinched away when he tried to take it in his.

She said something, which of course he didn't understand, and ran out the door.

Anamaya ran through the groaning night, a night with ghostly tears rising from the blood-soaked ground like smoke. She ran confidently, sure of her footing despite the slippery mud and the marsh, despite the scalding waters. The sun had gone, but now Quilla guided her.

The courtyard outside the Inca's lodgings was a scene of unbelievable devastation. The strangers had come here on their horses and destroyed what they hadn't been able to pillage. They had carried away everything that was made of gold. They had defiled life. Their shouts could be heard occasionally in the night. They prowled about, bringing death to any they found still alive.

The hammock in which the Inca had lain that morning now floated in the bath of mixed waters like an old, discarded cloth.

'You're not dead . . .'

Inti Palla. Anamaya turned to face her. Her face was red, her clothes ripped – she was only a shadow of her former proud self. To think that Anamaya had once been frightened of her.

'No, I'm not dead, Inti Palla. I've come back to complete the inevitable.'

'You are the reason for all this destruction.'

'Shut up. You're a silly idiot. Our Emperor is captured because of the likes of you, unthinking fools with no courage . . .'

Inti Palla said nothing. She had no more strength to cause harm. She cried warm tears. Her arms shook like the wings of a bird hit by an arrow.

'The sun has disappeared,' she blubbered. 'There's nothing left . . .'

'The world is still here,' murmured Anamaya to herself, moving away, 'and a child to see it reborn . . .'

'We've got to run away,' cried Inti Palla.

'We've got to live.'

'You're right about that, little sister,' said another familiar voice. And his powerful arms hugged her tight.

By God it's a hot night, by God how quickly loneliness and fear overcome me, how danger seems to lurk in every shadow . . .

From time to time, Gabriel touched his head to check that he still existed. His head throbbed with pain, but he felt the curious plaster that the girl had put on his wound before disappearing . . .

She's coming back.

He had repeated this many times to himself. But so many hours had passed since she had left, he was no longer so sure.

Earlier, he had had the warmth of her skin, the tenderness of her hands, the giddiness he felt when she was near. But what did he have now?

He had the old matting that he was lying on, he had pain in his back, he had his ebbing consciousness . . .

He saw ghosts. He remembered the reproachful look on Sebastian's face and the fury on Pizarro's as he had left them. He had abandoned them, betrayed them at the crucial moment.

What would be his punishment? Death.

He realized that he wasn't scared when he thought of death. *Death: well, wasn't Death with me in the Inquisition's jail? Wasn't an early death what my father damned me to? And wasn't she there, whispering in my ear in the square?*

But still, I don't see myself dying in a reed hut lost in a marsh only a league from Cajamarca.

He remembered the tone of what she had said before leaving. *Wait here for me.* That's what she had told him. He was sure of it.

And so he waited, his heart now at peace.

'When Villa Oma told me that you had asked for the Sacred Double,' said Manco, 'I felt like it was me that you were calling . . .'

They were in each other's arms in what had been Atahualpa's bed-chamber until that morning. It had been ransacked.

'He spoke to me about you,' whispered Anamaya.

'Who?'

'I begged him night after night to speak to me, but he never came. People still called me *Coya Camaquen*, but more out of habit, I guess, because I saw nothing. Your father, Huayna Capac, told me nothing for ages. I had almost forgotten that he had promised to watch over me from the Other World.'

'We were on the long road from Cuzco, hiding whenever we came across troops. My brother Atahualpa had sworn an atrocious revenge on all the Cuzco clans. I saw—'

He fell silent. She squeezed his hand tenderly.

'. . . I saw what a man should never see, Anamaya. I saw babies suckling on the breasts of women with their throats slit . . .'

'What happened to Villa Oma?'

'The priests hid him.'

'And the dwarf?'

She had blurted this out unthinkingly. Manco looked at her, astonished.

'The dwarf? Why are you asking me about him?'

'It's a long story, too long to tell tonight. Please just tell me if you know where he is.'

'I saw him taken into Cuzco in chains.'

'And then?'

'I don't know what happened to him. The palaces of the most ancient *panacas* were defiled, the temples searched, my brother Paullu only just escaped death . . . I saw all the cruelty of the world, Anamaya, and that made me more of an adult than the *huarachiku* ever did. As for what happened to the dwarf in all that chaos . . .'

'Atahualpa was advised by liars, by false prophets, by cowards . . .'

'But he listened to them. Now there are no more clans – but it doesn't matter. You say that they laid their hands on him? They actually dared touch the Emperor?'

'They touched him, grabbed him, their hands were all over him . . .'

'Who are these strangers? Are they gods?'

Her mouth was dry. She replied:

'No. They're just men.'

Manco said nothing. She sensed a fresh gravity in him as he considered this. But that didn't dispel his rage.

'When you were approaching with the Sacred Double last night, he finally spoke to me. He came to me as a child and said: 'Look after my son who you saved from the snake, because he is the first knot of the future strand . . .'

'It was just before dawn,' said Manco. 'I was alone with him in the tent. I woke with a start to find a snake slithering across my gold bracelet, a snake like the one that you lured away from me during the race all those years ago . . . I went out to watch the dawn over the mountains. War was everywhere. Yet I felt a strong force within me, and then a light appeared before my eyes, a golden globe that burned on the horizon . . .'

'You are the one, Manco. There is no one left but you . . .'

He didn't reply. He put his arms around her and mur-mured:

'I remember the day you told us that you would never leave us . . . I remember the day that my brother Paullu and I couldn't decide whether you were ugly or beautiful . . .'

Anamaya stiffened instinctively in his hold.

'What's wrong?' he asked.

She said nothing. She saw his gaze trying to read hers. She sensed his strength, like that of a young puma . . .

'It's time to go, Manco, to Cuzco, with the Sacred Double . . .'

'I know,' he said. 'Why do you think I've come? Why do you think I dodged Ruminahui's troops and avoided the strangers to get here?'

'Why?'

'To take you away.'

She drew a breath before saying:

'I will always be with you, Manco, but I'm not going with you now.'

'I don't understand.'

'Something's happened . . .'

She wanted to tell him the truth. There was no more room for lies in the new troubles of her heart than there had been before. Yet a great weariness came over her. What was more, she would have to find words to describe what had only been looks, touches, a truth that was clouded by uncertainty. So she kept her lips closed.

She heard his heavy breath, and his stare was burning. But he said nothing. He asked nothing of her. He stood up.

'I said that I had grown up,' he told her. 'I accept what you give to me, and respect what you hold back. My destiny has been written on a dawn of blood, and as one mystery is revealed to me, another takes its place. Tomorrow I shall be in the mountains and I will escort the Sacred Double, drawing my strength from him. But I will never forget that it was through you . . .'

'I'll never forget it either, Manco.'

'Look after yourself, little sister.'

He stroked her cheek, then disappeared into the night. She shivered uncontrollably.

Then she too walked away into the dark, her heart beating fast. She headed towards the man who was her destiny.

Gabriel was hot, so he removed first his padded coat of mail, then his shirt. Sweat had dried on his body and he was covered with dust and blood. He put his lips to his arm and tasted its bitter saltiness. He felt the biting pain of all the blows he had received. He felt a drowsiness come over him, a numbness that he couldn't shake off.

The girl had slipped almost noiselessly into the hut, but he didn't move. He kept his eyes closed to savor this moment a little longer.

All his cries and complaints evaporated, leaving a peaceful silence in their place.

There was only the quiet and eternal fragility that made them one.

Sometimes, he thought, *'for a night' means for ever, a burning, black hour with no tomorrow* . . .

He opened his eyes. She was leaning over him with a worried look. Her hand touched his lips, and wandered to his cheeks, tracing shapes on them. He forced himself to remain still, using all his strength to resist the urge to take her in his arms.

Now her hand was on his front, and she traced his muscles with her fingers, and played with the hair on his chest.

Her hand traveled back up to his shoulder, and she touched it as though she were discovering it for the first time.

She prodded him gently. He understood that she wanted him to lie on his stomach, so he turned over, sighing, feeling the well-being that her caresses brought, despite his wounds.

Suddenly, she cried out.

*   *   *

'No, they're just men.'

That was what Anamaya had told Manco, and what she had said then with words she now discovered to be real with her hands. The strength and softness of this man, and the way he quivered when she touched him.

She remembered, of course, and all the doors of her emotions opened simultaneously, as though blown open by a great wind, all that she had tried to hide in the depths of her heart, all her fears, all the tears that she had shed, all those moons that had passed, everything evaporated. And now everything was simple.

It wasn't a vision, because the Sacred Double wasn't with her. It didn't come from the Other World, and no priest or sage had taught it to her.

It came from within herself.

It was the most powerful emotion that she had ever known.

If it was a fear, then it went beyond any fear that she had ever known.

If it was a god, then it was the most mysterious and demanding of gods.

It made her want to both laugh and cry, to sprint through the fields and turn into a stone, to shout out and be silent.

He obeyed her hands, and showed her his wounded back.

And then she saw it: the dark stain of the puma hidden on the back of his shoulder, coiled, about to spring.

She cried out.

She remembered the words the Inca Huayna Capac had told her, already so many years ago: 'Trust the puma . . .' She remembered the Ancestors' stone where the puma's eyes had been waiting for her. She remembered the child who had told her the previous night: 'Have no fear for the future: the puma is with you.'

Her fingers traced the shape of the puma – powerful, free, gathered to spring – on the man's shoulder.

She gently lowered herself to him.

She had only to kiss the gentle, quivering man who had always been her destiny.

CHAPTER 47

Cajamarca: dawn of 17 November 1532

AT DAWN, THEY BOTH WENT OUT ONTO THE PLAIN. Everything was smothered in vapour: fingers of fog had settled like gauze; steam rose from the springs of boiling water; ghosts emerged from the corpses that were strewn on the causeway, in the marsh, in the pools, ghosts fleeing to other worlds with one last breath.

The man and the girl were alone.

Gabriel helped Anamaya into the saddle and hauled himself up behind her. He nestled his head against her neck and together they looked at the town.

Soon he would have to talk. He would have to explain himself, prove his loyalty and justify what his countrymen would call his treason. They had to survive in this strange new world, a world born of the great upheaval the day before.

Soon they would have to accept that the world was more than a refuge where lovers could see each other, touch and love one another without having to say a word.

Soon. But not now.

ACKNOWLEDGEMENTS

Our thanks of course go out to all the team at Editions XO. Anne Gallimard, Édith Leblond, Catherine de Larouzière and Chantal Théolas, Véronique Podevin and Julia Cavanna.

We are grateful to Susanna Lea for 'giving us wings', by enabling this story to travel all over the world.

Establishing locations in Peru was made easier by Enrique 'Kike' Polack (Kantu Agency at Cuzco) and his team. Thanks to Marvin for his help and to René for driving us over all kinds of terrain. The knowledge and passion of our guides, Manuel Portal Cabellos at Cajamarca and Roger Valencia at Cuzco, gave us much material for reflection.

Comments by Alex Gilly, who carried out the translation of the text into English, meant a great deal to us.

Finally, we would like to thank our reader-testers, whose support and coments were with us constantly: Edica, Mélanie and Carolina Houette, Alexandre Audouard and Guillaume Fixot.

Antoine B. Daniel